PgMP® Study:
Two Complete Exams

340 Questions and Answers

First Edition

based on PMI Standards for Program Management – 4th edition

by
Leithy Mohamed Leithy

MBA, PfMP, PgMP, PMP, PMOC, COBIT, ITIL, CSSGB

Copyright © 2018 Leithy Mohamed Leithy

All rights are reserved. This book or any portion thereof may not be reproduced or used in any manner whatsoever without the express written permission of the publisher except for the use of brief quotations in a book review.

For permission to use material from this text or product, contact us by:
e-mail: support@6p-Consulting.com,
Website: www.6p-Consulting.com

ISBN: 9781719869980

Discover other titles by Leithy Mohamed Leithy:

- **Passing the PfMP® Exam: A Study Guide**
- **Passing the PgMP® Exam: A Study Guide**
- **Passing the PMP® Exam: A Study Guide**

Discover PgMP online training courses by Leithy Mohamed Leithy on Udemy and Skillshare with big discount at www.6p-consulting.com

About the Author

Leithy Mohamed Leithy is a certified Portfolio Management Professional (PfMP®), Program Management Professional (PgMP®), and Project Management Professional (PMP®). He also has the certification of Project Management Office (PMOC), ITIL, COBIT, and CSSGB.

Leithy is originally an engineer of computer and automatic control, graduated from Ain Shams University in Egypt in 1989. Later, he upgraded his educational level and got his master (MBA) in IT Management from Leicester University in the UK.

Leithy has extensive experience in portfolio management, program management, project management and PMO. He practiced the implementation of project management office, program management office, and portfolio management office for the different models: Supportive, Directive and Controlling.

He has practical experience in delivering sensitive projects and programs under high pressure, harsh target deadlines, and budget challenges. He developed project and program management methodologies and implemented them in large multi-national organizations.

He acquired excellent practical portfolio management experience while managing multiple portfolios and guided the portfolio managers to achieve their target strategic and financial objectives.

He worked mainly in the Arabian Gulf over the last twenty-five years with big firms and international enterprises, strengthening his practical experience and adding a lot to his pragmatic thinking. While concentrating on information technology, he interfered with different industries; educational, health, financial, telecommunication, utilities, and oil and gas.

Combining the practical experience with the academic knowledge and international certifications creates an excellent understanding of the best practice and world-class standards.

Leithy is the founder of the 6P-Consulting management services company, which is specialized in project, program, portfolio, and PMO management services, www.6P-Consulting.com

Leithy is a Udemy instructor and Skillshare instructor for many online training courses in project, program, portfolio, and management. You can review his list of courses and you can get benefits from the coupon codes and existing discount on: www.6P-Consulting.com

Contents

About the Author 4
Introduction 8
1. Exam 1 - Questions 10
2. Exam 1 – Questions and Answers 56
1. Exam 2 - Questions 154
2. Exam 2 – Questions and Answers 200
Appendix (A) – Questions Mapping per Domain 294
1. Exam 1 – Question Reference 296
2. Exam 2 – Questions Reference 302

Introduction

This book is developed to help you in passing the Program Management Professional Certification PgMP® Exam on your first attempt. It is your tool to discover your weak points and areas the needs more concentration before entering the actual exam. I am sure that no one wants to enter a PgMP testing exam without total reassurance that he has become familiar with the actual certification exam.

The book is created based on the "The Standard for Program Management – Fourth Edition," which was PMI certified in 2017. This book adopts all PMI publications related to the Program Management that were created before the publication date of this edition.

This book contains two full PgMP® sample exam with its detailed answer and explanation, i.e.; it has a total of 340 questions and answers. The questions were created based on the "PMI Program Management Professional (PgMP)® Handbook" published in October 2017 and the Program Management Professional (PgMP)® Examination Content Outline.

This book is different from others as it is created by an author who passed the PfMP®, PgMP® and PMP® Exams on his first attempt, so, the author knows how to pass the different exams from the PMI on the first attempt. This reflects the flavor of the questions that you are going to see on the exam. Besides, it covers different examples of each type of the commonly found questions on the PMP® Exam model; including the regular question, table question, and question set.

PMP, PgMP, and PfMP are registered trademarks by PMI.

Although the two exams include the questions randomly from the different domains as you will in the real exam, you can still access the questions for a specific domain for studying purposes by referring to the tables in the Appendix(A).

Please note that each question answer has the following details:

- **The right answer**
- **Question Reference**: this is referring to the Standard Guide: "The Standard for Program Management – Fourth Edition," which was PMI certified in 2017. If the question reference section from the Standard Guide span over few pages, I will mention the page number that is directly related to the subject question
- **Clarification and Tips**: this is the most important part of the answer that describes the reasons for selecting the right answer and eliminating the three other choices
- **Domain**: the name of the program management performance domain covering this question
- **Phase / Element**: the phase or element of the performance domain from which the question is coming

For any query, please contact us at support@6P-Consulting.com

1. Exam 1 - Questions

Q1 - Marcos is suffering from low participation from the stakeholders in his program. He wants to identify potential risks caused by a lack of participation from stakeholders. What should he do?

(a) He should review stakeholder metrics regularly
(b) He should review the stakeholder engagement plan regularly
(c) He should review the stakeholder register regularly
(d) He should review the stakeholder map regularly

Q2 - Kathy is looking for some help to engage the stakeholders to address the change the program will bring. What is your best advice to her?

(a) Review the change request log regularly with the stakeholders
(b) Submitting program status reports to the stakeholders
(c) Engaging stakeholders to assess their readiness for change, facilitating or negotiating the approach to implement change, and obtaining and evaluating the stakeholders' feedback on the program's progress
(d) Share open issues and emerged high risks with stakeholders

Q3 - As a program manager, what is the most important reason that drives you to conduct environmental analysis?

(a) Environmental analysis can be used to assess the validity of a program's business case and program management plan
(b) Environmental analysis can be used to validate the program assumptions
(c) Environmental analysis can be used to assess the program benefits realization plan
(d) Environmental analysis can be used to ensure accurate program reporting

Q4 - Lee is working on the definition phase and is executing the program infrastructure development activity. What is meant by infrastructure in this context?

(a) The infrastructure refers to the work breakdown structure
(b) The infrastructure refers to risk breakdown structure
(c) The infrastructure refers to both personnel and to program specific tools, facilities and finances used to manage the program
(d) The infrastructure refers to the program organization chart

Q5 - Which of the following is not included in the program business case?

(a) Details about the program outcomes
(b) The extent to which the program aligns with the organization's strategic objectives
(c) Market demand or barriers
(d) Major milestones

Q6 - Lucas concentrates on the program schedule to define any slippage that may delay the benefits realization. He did not pay attention to the possibility of early delivery. What is your advice to Locus?

(a) I will advise Locus to continue what he is doing as the early delivery is only a dream for the program managers which never happens
(b) I will advise Locus to concentrate on early delivery as it will compensate any slippage in the program
(c) I will advise Locus to consult the program sponsor first to see if he will accept early delivery or not
(d) I will advise Locus to identify both slippages and early deliveries as they are necessary as part of the overall program management function

Q7 - Which of the following can be used to achieve benefit sustainment after the program is closed?

(a) Operations and maintenance
(b) New projects
(c) New programs
(d) All the above

Q8 - Ahmed is a program manager who is currently executing the activity of evaluating overall program quality on a regular basis to provide confidence that the program will comply with the relevant quality policies and standards. Which activity is he executing?

(a) Program quality planning
(b) Program quality control
(c) Program quality assurance
(d) Program quality audit

Q9 - Which of the following is an example of a tangible benefit?

(a) Profit increased
(b) Brand recognition
(c) Public benefit
(d) All the above

Q10 - Omar is a program manager who has created a strong resource plan with his component managers. During program execution, he found some needs to change the resources according to certain practical situations. What should Omar do to prioritize the resource requirements within his program?

(a) Omar should consult his component managers for resource conflict and add a new issue to the register
(b) Omar should manage the resources at the program level and should work with the component managers who manage resources at the component level to balance the needs of the program with the availability of resources
(c) Omar should concentrate only on the program level resource requirements and should not be dragged to the project level resource management
(d) Omar should review the created resource plan

Q11 - James is managing a program in your organization from the vendor side. He monitors the schedule to identify the slippages in order to work on their recovery, but he ignores the opportunities that may exist in the schedule. What is your view on what James is doing?

(a) James is doing a good job and he should continue focusing on slippages and ignore the opportunities
(b) James is doing a bad job. He should focus on opportunities and ignore the slippages
(c) James should identify not only schedule slippages but also opportunities to accelerate program schedule
(d) James should involve the PMO to report the schedule status

Q12 - Jim is developing a plan that describes how, when and by whom information will be administered and disseminated. Which plan is this?

(a) The program information management plan
(b) The program communications management plan
(c) The program quality management plan

(d) The program change management plan

Q13 - Question Set (1/2) - Jim is appointed to manage one of your organization programs. He started to review the program alignment with the organization strategy. Which of the following options has the dominant reason for organizations to build strategy?

(a) Organizations need to build a strategy to define ways to execute their initiatives
(b) Organizations need to build a strategy to create plans on how to achieve their initiatives
(c) Organizations need to build a strategy to define how their vision will be achieved
(d) Organizations need to build a strategy to define how resources will be utilized

Q14 - Question Set (2/2) - Jim is appointed to manage one of your organization programs. He started to review the program alignment with the organization strategy. Which of the following options may influence the organizations initiatives?

(a) Market dynamics
(b) Customer and partner requests
(c) Competitor plans and actions
(d) All the above

Q15 - Who is responsible for reviewing and approving the approach to program quality management and the standards by which quality will be measured?

(a) The component managers
(b) The PMO
(c) The governance participants
(d) The organization governance team

Q16 - The lessons learned are critical assets to be reviewed in all the following cases, except:

(a) When updating the program stakeholder register
(b) When considering major changes to the program management plan
(c) When introducing a new program component
(d) When announcing the closure of one of the program components

Q17 - Because people have the propensity to resist change whenever they have not directly requested it, the program manager is exerting effort to engage the stakeholders. Which of the following actions may help to engage the stakeholders?

(a) The program manager should be the champion for change in the organization
(b) The program manager and the program team members need to understand the attitudes and the agendas for each stakeholder throughout the duration of the program
(c) The program manager should understand the motivations of each stakeholder who could attempt to alter the course of the program
(d) All the above

Q18 - How often do programs use the satisfaction surveys?

(a) As a quality assurance measurement
(b) As a quality control measurement
(c) As inputs to requirement gathering
(d) As a base for rewarding the team

Q19 - The program manager Chung has been notified by the board meeting that his program is canceled due to changes in the organizational environment which have resulted in diminished program needs. Which of the following activities should be executed by Chang?

(a) Identify areas for improvement
(b) Issue the final program report
(c) Document the lessons learned
(d) All the above

Q20 - Jacob is working in program financial management and he confuses the program financial framework with the financial management plan. How can you help him?

(a) The program financial management plan expands upon the program financial framework and describes the management of items such as risk reserves, potential cash flow problems and international exchange rate fluctuations
(b) The program financial management framework expands upon the program financial plan and describes the management of items such as risk reserves, potential cash flow problems and international exchange rate fluctuations
(c) The program financial framework is a subsidiary element of the program management plan, but the financial management plan is not
(d) The program financial framework is the same as the financial management plan

Q21 - Your program in the Sab organization has five components, three projects and two subsidiary programs. What is the suitable level to govern the quality management planning?

(a) Quality management planning is governed at the program level
(b) Quality management planning is often performed at the component level and is therefore governed at that level
(c) Quality management planning is governed at the organization level
(d) Quality management planning is governed at the PMO level

Q22 - The program sponsor of the program that you are managing is discussing with you the appropriate way to oversee the program. He was thinking about having three steering committees to oversee the program from different dimensions; the benefits, the financial and the strategic objectives. What is your recommendation to the program sponsor?

(a) I will agree with his suggestion of having these three committees
(b) I will suggest adding a fourth steering committee to oversee the program from the risk standpoint
(c) I will recommend having only one steering committee for the program as this is more efficient
(d) I will recommend having no steering committee as having the program sponsor should be sufficient

Q23 - Ravi is appointed to manage a running program after the program manager left. Ravi started to gather information to understand the program details by reviewing the program documentation and meeting the key stakeholders. During his review for the resource management plan, Ravi found that the sum of human resources needed to successfully complete each component is less than the total quantity of human resources needed to complete the program. What is the most probable reason for this difference?

(a) The sum of human resources needed to successfully complete each component is less than the total quantity of human resources needed to complete the program because the resources can be reallocated between components as the components are completed
(b) The sum of human resources needed to successfully complete each component is less than the total quantity of human resources needed to complete the program because the resources can work more than eight hours a day
(c) This difference indicates wrong human resource calculation, so Ravi should review the human resource planning in detail
(d) This difference indicates wrong human resource calculation, so Ravi should report this problem before he starts managing the program

Exam 1 - Questions

Q24 - Which of the following documents include the stakeholder engagement guidelines and a detailed strategy for effective stakeholder engagement?

  (a) Stakeholder map
  (b) Stakeholder register
  (c) Stakeholder engagement plan
  (d) The power/interest grid

Q25 - Allan worked for a week with his management team to collect important information for the program charter creation. He requested the charter approval during the steering committee meeting. Unfortunately, the charter was not approved and the program was not authorized. What should Allan do with the collected information?

  (a) This information is ignored as the program charter was not approved
  (b) This information is added to the rejection report
  (c) This information is recorded and captured in a lessons learned repository
  (d) This information is captured in the issue log

Q26 - The following items are shared between the stakeholders and the risks, except:

  (a) They should be identified, studied, categorized, and tracked
  (b) They can be managed by the program team
  (c) They may be internal or external to the program
  (d) They may have a positive or negative impact on the outcome of the program

Q27 - Your program faced a hard quality audit where the auditors created a long list of non-conformances that include some quality changes.
Who is responsible for implementing all required quality changes?

  (a) The program manager
  (b) The program management office
  (c) The program component managers
  (d) The program management team

Q28 - The following statements may specify program charter, except:

  (a) The program charter formally expresses a chronological representation of a program's intended direction

(b) The program charter formally expresses the organization's vision, mission, and benefits expected to be produced by the program
(c) The program charter provides the program manager with authority for leading other subsidiary programs, projects, and related activities to be initiated
(d) The program charter defines program-specific goals and objectives in alignment with the organization's strategic plan

Q29 - Jimmy is working in his program and is facing reluctance while driving changes in the organization. He is looking for support in driving these changes, who should provide him with the required support?

(a) The component managers
(b) The program management office
(c) The subject matter experts
(d) The program sponsor

Q30 - Adam is managing a serious program in your organization. He is an experienced program manager who closed a few programs successfully in your organization. Adam is preparing to rebaseline his program. When should the program budget be rebaselined?

(a) When a new program sponsor is assigned
(b) When a new program manager is assigned
(c) When the program is cancelled
(d) When there are changes which are approved and have significant cost impacts

Q31 - Fatma is calculating the total cost of ownership for her starting program. She conducted few meetings with the projects managers and the subsidiary program managers to gather their input. She collected the development and implementation costs for all the program components and the program management costs. Which cost is she missing?

(a) The risk management cost
(b) The transition and sustainment cost
(c) The quality management cost
(d) The third-part cost

Q32 - As a program manager, and during the financial management planning, you identified financial risks.
Where should you document these risks?

(a) In the financial management plan
(b) In the risk management plan
(c) In the program financial framework
(d) In the program risk register

Q33 - Which of the following documents may contain politically and legally sensitive information, and may have access and review restrictions placed on it by the program manager?

(a) Program roadmap
(b) Stakeholder register
(c) Program management plan
(d) Transition plan

Q34 - James is writing his first program governance plan. He asked you to provide him with some examples. Which of the following may be included in your example of the program governance plan?

(a) A schedule of anticipated program-related governance meetings
(b) The structure and composition of the group of governance participants and the definitions of the roles and responsibilities of key stakeholders
(c) List of governance key dependencies, assumptions, and constraints
(d) All the above

Q35 - Chao has just finished the transition activities of his program after three years of hard working. He is currently working on getting the official program closure. Which of the following factors may he consider to obtain the formal closure?

(a) The clearance of all opened program issues
(b) The mitigation of all opened risks with high impact and high probability
(c) The judgment of the approved business case, actual program outcomes, and the current goals and strategic objectives of the organization
(d) The clearance of all the requested change requests

Q36 - The Sodim organization is thinking about creating a program to manage the organization transformation. Because of the limited information, time and resources available, it is difficult to develop a highly detailed or accurate cost estimate for this program. Therefore, Sodim uses a rough order of magnitude to estimate the program cost. What is your advice to Sodim?

(a) This initial rough order-of-magnitude estimate is a good option as it allows financial decision makers in Sodim to decide if the program should be funded
(b) This initial rough order-of-magnitude estimate is misleading and should be avoided for a proper estimate
(c) Sodim should find internal resources to execute the required analysis and create an accurate estimate
(d) Sodim should recruit external resources to execute the required analysis and create an accurate estimate

Q37 - John is a program manager in your organization, he is creating a procurement management setup to control all the component procurements at the program level. One of the component managers was not happy with this process and wanted to control the procurement of his component on the component level. He came to you asking for advice. What is your advice to him?

(a) I will advise him to reject the procurement process imposed by the program manager on his component level
(b) I will advise him to escalate the subject to the program sponsor
(c) It is common to direct, centralize and conduct all the procurements on the program-level team rather than to individual components
(d) It is not usual that all procurements are centralized on the program level as some components may have their own procurements special requirements

Q38 - All the following activities belong to benefits sustainment, except:

(a) Monitoring the performance of the product, service, capability, or results from reliability and availability-for-use perspective
(b) Monitoring the continued suitability of the deployed product, service, capability, or results
(c) Review of applicable contractual agreements
(d) Implementing the required change efforts to ensure that the capabilities provided during the course of the program continue when the program is closed

Q39 - All the following are considered part of the effective program governance, except:

(a) Executing reviews and health checks of the program progress
(b) Evaluating opportunities and threats affecting benefits, including updating the benefits register for new opportunities and risks affecting benefits

(c) Facilitating the engagement of program stakeholders by establishing clear expectations for each program's interactions with key governing stakeholders throughout the program
(d) Making decisions to transition between phases, terminate, or close the program

Q40 - George is developing a document that graphically depicts dependencies between major milestones and decision points. Which document is this?

(a) The program schedule
(b) The milestone list
(c) The program roadmap
(d) The program management plan

Q41 - Question Set (1/2) - Ahmed is assigned as a program PMO and he is looking after the Ad-Val program which is a critical program in his organization. He noticed that the program team is confused about their roles and responsibilities. So, he decided to review all the program roles and responsibilities, which document should Ahmed review?

(a) Program Communication Plan
(b) Stakeholder Engagement Plan
(c) Program Governance Plan
(d) Program Organization Chart

Q42 - Question Set (2/2) - Ahmed is assigned as a program PMO and he is looking after the Ad-Val program which is a critical program in his organization. He noticed that the program team is confused about their roles and responsibilities. After he reviewed the roles and responsibilities, he decided to update them with the program team main players and then get the required approval.
Who should approve these roles and responsibilities?

(a) Program steering committee
(b) Program sponsor
(c) Program management office
(d) Corporate PMO

Q43 - When is the program manager usually selected and assigned?

(a) During the formulation subphase
(b) During the planning subphase

(c) During the delivery phase
(d) Before the program is initiated

Q44 - You have five phase-gates in your program as follows:
Phase-gate 1 in Jan-2019, Phase-gate 2 in Apr-2019, Phase-gate 3 in Dec-2019, Phase-gate 4 in Jan-2020, and Phase-gate 5 in Feb-2020.
You have a request from the governing body in your organization to add a health check in your governance plan. Where is the best schedule to add a program health check?

(a) Between phase-gate 1 and phase-gate2
(b) Between phase-gate 2 and phase-gate3
(c) At phase-gate 4
(d) At phase-gate 5

Q45 - Lee, the project manager, is managing a component in your program came asking you to provide him with a component contingency reserve to handle risk responses. What is your right answer to Anil?

(a) I will provide him with a reasonable contingency reserve to handle component-level risk responses
(b) I will tell him that the component-level risk responses will be handled by the contingency reserves at the program level
(c) I will tell him that he does not need to have a contingency reserve to handle risks as this should be included in the component budget
(d) I will ask him to raise a change request

Q46 - Omar is a program manager executing a program whose main objective is to create a very competitive thermal camera. During the program phase-gate review, the program steering committee found that the program is not likely to deliver its expected benefits due to rapid technology change in the competitive market of the thermal cameras. What decision should be taken by the steering committee?

(a) The steering committee should request the program manage to activate the change management process
(b) The steering committee should request a business case review
(c) The steering committee should take the hard decision to terminate the program
(d) The steering committee should request the program manager to create a recovery plan for the situation

Q47 - Lee is working in the program schedule management planning where he just created the initial program master time schedule.
What is usually expected in the initial program master time schedule?

(a) The order and start/end dates of components and their key interdependencies with other components
(b) The detailed component benefits realization
(c) The program transition plan details
(d) The initial component schedules including the component deliverables

Q48 - Miguel is managing a program that is related to public works in order to create roads between three major cities. The benefits to be realized by this program are examples of:

(a) Benefits to be realized at the end of the program
(b) Benefits to be realized incrementally during the program life cycle
(c) Benefits to be realized after the program is closed
(d) Benefits to be realized at the beginning of the program

Q49 - You are appointed to manage a program which is a joint effort between the Happy organization and its competitor Driving organization. It was agreed between the two organizations that Happy will fund 60% of the required funding and Driving will fund 40%. You are defining the governance plan and working with the senior management in both organizations to establish steering committee(s) for the program. What is your best recommendation?

(a) I will recommend having one joint steering committee for both Happy and Driving organizations
(b) I will recommend having one steering committee for the Happy organization as it is funding 60% of the program funding
(c) I will recommend having three steering committees; one for the Happy organization, another for the Driving organization, and the third as a joint steering committee for both Happy and Driving organizations
(d) I will recommend having only one steering committee for the program as this is more efficient

Q50 - Which of the following documents is approved first?

(a) The program charter
(b) The program management plan

(c) The program roadmap
(d) The program business case

Q51 - Who should evaluate the fitness for use of the benefits delivered by the program?

(a) The program manager
(b) The testing team
(c) The staff who receive it
(d) The PMO

Q52 - Ahmed was one of the executives who had high interest in your program and high level of power. During the last organization change, Ahmed was promoted to the board level role where he became less interested in your program.
According to the stakeholder map, how should you interact with Ahmed?

(a) Manage closely
(b) Keep satisfied
(c) Keep informed
(d) Monitor

Q53 - Assume that your organization is specialized in producing and exporting specific goods and services efficiently and at a lower opportunity cost than other companies. This is an example of:

(a) Opportunity cost
(b) Comparative advantage
(c) Positive risk
(d) Negative risk

Q54 - All the following tools may help in environmental analysis while managing a program, except:

(a) SWOT analysis
(b) Document analysis
(c) Assumptions analysis
(d) Historical information analysis

Q55 - Richard got the program management plan completed and approved. He started the delivery phase of his program and while going into planning details related to one of the program components, he discovered some conflicting priorities, assumptions and constraints that will influence the approved program management plan. What should he do?

(a) He should not update the program management plan as it was approved by the steering committee
(b) He should not update the program management plan as he already started the delivery phase
(c) He should not update the program management plan as he closed the planning subphase where he developed the program management plan
(d) He should apply the required updates and revisions to the program management plan and its subsidiary plans, then request approval through the Program Governance Performance Domain

Q56 - Myra, the program manager in your organization, confuses the program payment schedules with the component payment schedules. How can you help her?

(a) The component payment schedules identify the schedules and milestones where funding is received, but the program payment schedules indicate how and when contractors are paid
(b) The program payment schedules identify the schedules and milestones where funding is received, but the component payment schedules indicate how and when contractors are paid
(c) The program payment schedules are related to the payments on the program level, but the component payment schedules are related to the payments on the component level
(d) There is no difference between the program payment schedules and the component payment schedules

Q57 - Sam, an experienced program manager, joined a new organization. He was assigned a few months ago to his first program in the new organization, but he is not happy about his granted degree of autonomy for oversight of his program's components. He requested your advice, which of the following will be your best advice?

(a) I will advise him to escalate the subject to the program sponsor and ask him to review the given responsibilities to the program manager role
(b) I will advise him to escalate the subject to the program governance participants and ask them to review the given responsibilities to the program manager role
(c) I will advise him to wait until he better understood the organization culture and the rationale behind the given authority as the degree of autonomy given to the program manager for oversight of his program's components are different among organizations
(d) I will advise him to assume the responsibility that he deserves and behave accordingly

Q58 - James is very concerned about the accuracy of the information distributed within the program, so he has many meetings with his management team stressing on the accuracy of the information. What is the impact of distributing incorrect information within a program?

   (a) Incorrect information has no effect as it will be filtered by the recipient
   (b) Incorrect information has a negative impact on the program manager reputation
   (c) Incorrect information may lead to errors and incorrect decisions
   (d) Incorrect information will not lead to incorrect decisions

Q59 - All the following are established as part of the program change management principles and procedures, except:

   (a) Evaluating each requested change
   (b) The approach for capturing requested changes
   (c) Identify the source of change
   (d) Determining the disposition of each requested change

Q60 - Alberto is a new program manager. He is currently preparing the program cost estimates and he needs to know how the program cost is attributed. How can you respond to his query?

   (a) The majority of the program's cost is attributable to managing the program itself and not to the individual components within the program
   (b) The majority of the program's cost is attributable to the individual components within the program and not to manage the program itself
   (c) The majority of the program's cost is attributable to both the individual components within the program and to managing the program itself
   (d) The program's cost is attributable to the program sponsor needs as he is responsible for the program funding

Q61 - When there is a significant change in the program master schedule, which of the following program artifacts should be assessed for potential revision?

   (a) The program mandate
   (b) The program roadmap
   (c) The program charter
   (d) The program management plan

Q62 - While you are executing your program delivery phase, you noticed that there is a minor overrun in the financial. What is expected to happen in your program?

   (a) This overrun is minor, so it will be neglected
   (b) This overrun is subject to audit and management oversight and should be justified
   (c) You will be requested to decrease the expenses to overcome this overrun
   (d) Your program will be subject to cancellation

Q63 - Which of the following statements describes precisely the difference between component-level risks and program risks?

   (a) Component-level risks should be dealt with within a relatively long time frame, while program risks may be applicable to short time frame
   (b) Component-level risks should be dealt with within a relatively short time frame, while program risks may be applicable at a point in the potentially distant future
   (c) Component-level risks and program risks usually have a similar time frame
   (d) The time scale is not a factor when comparing Component-level risks and program risks

Q64 - Sam, the program manager, is preparing an announcement for the past and future customers who will be watching intently to see how well the program delivers the stated benefits. What are these customers called?

   (a) Important customers
   (b) New customers
   (c) Old customers
   (d) Potential customers

Q65 - Halinka has a financial review from the organization on the program payments. She was asked by the review team how did she make the program payments, what is the right answer of Halinka?

   (a) In accordance with the achieved benefits
   (b) In accordance with the contracts
   (c) In accordance with the invoices
   (d) In accordance with the progress

Q66 - Which of the following elements are expected to appear in the financial management plan?

   (a) Funding schedules and milestones

(b) Financial reporting activities and mechanisms
(c) Financial metrics
(d) All the above

Q67 - The FLX program is very crucial to the Good Day organization. During the program kick-off meeting, some stakeholders stressed that they need to assess the overall health of the program and take appropriate action to ensure successful benefits delivery. What is the most important action that should be done by the program manger to fulfil this request?

(a) The program manager should refine program benefits risks
(b) The program manager should ensure having a strong communication management plan
(c) The program manager should send the new status of the benefits register to the key stakeholders
(d) The program manager should consistently monitor and report on benefits metrics to the stakeholders

Q68 - Kristin is writing a document that contains the explanation defining the processes for creating, maximizing, and sustaining the program benefits. What document is Kristin writing?

(a) The benefits register
(b) The benefits management plan
(c) The benefits delivery schedule
(d) The program transition plan

Q69 - Omar is managing an Organization transformation program in the Zenon organization, one of the IT leading organizations in Silicon Valley. While working on the benefits register, Omar found one benefit which is related to consolidation of positions in the operation division, which may have a negative impact on the division staff. What should Omar do as a program manager?

(a) Omar should neglect the negative impact of the benefits as the benefits are related to the program objectives
(b) Omar should minimize the negative impact of the benefits and he should manage, measure, and properly communicate the negative impact to the organization's leadership
(c) Omar should escalate the negative impact to the program sponsor
(d) Omar should protect this information of negative impact from reaching the impacted staff

Q70 - Jason was estimating the costs of his program components. He has high uncertainty for one program component. Therefore, he calculated the component estimate as close to the beginning of a work effort as possible. A few months later, he found that the cost of the output of this component is lower than originally planned. What is the best action he can do?

(a) He should wait until he closes this component and then he can ask for a reward for the saved budget
(b) He can present an opportunity to the program sponsor for additional products that would be acquired later in the program
(c) He should open an opportunity on the risk register for the extra money
(d) He should wait until he closes this component and then he can use the budget to help the other components with budget deficiency

Q71 - Jimmy is confused about how the resources and program costs are managed on both the program level and component level, what is your advice to Jimmy?

(a) The majority of resources and program costs are managed at the program level
(b) The majority of resources and program costs are managed at the component level instead of the program level
(c) All the resources and program costs are managed at the program level
(d) All the resources and program costs are managed at the component level instead of the program level

Q72 - During your work to manage the ABC program, you noticed one stakeholder did not participate in any activity although there are three benefits that are going to affect his department. Your project manager dealing with this department assumed that he is a satisfied stakeholder and he did not participate in the program activities as he is confident about the program progress.
Incorrect assumptions about stakeholder behaviour may lead to all the following, except:

(a) Satisfied stakeholder
(b) Unanticipated issues
(c) Poor program management decisions
(d) Unhappy stakeholder

Q73 - Peter is in the definition phase of his program, he started to gather the communication requirements in order to create his communication plan. He got advice from a more experienced program manager to ensure that the communications requirements are clearly defined. What is the best reason for this advice?

(a) To create a strong communication plan

(b) To create a strong stakeholder engagement plan
(c) To facilitate the transfer of information from the program to the proper stakeholders with the proper content and delivery methods
(d) To ensure alignment between the program roadmap and the program charter

Q74 - Per is a program manager who has just created his stakeholder engagement plan including the stakeholder metrics. When should Per review the stakeholder engagement metrics?

(a) Regularly
(b) During the program closure to record the lessons learned
(c) At the time of accepting a benefit delivery
(d) In the Transition and Closure subphase

Q75 - During the last steering meeting, a decision was made to cancel the Mody program in your organization. The program manager was very disappointed as he exerted big effort to work towards achieving the program objectives. Which of the following may be the reason to cancel the Mody program?

(a) The change in technology made the product, which is delivered by one of the program components, has an obsolete architecture
(b) The change in technology made the program business case incorrect with wrong targets
(c) The program is suffering a high number of change requests
(d) The program has many open issues with high impact

Q76 - Kim is working as a program manager to the X-Tel program. He has five components which are managed by contractors. How is the baseline budget created in this case of contractors' involvement?

(a) The details of the budget come from the contracts, then the program overhead is added to the initial budget figure before a baseline budget can be prepared.
(b) The contracts constructed the baseline budget
(c) The program manager prepared his bottom-up cost regardless of the contracts
(d) The program sponsor is consulted to agree on the best approach to defining the baseline budget

Q77 - John is conducting a risk identification session in his program where he invited the program team, subject matter experts from outside the program team, and component managers. Who else should he invite?

(a) No need to invite more people, the current group is enough
(b) He should invite the program sponsor, customers, end users, stakeholders and risk management experts
(c) He should invite the program sponsor and risk management experts
(d) He has more staff than required, so he should remove the invitation for the subject matter experts from outside the program team

Q78 - Which of the following plans may have updates to reflect the needs of the program sponsor and the funding organizations' representatives with regard to financial arrangements?

(a) The program communications management plan
(b) The stakeholder engagement plan
(c) The quality management plan
(d) Options (A) and (B)

Q79 - _____ is the measure of the degree of acceptable variation around a program objective that reflects the risk appetite of the organization and program stakeholders.

(a) Risk appetite
(b) Risk exposure
(c) Risk register
(d) Risk threshold

Q80 - Milan has multiple change requests in the program that he is managing. One change request has multiple ways to implement the change, what should Milan do to select the best way?

(a) Milan should assess the costs, risks, and other aspects of each option to enable selection of the approach most likely to deliver the program's intended benefits
(b) Milan should assess the costs of each option to enable selection of the best way to execute the change
(c) Milan should assess the schedule impact of each option to enable selection of the best way to execute the change
(d) Milan should call the organization change management team to assess the different ways and provide advice

Q81 - Sam is managing a program in a Y5 organization. During his work in the delivery phase, he started to review more details regarding the program components with his team. Unfortunately, he discovered that one of the program components has more scope than planned which will affect the integration with two other components. He was angry with the component manager and came to you asking for advice, what is your best advice to him?

   (a) I will advise him to go back to the planning subphase to review all the component planning activities before continuing in the delivery phase
   (b) I will tell him that he needs to continually oversee the components throughout the delivery phase and when necessary, replan for their proper integration or realign to accommodate changes
   (c) I will tell him that he needs to continually oversee the components throughout the delivery phase and collect the pitfalls to be escalated to the steering committee
   (d) I will advise him to ignore this change as it is the mistake of the component manager

Q82 - Ahmed is preparing for a program review in which a decision will be made to end one of the program components. What is the name of the review that Ahmed is preparing?

   (a) Independent Review
   (b) Peer review
   (c) Phase-gate review
   (d) Walkthrough

Q83 - Sam is working on the program planning activity with his program management team. He started to plan for the resource management, so he conducted a meeting with the concerned stakeholders including the program quality manager.
What is the role of the program quality manager in developing the resources management plan?

   (a) The program quality manager has no role in developing the resources management plan
   (b) The program quality manager participates in the planning activity of the program resource management plan to verify that quality activities and controls are applied and flow down to all the components
   (c) The program quality manager participates in the planning activity of the program resource management plan to verify that the quality assurance and control added to the quality plan comply with the resource management plan
   (d) The program quality manager participates in the planning activity of the program resource management plan to define the changes required in the quality management plan to be aligned with the resource management plan

Q84 - Jack is a program manager in the First company. He manages an IT program to be delivered to the Healthy, which is a leading pharmaceutical organization. He is currently in the program transition phase. All preparation processes and activities within the Healthy organization that are related to ensuring that the service is received and incorporated as planned, are still not finished. Who should be responsible for completing them?

(a) Jack, the program manager
(b) Healthy organization team
(c) First company team
(d) Program steering committee

Q85 - Anil is managing his first program in your organization. He is suffering from the changes requested by some stakeholders that may affect the program schedule. Which of the following bounds the changes authorized for a program?

(a) The program scope
(b) Organizational strategy
(c) The organization risk exposure
(d) The program schedule

Q86 - Which of the following dimensions may the organization consider during the feasibility study process to decide on the proposed program?

(a) The organization's sourcing
(b) The organization's complexity
(c) The organization's financial
(d) All the above

Q87 - Michelle is working in the program closure activities in the MeanWel organization. She found some risks that are still open and may affect the realized benefits during the sustainment period which is covered by another organization; the Mena organization.
What should Michelle do to these opened risks?

(a) She should ignore them as the program activities are closed
(b) She should transfer them to the operation team of the Mena organization
(c) She should transfer these risks, along with any supporting analysis and response information, to the Mena organizational risk register
(d) She should keep them as part of the MeanWel organization risk register even if the project is closed

Q88 - While managing his program in the ABC organization, John is looking for the assessment of the ABC organization's willingness to accept and deal with risks. Which of the following is John looking for?

(a) Risk threshold
(b) Risk appetite
(c) Risk exposure
(d) Risk audit

Q89 - Which of the following areas of expertise may help the program manager in stakeholder engagement?

(a) Enterprise resource management (ERP)
(b) Customer relationship management (CRM)
(c) Knowledge management system (KMS)
(d) Information management system

Q90 - VK is a program manager who detected some changes in his program. He started to update the benefits management plan, what is the other important document that he should update with the benefits management plan update?

(a) Program Roadmap
(b) Benefits register
(c) Program governance
(d) Business case

Q91 - The following items are included in the program business case, except:

(a) Financial analysis
(b) Stakeholders influence
(c) Intrinsic and extrinsic benefits
(d) Market demands or barriers

Q92 - Santiago is the program manager assigned to manage one program in your organization that has three projects and one subsidiary program. He executed the program planning subphase and now he wants to initiate his first program component, which is the Leen project. He is seeking your help to advise him about the proper action. What is your advice?

(a) Wait until all the components are ready, then request their authorization from the steering committee

(b) Wait until he has all the components ready, then request their authorization from the program management office
(c) Request the authorization for the new program component from the steering committee
(d) Request the authorization for the new program component from the program management office

Q93 - When are the program benefits expected to exceed program costs?

(a) Program benefits are expected to exceed program costs at the project completion
(b) Program benefits are expected to exceed program costs at the project completion if the program is successful
(c) Program benefits are expected to exceed program costs over the time, as specified in the business case
(d) Program benefits are expected to exceed program costs over the time, as specified in the transition plan

Q94 - After you approve the program change request, which of the following activities should be executed?

(a) Communicate the change request to appropriate stakeholders
(b) Record the change request in the program change log
(c) Reflect in updates to component plans
(d) All the above

Q95 - Ahmed is working on his program closure. He has three components which are officially closed. He is transferring the responsibility of the operation and maintenance or the program benefits to the operation team who lack the skills of the new technology used in one of the program components. If Ahmed needs to release the resources of the program components as part of the program closure. What is the best choice that he should do for these resources?

(a) He should try to transfer some of the resources who have the skills of the new technology to the operation team
(b) He will release the resources from the program components regardless of their next move
(c) He will release the resources from the program components and transfer their allocation responsibility to the program sponsor
(d) He will release the resources from the program components and transfer their allocation responsibility to the operation team

Q96 - Prior to program closure, Fatma, the program manager, is developing a document to identify the program risks, processes, measures, metrics, and tools necessary to ensure the continued realization of the benefits delivered. Which document is this?

(a) Benefits register
(b) Benefits management plan
(c) Benefits sustainment plan
(d) Benefits transition plan

Q97 - Mustafa is assigned to manage the Yen program after the previous program manager was promoted to another position in your organization. Mustafa is looking for the list of planned benefits for the Yen program. Which document should Mustafa refer to?

(a) The benefits management plan
(b) The program management plan
(c) The benefits register
(d) The program charter

Q98 - Aisa is writing the program governance and is adding some elements related to the program success criteria. Which of the following is the best description of these criteria?

(a) The criteria describe the definition of success consistent with the expectations and needs of key program stakeholders
(b) The criteria describe the definition of success consistent with the program objectives
(c) The criteria describe the definition of success consistent with the needs of key program stakeholders
(d) The criteria describe the definition of success consistent with the expectations and needs of key program stakeholders, and reinforce the program alignment to deliver the maximum attainable benefits

Q99 - Per is working with a stakeholder analysis tool that groups the stakeholders based on their level of authority and their level of concern regarding the project outcomes. Which tools is this?

(a) The stakeholder map
(b) The stakeholder register
(c) The power/interest grid
(d) The stakeholder cube

Exam 1 - Questions

Q100 - Oscar is working on a component of the program management plan that includes the information management policies and distribution lists, which subsidiary plan is this?

(a) The program communication management plan
(b) The program information management plan
(c) The program change management plan
(d) The program schedule management plan

Q101 - Ahmed is managing his first program in the Uni-Corn organization. His program is the only program managed as stand-alone outside the existing two organization portfolio structures. Ahmed started to develop his program governance plan. He wants to align the program governance with the governance of the organization governing body, but he got an advice from an older program manager to align the program governance with one of the existing two portfolios governance.
What should Ahmed do?

(a) Ahmed should align his program governance with any of the existing portfolio governance
(b) Ahmed should align his program governance with the more complicated existing portfolio governance
(c) Ahmed can align his program governance with any of the existing portfolio governance or with the governance of the organization governing body
(d) Ahmed should align his program governance with the governance of the organization governing body

Q102 - Ahmed started to review and evaluate the acceptance criteria applicable to delivered components, review operational and program process documentation, and review training and maintenance materials. Which phase of the benefits delivery is he working on?

(a) Benefits identification
(b) Benefits transition
(c) Benefits delivery
(d) Benefits sustainment

Q103 - How should the program manager deal with resources which are no longer necessary for the program?

(a) The program manager should create work for these resources to make their work necessary for the program

(b) The program manager should seek consultation or advice from the program sponsor
(c) The program manager should keep the resources until the program ends even if they are no longer necessary for the program
(d) The program manager ensures resources are released for other programs when they are no longer necessary for the current program

Q104 - Linda is working on a program activity that creates the program change thresholds, which activity is this?

(a) Program change management planning
(b) Program change assessment
(c) Program change monitoring and controlling
(d) Program scope assessment

Q105 - Governance of programs in the diverse fields may have remarkably different needs based on the unique political, regulatory, legal, technical, and competitive environments in which they operate. In such cases, what is the most important common rule of governance between the different fields?

(a) The risk management
(b) A sponsor organization seeks to implement governance practices that enable the organization to monitor the program's support of the organizational strategy
(c) A sponsor organization seeks to implement governance practices that enable the organization to manage the risks properly
(d) The benefits realization to be assured

Q106 - How do usually the program stakeholders view the program benefits?

(a) As a positive risk
(b) As a change
(c) As an opportunity
(d) As an issue to be resolved

Q107 - What of the following are valid program funding models?

(a) Supported by internal and external sources of funding
(b) Funded entirely within a single organization
(c) Managed within a single organization but funded separately

(d) All the above

Q108 - How often does the program management deal with the program resources?

(a) Resources are often shared among different components within a program
(b) Resources are often fully dedicated to one component
(c) Resources are often dedicated to a maximum of two components
(d) Resources are often shared between maximum two components within the program

Q109 - How do the organizations consider their resources?

(a) Organization assets to execute the programs, projects, and operation
(b) One of the organization limiting factors
(c) Organization constraint
(d) All the above

Q110 - Who is responsible to ensure alignment of the individual component plans with the program's goals and intended benefits in support of the achievement of the organization's strategy?

(a) The program manager
(b) The component manager
(c) The program sponsor
(d) The whole program team

Q111 - Anil is writing the program charter for his first time and needs some help. Which of the following items can you suggest to Anil to include in the charter?

(a) High-level benefits
(b) Assumptions and constraints
(c) Key stakeholders
(d) All the above

Q112 - Anil is part of the strategy board in your organization. He is working with his board members to define the organization's strategic plan. Which of the following factors may influence the strategic plan?

(a) Shareholders

(b) Competitor plans and actions
(c) Customer and partner requests
(d) All the above

Q113 - All the following information is expected to appear in the stakeholder register, except:

(a) Stakeholder's name and role in the program
(b) Stakeholder's degree of support for the program
(c) Stakeholder's span of control
(d) Stakeholder's ability to influence the program outcome

Q114 - Omar is working as a program manager to manage a program that consists of four projects and one subsidiary program. During the execution of this program, some changes were applied to the industry regulations that mandates changes to three components.
What is your best choice to have an optimal contract(s) that supports your program to comply with these regulations?

(a) It is good to have three different contracts with three different companies for the three different components to implement the required changes
(b) It is optimal to have three different contracts with one company for the three different components to implement the required change
(c) It will be optimal to award one complete contract to implement the required changes in the three components
(d) I will check with the program sponsor to get his advice to have one contract or three contracts

Q115 - Santiago is a program manager in your organization, he created a strong procurement management to control all the component procurements at the program level. He decided to administer all the program contracts at the program level. What will be the role of the component managers in contract administration?

(a) Component managers have no role in the contract administration if the program contracts are administered at the program level
(b) Component managers accept invoices for component contract payments
(c) Component managers report deliverable acceptance and contract changes
(d) Component managers pay for the contract changes

Q116 - Miguel is expecting turbulences in his program coming from the anticipated regulation changes that will lead to major changes in two of his program components. He arranged a meeting with the two component managers and the EPMO to discuss the subject and agree on a decision. Which of the following is the best decision that they can make?

- (a) Ignore the anticipated change as it is still not happening
- (b) Take the anticipated change into account to continue alignment with the organization's strategic goals and objectives
- (c) Register this expected change as a risk in the relevant program component
- (d) Escalate the problem to the next program steering committee

Q117 - What is the primary objective of stakeholders' engagement?

- (a) Gain and maintain stakeholder buy-in for the program's objectives, benefits, and outcomes
- (b) Involve stakeholders in quality analysis reviews
- (c) Involve stakeholders in goal setting
- (d) Establish direct and indirect communication among the stakeholder and the program's leaders and team

Q118 - You are currently creating your program stakeholder engagement plan, which of the following aspects should be considered for each stakeholder?

- (a) His culture to deal with his subordinates
- (b) Attitudes about the program and its sponsor
- (c) His span of control
- (d) All the above

Q119 - After being assigned as program manager for X-Tel program, Per is reviewing the program major artifacts and started to document factors that, for planning purposes, are considered true, real, or certain. What are these factors?

- (a) They are the program assumptions
- (b) They are the enterprise environmental factors
- (c) They are the program constraints
- (d) They are the program risks

Q120 - The program sponsor is writing a document to authorize the program management team to use organizational resources, in order to execute the program. Which document is this?

- (a) The program mandate

(b) The program business case
(c) The program charter
(d) The program roadmap

Q121 - Sam is writing a risk to the risk register that arises as a direct outcome of implementing the risk response. What is the name of this risk?

(a) Secondary risk
(b) Residual risk
(c) Positive risk
(d) Black swan risk

Q122 - Simon defined his components cost estimation during the program Definition phase. Now during the Benefits Delivery phase, Simon discovered that his estimation is not accurate enough for one of his components and he found that the budget for this component is more than required. What is the best choice for Simon?

(a) Simon will discuss the subject with the component manager to get a solution
(b) Simon may present an opportunity to the sponsor for additional products that would be acquired later in the program
(c) Simon should create a positive risk in the risk register
(d) Simon may use this extra budget to reward the good performance program team

Q123 - Jack is managing a program in the Hola organization. During his planning activities, he found some of the services required for his program are offered by the Hola organization. He came asking you for advice on how to acquire this service, what is your best reply?

(a) I will advise him to follow the program procurement management plan
(b) I will advise him to follow the organization procurement management plan
(c) I will advise him to contact the service owner in Hola and agree with him on how to acquire the services as per the policies and procedures within the Hola organization
(d) I will advise him not to acquire service from within the organization

Q124 - A program is closed either because the program charter is fulfilled or internal/external conditions arise that bring the program to an early end. Which of the following may be one of these conditions?

(a) Open issues that need to be contained during the sustainment phase
(b) Missed milestones that were rescheduled after the transition to production

(c) Changes in the business case that no longer make the program necessary
(d) Some major risks that cannot be mitigated and the program management decided to accept them

Q125 - Sylwia is a program manager who managed many programs during her experience. She noticed that the timing of funding has a direct impact on a program's ability to perform, but she did not grasp the objective of financing in program development. What is your explanation to Sylwia?

(a) The objective of financing in program development is to minimize the risk if the program fails
(b) The objective of financing in program development is to share the risk of failure with another entity
(c) The objective of financing in program development is to share the profit with another entity
(d) The objective of financing in program development is to obtain funds to bridge the gap between paying out monies for development and obtaining the benefits of the programs

Q126 - Aisa is working to establish common high-level expectations for the program stakeholders regarding the delivery of the program's benefits. Which of the following actions is the best to be done by Aisa?

(a) Provide stakeholders with detailed program status on a regular basis
(b) Provide stakeholders with summary information from the program charter and program business case
(c) Provide stakeholders with appropriate information contained in the program charter and program business case, and provide an accompanying executive brief to summarize the details of the risks, dependencies, and benefits
(d) Provide the stakeholders with the details of the benefits register

Q127 - Harish started to establish the benefits management plan, define and prioritize program components, and define the key performance indicators required to monitor the delivery of program benefits. Which stage or phase of the benefits management is he executing?

(a) Benefits delivery
(b) Benefits identification
(c) Benefits analysis and planning
(d) Benefits transition

Q128 - Pierre is a new appointed program manager. He is managing his first program in the X-Com organization. Pierre started to meet the program stakeholders to gather their expectations. He was confused and came to you asking how to manage the stakeholders. What is your advice to him?

(a) My advice to Pierre is to create a strong stakeholder management plan
(b) My advice to Pierre is to create a stakeholder engagement plan
(c) My advice to Pierre first is to categorize the stakeholders before developing the stakeholder management plan
(d) My advice to Pierre is that he should manage the stakeholder expectations rather than the stakeholders themselves

Q129 - When is usually the stakeholder engagement active during the different phases of the program life cycle?

(a) Stakeholder engagement is active during the planning phase of the program
(b) Stakeholder engagement is a continuous program activity, so it is running during the whole program life cycle
(c) Stakeholder engagement is active during the program planning subphase
(d) Stakeholder engagement is active during the stakeholder engagement planning

Q130 - Chao is working in the program planning activities with his program team. He is creating the program work breakdown structure with the help of the component managers and technical leads. He went deep in the WBS decomposition even to the fifth level of the components. What is your advice to Chao?

(a) I will advise him to stop decomposition as level five of the components is good enough
(b) I will advise him to stop decomposition at the first two levels of the components
(c) I will advise him to continue decomposition to level ten of the components
(d) I will advise him to review the subject with the component managers and agree on the decomposition level

Q131 - During the benefits realization, there may be a window of opportunity for the realization of a planned benefit and for that benefit to generate real value.
Who may determine if the window of opportunity was met or compromised by actual events in the program or component?

(a) The program manager
(b) The program steering committee

(c) The key stakeholders
(d) All the above

Q132 - You are managing the O3 program in your organization. During the regular team meeting, you were informed that the purchasing department manager is reluctant to send his team for the training session as per the agreed upon schedule. The subsidiary program manager added that this is not the first time that this manager represents a negative contribution to the O3 program. What should be your right action?

(a) I should meet the purchasing department manager and put some pressure on him to recover the missed training session
(b) I should meet the purchasing department manager, work to minimize any negative impact on him as a result of the O3 program and work to mitigate the effect of his negative contribution
(c) I should meet the purchasing department manager and threaten him to escalate the subject to the steering committee
(d) I should escalate the subject to the steering committee and use the committee power to enforce this stakeholder to respect the program schedule activities

Q133 - Marcie is managing the REF program in her organization. She has a meeting with a group of participants representing various program-related interests with the purpose of supporting the program under its authority by providing guidance, endorsements, and approvals through the governance practices. Which group is this?

(a) Change control board
(b) Board of director
(c) Program steering committee
(d) Regulatory agencies

Q134 - The program manager should deal with the stakeholders using all the following options, except:

(a) Be aware of the stakeholders' impact
(b) Understand the stakeholders' level of influence
(c) Manage the stakeholders' expectation
(d) Manage the stakeholders

Q135 - You are assigned to execute a critical program in your organization, the program infrastructure includes a risk manager who was appointed by the governing body. When you started to apply major program scope change, the risk manager requested to repeat the risk management planning in order to accommodate this change. What is your reply to him?

(a) I will tell him that risk management planning is executed once during the program definition phase and there is no need to repeat it again
(b) I will escalate the subject to the governing board to get their feedback
(c) I will let him repeat the program risk planning to accommodate the major change introduced to the program
(d) I will involve the PMO to judge if there is a need to repeat the risk management planning again

Q136 - Ahmed is working in the risk management activities of Program JEK. He executed the risk identification for the third time in the program and added the identified risks to the risk register. Which of the following statements describes the iteration of the risk identification correctly?

(a) Risk identification is an iterative activity where the frequency of iteration is ten times maximum in any program
(b) Risk identification is an iterative activity where the frequency of iteration and involvement of participants may vary
(c) Risk identification is an iterative activity where the involvement of participants is usually the same within the same program
(d) Risk identification is an iterative activity that may be repeated within the definition and delivery phases only

Q137 - Santiago is managing an important program in your organization. He was working on the program scope monitoring and controlling where he went down to the program level to see the impact of the suggested change on the component scope. What is your advice to Santiago?

(a) I will advise Santiago to manage the scope of the components as well as he manages the scope of the program to ensure program benefits realization as planned
(b) I will advise Santiago to restrict his activities to managing scope only to the allocated level for components and avoid controlling component scope
(c) I will advise Santiago to restrict his activities to managing scope only to the allocated level for components and should avoid controlling component scope unless there is a major change
(d) I will advise Santiago to restrict his activities to managing scope only to the program level and not to look at the component levels as they are managed by the component managers

Q138 - Simon is working in the program schedule management planning activities. He created the program high level schedule and is looking for some documents to help him with the delivery dates and major milestones. Which document(s) do you suggest to Simon?

(a) The program roadmap
(b) The program charter
(c) The program roadmap and the program charter
(d) The component schedules

Q139 - Which of the following stakeholder aspects are important for the stakeholder analysis and engagement planning?

(a) Attitudes about the program and its sponsors
(b) Relevant phase(s) applicable to stakeholders' specific engagement
(c) The expectation of program benefits delivery
(d) All the above

Q140 - Richard is the program manager for one critical program in his organization. Richard requested his program management team to send him the communication that they want to distribute to certain key stakeholders. Richard wants to review these communications and provide his team with his input before the distribution. Why is Richard doing that?

(a) He is doing that because an incorrect message to an audience may cause problems for the program and in some cases, lead to the stoppage of a program
(b) He is doing that because he is applying the quality assurance processes
(c) He is doing that because he is applying an autocratic leadership style
(d) He is doing that because he is not trusting his team

Q141 - Ming is currently in the program closure phase, he found that the charter is fulfilled and operations are not necessary to continue realization of ongoing benefits. What should he do for the transition activities?

(a) Ming should review the program roadmap to see what he has to do
(b) Ming should terminate the program with no transition to operations
(c) Ming should terminate the program after executing the transition to operations
(d) Ming should consult the program management office on what he should do

Q142 - Nilson is working on the Kom program which is expected to run for three years. After one year of hard working in the program, Nilson found that the initial cost estimates for the Geo project, which is one of the program components, is less than what it should be. This was discovered after practical understanding for the program current environment. What should Nilson do?

(a) Nilson should halt the program execution until he audits all the components estimated costs
(b) Nilson should update the cost estimate to reflect the current environment considerations
(c) Nilson should ask the PMO to review all the program components costs
(d) Nilson should ask the team who originally estimated the program cost to meet and review again all of their estimations

Q143 - The business case of the GenWin program was developed by the portfolio organization. During the program formulation and after the program manager is assigned, more analysis was executed to determine the priority of the GenWin program and the program manager found elements to be updated in the business case. What is the right action to be done?

(a) Keep the business case as it is because it was developed by the portfolio management which is a higher authority than the program management
(b) The business case should be revised and updated according to the new information
(c) Hold the update as more updates may be collected during the planning subphase of the delivery phase
(d) The business case should not be updated, the requested update will be included in the program charter

Q144 - Fatma is performing the initial program planning with her team, during the initial program risk assessment, she identified risk related to strategy alignment. Which of the following risks may be related to strategy alignment?

(a) Program roadmap not aligned with organizational roadmap
(b) Program roadmap not supportive of portfolio roadmaps
(c) Program objectives not supportive of organizational objectives
(d) All the above

Q145 - Chung was preparing a plan that is used as a response to a risk that has occurred and the primary response proves to be inadequate. Which plan is this?

(a) Risk management plan
(b) Fallback plan
(c) Contingency plan

(d) Financial management plan

Q146 - Milan wants to measure the performance of the stakeholders' engagement. He met his project managers and subsidiary program manager to create some metrics.
What are the primary metrics for stakeholder engagement should he consider?

(a) Stakeholder participation
(b) Frequency or rate of communication with the program team
(c) Positive contributions to the realization of the program's objectives and benefits,
(d) All the above

Q147 - Chao has completed his first program a few months ago. That program was created to develop the benefits at one time which is at the program completion. Now, Chao is requested to manage a new program that will deliver benefits on a regular basis. Chao is planning to utilize the same governance that he applied in the first program and he is asking you for advice. What will you recommend to him?

(a) I will advise him to change the governance of the old program before applying it to the new program as the benefits realization are coming in increments in the new program rather than one time as the old one
(b) I will advise him to keep the governance of the old program and to apply it to the new program with minor changes if needed
(c) I will advise him to keep the governance of the old program and to apply it to the new program as there is no expected difference in governance between the two programs because of the different benefits realization plans
(d) I will advise him to use the governance of the old program as it was proved to be successful in the execution of the first program

Q148 - After Kathy had created the benefits register in her program with the help of the component managers and key team members, what is the next step to be done?

(a) Review the benefits register with the program sponsor
(b) Review the benefits register with the key stakeholders to develop the appropriate performance measures
(c) Develop the benefits management plan
(d) Start the benefits delivery phase

Q149 - Which of the following statements is describing the program benefit accurately?

(a) A benefit is the gains and assets realized by the organization only as the result of outcomes delivered by the program
(b) A benefit is the outcome of the program
(c) A benefit is the gains and assets realized by the organization and other stakeholders as the result of outcomes delivered by the program
(d) A benefit is produced by the output as a desired operational result

Q150 - Which of the following artifacts serves as the framework for developing the program master schedule and defines the program manager's management control points?

(a) The program WBS
(b) The program component schedule
(c) The program charter
(d) The program benefits realization plan

Q151 - The program manager is further defining program benefits and adding more details. Which of the following aspects is the most important for him/her to consider?

(a) The program manager should refine program benefits risks and quantify new benefits risks
(b) The program manager should review the benefits register
(c) The program manager should send the new status of the benefits register to the key stakeholders
(d) The program manager should freeze the changes to the benefits register

Q152 - Adrian was assigned to one program in his organization. He created his program communication management plan and started to execute it. After he distributed his program weekly report, he got some communication from one of the program stakeholders asking for more details about one specific deliverable. In general, what should be the response of Adrian when he got communication from one or more of the stakeholders?

(a) Communication should be a one-way information flow with the stakeholder. So, Adrian should ignore the stakeholder's communication unless he has a query to be answered
(b) Adrian should review his program communication plan and respond accordingly
(c) Adrian should gather, analyze and distribute the communications received from the stakeholders back within the program as required
(d) Adrian should consult his program key influencer to reach an agreement on his probable feedback in similar cases

Q153 - Adam is preparing the program reporting to send it to the key stakeholders as per the communications management plan. One of his component managers was confused with the purpose of having the program reporting. What should Adam tell him?

(a) He should tell him that the program reporting provides the stakeholders with information about major program change requests
(b) He should tell him that the program reporting provides the stakeholders with information about milestone status
(c) He should tell him that the program reporting provides the stakeholders with information about how resources are being used to deliver program benefits
(d) He should tell him that the program reporting is part of the communications governance that should be followed

Q154 - What do we call those risks that have been deliberately accepted?

(a) Secondary risks
(b) Negative risks
(c) Positive risks
(d) Residual risks

Q155 - Which of the following statements describes the responsibilities of the program manager and the component manager in resource management?

(a) The program manager manages resources at the program level only
(b) Only the component managers are working in managing resources at the component level
(c) The program manager manages resources at the program level and at the component level
(d) The program manager manages resources at the program level and works with the component managers who manage resources at the component level

Q156 - Why is the stakeholder engagement a continuous program activity?

(a) Because the change requests are affecting the program scope
(b) Because the list of stakeholders and their attitudes and opinions change as the program progresses and delivers benefits
(c) To accommodate any new requirements
(d) To deal with the changing environment around the program

Q157 - Ahmed is currently in the Benefits Delivery phase of his program where he aggregates all performance information across projects and non-project activity to provide a clear picture of the program performance as a whole. Which activity does Ahmed execute?

(a) Program information distribution activity
(b) Program reporting activity
(c) Components reporting activity
(d) Program audit

Q158 - After Hong, the program manager, got the steering committee approval on the program charter, which phase or subphase should she start?

(a) She should start the component oversight and integration
(b) She should start the program delivery
(c) She should start the program formation
(d) She should start the program planning

Q159 - Mohamed started to manage his first program in the Fajr organization. He started to create a document that justifies the need for a program by defining how a program's expected outcomes would support the organization's strategic goals and objectives. Which document is Mohamed working on?

(a) Mohamed is working on the program charter
(b) Mohamed is working on the program business case
(c) Mohamed is working on the program roadmap
(d) Mohamed is working on the program management plan

Q160 - What is the most important reason for you as a program manager to define a robust program risk management strategy?

(a) Program risk management strategy defines ways to control risks in the watch list
(b) Program risk management strategy drives consistency and effectiveness in program risk management activities throughout the program as part of program integration and supporting activities
(c) Program risk management strategy assesses the required risk categories to be used through-out the program life cycle
(d) Program risk management strategy defines the risk responses required for major risks

Q161 - If your program received the required budget and now begins paying expenses, what is the role of the financial activities?

(a) No need for financial activities as the budget was approved
(b) The financial effort will focus on reporting
(c) The financial effort moves into tracking, monitoring, and controlling the program's funds and expenditures
(d) The financial effort will focus on the component level

Q162 - Sam, the program manager, is working closely with the program sponsor and key stakeholders to develop a document that is used to assess the program's investment against the intended benefits. Which document is Sam working on?

(a) The program charter
(b) The program management plan
(c) The program business case
(d) The program stakeholder register

Q163 - Which of the following are factors to be considered when optimizing and tailoring program governance?

(a) Decision-making hierarchy
(b) Program funding structure
(c) Risk of failure
(d) All the above

Q164 - Question Set (1/2) - Your organization assigned you to manage a program that is required to develop the matching engine for a stock exchange. One of your stakeholders is curious about the program and often raises many questions. You as a program manager, are preparing efficient answers to his question. As a program approach how should you deal with these communications with the very active stakeholder?

(a) These communications with the active stakeholder should be captured and published in a way that will allow multiple stakeholders to benefit from them
(b) Only the part of these communications which is reviewed and accepted by the program sponsor will be published in a way that will allow multiple stakeholders to benefit from them

(c) Only the part of these communications which is reviewed and accepted by the program governance board will be published in a way that will allow multiple stakeholders to benefit from them

(d) These communications are between specific stakeholders and the program manager and should be kept private to these stakeholders

Q165 - Question Set (2/2) - Your organization assigned you to manage a program that is required to develop the matching engine for a stock exchange. One of your stakeholders is curious about the program and often raises many questions. You, as a program manager, are preparing efficient answers to his question. If you decide to share these communications with other stakeholders, what is the best approach to deliver this information?

(a) These communications need to be formatted and presented in two packages; one for an internal group and another for an external group
(b) These communications need to be formatted and presented in one package for all stakeholders
(c) These communications need to be formatted and presented differently for certain stakeholder groups to keep their interest in reviewing them
(d) As stated earlier, there is no need to share this information

Q166 - Fatma is managing a program in the Cell organization. She is executing the program delivery phase and working on the risk management. Fatma wants to determine whether program assumptions are still valid. Which risk activity is she working on?

(a) Risk response planning
(b) Risk categorization
(c) Risk monitoring
(d) Risk identification

Q167 - Alex is managing a program that has five projects. He finished the definition phase and is currently working in the delivery phase. Alex noticed that projects are creating deliverables, but the associated benefits are not realized at the program level, he was trying to understand the reason behind this problem. What is the most probable reason to have this problem?

(a) The program is missing the consolidation of the integration efforts of the program components
(b) This program has no benefits to realize, but it has deliverables at the component level
(c) The program benefits are usually realized at the end of the program
(d) The program is missing the roadmap

Exam 1 - Questions

Q168 - Omar is in the execution of the Benefits Delivery phase, he knows that the resulting benefits review requires analysis of the planned versus actual benefits across a wide range of factors, but he doesn't know which item is most important to start with. How can you help him?

(a) Value delivery
(b) CPI and SPI values for the program components
(c) Program Change request status
(d) Program performance status

Q169 - Zia is executing his first program ABC in Q-Lon company. He is executing the program strategy alignment process and became confident that the charter, business case, and roadmap are all aligned together. He asked you when to end the program strategy alignment process, what is your right answer?

(a) As the charter, business case and roadmap are all aligned together, Zia can end the program strategy alignment process immediately
(b) The program strategy alignment process should run until the end of the program life cycle
(c) The program strategy alignment process is performed during the formulation subphase, then it can be terminated
(d) Zia should wait until the program management plan is created to ensure that no updates are required which could affect the strategy alignment

Q170 - Jacob presented one of his program components to the steering committee in order to approve the component initiation. After reviewing the details of the component authorization, the steering committee approved the component authorization. After the meeting, Jacob started to redefine the priorities of existing program components. Why did Jacob start this redefinition?

(a) To ensure optimal resource allocation and management of interdependencies
(b) To review the dependencies between the new component and the other existing components
(c) To ensure that none of the existing components should be closed
(d) To review the progress of the existing components and select the right timing to present the new component

2. Exam 1 – Questions and Answers

Q1 - Marcos is suffering from low participation from the stakeholders in his program. He wants to identify potential risks caused by a lack of participation from stakeholders. What should he do?

   (a) He should review stakeholder metrics regularly
   (b) He should review the stakeholder engagement plan regularly
   (c) He should review the stakeholder register regularly
   (d) He should review the stakeholder map regularly

Question Category: Difficult
The right answer is Option (A)
The Standards for Program Management - 4th Edition - reference: Chapter (5), Program Stakeholder Engagement, 5.4 PROGRAM STAKEHOLDER ENGAGEMENT, page 65
Clarification and Tips:
The program manager should review stakeholder metrics regularly to identify potential risks caused by a lack of participation from stakeholders, so Option (A) is the right answer.
Options (B), (C), and (D) are wrong suggestions to identify potential risks caused by a lack of participation from stakeholders.
Domain: Stakeholder Engagement
Phase or Element: PROGRAM STAKEHOLDER ENGAGEMENT

Q2 - Kathy is looking for some help to engage the stakeholders to address the change the program will bring. What is your best advice to her?

   (a) Review the change request log regularly with the stakeholders
   (b) Submitting program status reports to the stakeholders
   (c) Engaging stakeholders to assess their readiness for change, facilitating or negotiating the approach to implement change, and obtaining and evaluating the stakeholders' feedback on the program's progress
   (d) Share open issues and emerged high risks with stakeholders

Question Category: Moderate
The right answer is Option (C)
The Standards for Program Management - 4th Edition - reference: Chapter (5), Program Stakeholder Engagement, page 60
Clarification and Tips:
The best advice to Kathy is to engage stakeholders to assess their readiness for change, facilitating or negotiating the approach to implement change, and obtaining and evaluating the stakeholders' feedback on the program's progress, so Option (C) is the right answer.

Options (A), (B) and (D) may help, but Option (C) is much better.
Domain: Stakeholder Engagement
Phase or Element: General

Q3 - As a program manager, what is the most important reason that drives you to conduct environmental analysis?

(a) Environmental analysis can be used to assess the validity of a program's business case and program management plan
(b) Environmental analysis can be used to validate the program assumptions
(c) Environmental analysis can be used to assess the program benefits realization plan
(d) Environmental analysis can be used to ensure accurate program reporting

Question Category: Moderate
The right answer is Option (A)
The Standards for Program Management - 4th Edition - reference: Chapter (3), Program Strategy Alignment, 3.4.2 ENVIRONMENTAL ANALYSIS, page 39
Clarification and Tips:
Environmental analysis can be used to assess the validity of a program's business case and program management plan, so Option (A) is the right answer.
Options (B) and (C) are considered indirect reasons to conduct the environmental analysis, but Option (A) is much better.
Option (D) is wrong as it is not a reason to use the environmental analysis.
Domain: Strategy Alignment
Phase or Element: ENVIRONMENTAL ASSESSMENTS

Q4 - Lee is working on the definition phase and is executing the program infrastructure development activity. What is meant by infrastructure in this context?

(a) The infrastructure refers to the work breakdown structure
(b) The infrastructure refers to risk breakdown structure
(c) The infrastructure refers to both personnel and to program specific tools, facilities and finances used to manage the program
(d) The infrastructure refers to the program organization chart

Question Category: Moderate
The right answer is Option (C)
The Standards for Program Management - 4th Edition - reference: Chapter (7), Program Life Cycle Management, 7.2.2.1 PROGRAM INFRASTRUCTURE DEVELOPMENT, page 99
Clarification and Tips:

Exam 1 - Questions and Answers

This infrastructure refers to both personnel and to program specific tools, facilities and finances used to manage the program. Therefore, Option (C) is the right answer.
Domain: Life Cycle Management
Phase or Element: Definition

Q5 - Which of the following is not included in the program business case?

(a) Details about the program outcomes
(b) The extent to which the program aligns with the organizations strategic objectives
(c) Market demand or barriers
(d) Major milestones

Question Category: Moderate
The right answer is Option (D)
The Standards for Program Management - 4th Edition - reference: Chapter (3), Program Strategy Alignment, 3.1 PROGRAM BUSINESS CASE, page 35
Clarification and Tips:
Options (A), (B), and (C) are items expected to appear in the program business case, but Option (D) is not. Therefore, the right answer is Option (D).
Domain: Strategy Alignment
Phase or Element: PROGRAM BUSINESS CASE

Q6 - Lucas concentrates on the program schedule to define any slippage that may delay the benefits realization. He did not pay attention to the possibility of early delivery. What is your advice to Locus?

(a) I will advise Locus to continue what he is doing as the early delivery is only a dream for the program managers which never happens
(b) I will advise Locus to concentrate on early delivery as it will compensate any slippage in the program
(c) I will advise Locus to consult the program sponsor first to see if he will accept early delivery or not
(d) I will advise Locus to identify both slippages and early deliveries as they are necessary as part of the overall program management function

Question Category: Difficult
The right answer is Option (D)
The Standards for Program Management - 4th Edition - reference: Chapter (8), Program Activities, 8.2.9 PROGRAM SCHEDULE MONITORING AND CONTROLLING, pages 136
Clarification and Tips:

www.6p-consulting.com

Identification of both slippages and early deliveries are necessary as part of the overall program management function.
Therefore, Option (D) is the right answer.
Domain: Life Cycle Management
Phase or Element: Delivery

Q7 - Which of the following can be used to achieve benefit sustainment after the program is closed?

(a) Operations and maintenance
(b) New projects
(c) New programs
(d) All the above

Question Category: Easy
The right answer is Option (D)
The Standards for Program Management - 4th Edition - reference: Chapter (7), Program Life Cycle Management, 7.2.2.4 BENEFITS SUSTAINMENT AND PROGRAM TRANSITION, page 101
Clarification and Tips:
Options (A), (B), and (C) can be used to achieve benefit sustainment after the program is closed. So the right answer is Option (D).
Domain: Life Cycle Management
Phase or Element: Closing

Q8 - Ahmed is a program manager who is currently executing the activity of evaluating overall program quality on a regular basis to provide confidence that the program will comply with the relevant quality policies and standards. Which activity is he executing?

(a) Program quality planning
(b) Program quality control
(c) Program quality assurance
(d) Program quality audit

Question Category: Moderate
The right answer is Option (C)
The Standards for Program Management - 4th Edition - reference: Chapter (8), Program Activities, 8.2.6 PROGRAM QUALITY ASSURANCE AND CONTROL, page 132
Clarification and Tips:
The description of the activity which is executed by Ahmed is the program quality assurance.

Program quality planning identifies the standards that are relevant to the program as a whole and specifies how to satisfy them across the program.

Program quality control is the activity of monitoring specific component project or component program deliverables and results to determine if they fulfill quality requirements that lead to adequate benefits realization.

Program quality audit concentrates on the program process and aims to answer the question Are we doing it right? This may be executed by external or internal as a benchmarking exercise. Therefore, the right answer is Option (C).

Domain: Life Cycle Management
Phase or Element: Delivery

Q9 - Which of the following is an example of a tangible benefit?

(a) Profit increased
(b) Brand recognition
(c) Public benefit
(d) All the above

Question Category: Moderate
The right answer is Option (A)
The Standards for Program Management - 4th Edition - reference: Chapter (4), Program Benefits Management, 4.2 BENEFITS ANALYSIS AND PLANNING, page 48
Clarification and Tips:
Profit increased is an example of a tangible benefit, but brand recognition and public benefit are examples of intangible benefits. Therefore, Option (A) is the right answer.
Domain: Benefits Management
Phase or Element: BENEFITS ANALYSIS AND PLANNING

Q10 - Omar is a program manager who has created a strong resource plan with his component managers. During program execution, he found some needs to change the resources according to certain practical situations. What should Omar do to prioritize the resource requirements within his program?

(a) Omar should consult his component managers for resource conflict and add a new issue to the register
(b) Omar should manage the resources at the program level and should work with the component managers who manage resources at the component level to balance the needs of the program with the availability of resources
(c) Omar should concentrate only on the program level resource requirements and should not be dragged to the project level resource management

(d) Omar should review the created resource plan

Question Category: Difficult
The right answer is Option (B)
The Standards for Program Management - 4th Edition - reference: Chapter (8), Program Activities, 8.2.7 PROGRAM RESOURCE MANAGEMENT, pages 133

Clarification and Tips:
The program manager manages resources at the program level and works with the component managers who manage resources at the component level to balance the needs of the program with the availability of resources.
Therefore, Option (B) is the right answer.
Please note the following:
Adding a new issue to the register or reviewing the resource plan will not help in resource prioritization.
Concentrating on the program level does not mean that the program manager is not involved to help the project problems which cannot be handled by the project manager, the program manager is still responsible to create the proper environment for the project manager to succeed and execute his job.
Domain: Life Cycle Management
Phase or Element: Delivery

Q11 - James is managing a program in your organization from the vendor side. He monitors the schedule to identify the slippages in order to work on their recovery, but he ignores the opportunities that may exist in the schedule. What is your view on what James is doing?

(a) James is doing a good job and he should continue focusing on slippages and ignore the opportunities
(b) James is doing a bad job. He should focus on opportunities and ignore the slippages
(c) James should identify not only schedule slippages but also opportunities to accelerate program schedule
(d) James should involve the PMO to report the schedule status

Question Category: Difficult
The right answer is Option (C)
The Standards for Program Management - 4th Edition - reference: Chapter (8), Program Activities, 8.2.9 PROGRAM SCHEDULE MONITORING AND CONTROLLING, pages 136

Clarification and Tips:
Schedule control involves identifying not only slippages but also opportunities to accelerate program or component schedules

Therefore, Option (C) is the right answer.
Domain: Life Cycle Management
Phase or Element: Delivery

Q12 - Jim is developing a plan that describes how, when and by whom information will be administered and disseminated. Which plan is this?

- (a) The program information management plan
- (b) The program communications management plan
- (c) The program quality management plan
- (d) The program change management plan

Question Category: Moderate
The right answer is Option (B)
The Standards for Program Management - 4th Edition - reference: Chapter (8), Program Activities, 8.1.2.2 PROGRAM COMMUNICATIONS MANAGEMENT PLANNING, pages 112
Clarification and Tips:
The program communications management plan is the component of the program management plan that describes how, when and by whom information will be administered and disseminated, so Option (B) is the right answer.
Domain: Life Cycle Management
Phase or Element: Definition

Q13 - Question Set (1/2) - Jim is appointed to manage one of your organization programs. He started to review the program alignment with the organization strategy. Which of the following options has the dominant reason for organizations to build strategy?

- (a) Organizations need to build a strategy to define ways to execute their initiatives
- (b) Organizations need to build a strategy to create plans on how to achieve their initiatives
- (c) Organizations need to build a strategy to define how their vision will be achieved
- (d) Organizations need to build a strategy to define how resources will be utilized

Question Category: Difficult
The right answer is Option (C)
The Standards for Program Management - 4th Edition - reference: Chapter (3), Program Strategy Alignment, 3.1 PROGRAM BUSINESS CASE, page 35
Clarification and Tips:
Initiatives are created after the strategy is defined in order to achieve this required strategy, so, options (A) and (B) are wrong.

Option (D) is wrong as resources will come to the picture after defining the strategy and creating the initiatives.
The right answer is an Option (C) as organizations build a strategy to define how their vision will be achieved.
Domain: Strategy Alignment
Phase or Element: PROGRAM BUSINESS CASE

Q14 - Question Set (2/2) - Jim is appointed to manage one of your organization programs. He started to review the program alignment with the organization strategy. Which of the following options may influence the organization's initiatives?

(a) Market dynamics
(b) Customer and partner requests
(c) Competitor plans and actions
(d) All the above

Question Category: Easy
The right answer is Option (D)
The Standards for Program Management - 4th Edition - reference: Chapter (3), Program Strategy Alignment, 3.4.1 ENTERPRISE ENVIRONMENTAL FACTORS, page 38
Clarification and Tips:
Options (A), (B), and (C) may influence the organization's initiatives. So the right answer is Option (D).
Domain: Strategy Alignment
Phase or Element: ENVIRONMENTAL ASSESSMENTS

Q15 - Who is responsible for reviewing and approving the approach to program quality management and the standards by which quality will be measured?

(a) The component managers
(b) The PMO
(c) The governance participants
(d) The organization governance team

Question Category: Moderate
The right answer is Option (C)
The Standards for Program Management - 4th Edition - reference: Chapter (6), Program Governance, 6.1.8 PROGRAM CHANGE GOVERNANCE, page 74
Clarification and Tips:
The governance participants are responsible for reviewing and approving the approach to

quality management and the standards by which quality will be measured, so Option (C) is the right answer.
Remember that this question describes a governance activity more than a quality activity.
Domain: Program Governance
Phase or Element: PROGRAM GOVERNANCE PRACTICES

Q16 - The lessons learned are critical assets to be reviewed in all the following cases, except:

(a) When updating the program stakeholder register
(b) When considering major changes to the program management plan
(c) When introducing a new program component
(d) When announcing the closure of one of the program components

Question Category: Moderate
The right answer is Option (D)
The Standards for Program Management - 4th Edition - reference: Chapter (8), Program Activities, 8.2.4.1 LESSONS LEARNED DATABASE, pages 130
Clarification and Tips:
Options (A), (B) and (C) are cases where the lessons learned are critical assets to be reviewed, but Option (D) is not. Therefore, Option (D) is the right answer.
Domain: Life Cycle Management
Phase or Element: Delivery

Q17 - Because people have the propensity to resist change whenever they have not directly requested it, the program manager is exerting effort to engage the stakeholders. Which of the following actions may help to engage the stakeholders?

(a) The program manager should be the champion for change in the organization
(b) The program manager and the program team members need to understand the attitudes and the agendas for each stakeholder throughout the duration of the program
(c) The program manager should understand the motivations of each stakeholder who could attempt to alter the course of the program
(d) All the above

Question Category: Moderate
The right answer is Option (D)
The Standards for Program Management - 4th Edition - reference: Chapter (5), Program Stakeholder Engagement, page 59
Clarification and Tips:
Options (A), (B), and (C) are actions that may help in stakeholders' engagement, so Option (D) is

the right answer.
Domain: Stakeholder Engagement
Phase or Element: General

Q18 - How often do programs use the satisfaction surveys?

- (a) As a quality assurance measurement
- (b) As a quality control measurement
- (c) As inputs to requirement gathering
- (d) As a base for rewarding the team

Question Category: Moderate
The right answer is Option (B)
The Standards for Program Management - 4th Edition - reference: Chapter (8), Program Activities, 8.2.6.1 PROGRAM QUALITY CONTROL, pages 132
Clarification and Tips:
Programs often use customer satisfaction surveys as a quality control measurement, so Option (B) is the right answer.
Domain: Life Cycle Management
Phase or Element: Delivery

Q19 - The program manager Chung has been notified by the board meeting that his program is canceled due to changes in the organizational environment which have resulted in diminished program needs. Which of the following activities should be executed by Chang?

- (a) Identify areas for improvement
- (b) Issue the final program report
- (c) Document the lessons learned
- (d) All the above

Question Category: Moderate
The right answer is Option (D)
The Standards for Program Management - 4th Edition - reference: Chapter (6), Program Governance, 6.1.12 PROGRAM CLOSURE, page 77
Clarification and Tips:
Regardless of the cause for termination, closure procedures should be implemented. As options (A), (B), and (C) are part of the closure procedure, so Option (D) is the right answer.
Domain: Program Governance
Phase or Element: PROGRAM GOVERNANCE PRACTICES

Exam 1 - Questions and Answers

Q20 - Jacob is working in program financial management and he confuses the program financial framework with the financial management plan. How can you help him?

(a) The program financial management plan expands upon the program financial framework and describes the management of items such as risk reserves, potential cash flow problems and international exchange rate fluctuations
(b) The program financial management framework expands upon the program financial plan and describes the management of items such as risk reserves, potential cash flow problems and international exchange rate fluctuations
(c) The program financial framework is a subsidiary element of the program management plan, but the financial management plan is not
(d) The program financial framework is the same as the financial management plan

Question Category: Difficult
The right answer is Option (A)
The Standards for Program Management - 4th Edition - reference: Chapter (8), Program Activities, 8.1.2.5 PROGRAM FINANCIAL MANAGEMENT PLANNING, pages 115
Clarification and Tips:
The program financial management plan expands upon the program financial framework and describes the management of items such as risk reserves, potential cash flow problems, international exchange rate fluctuations, future interest rate increases or decreases, inflation, currency devaluation, local laws regarding finances, trends in material costs, and contract incentive and penalty clauses.
Therefore, the right answer is Option (A).
Please note that Options (B) and (C) are reversed.
Domain: Life Cycle Management
Phase or Element: Definition

Q21 - Your program in the Sab organization has five components, three projects, and two subsidiary programs. What is the suitable level to govern the quality management planning?

(a) Quality management planning is governed at the program level
(b) Quality management planning is often performed at the component level and is therefore governed at that level
(c) Quality management planning is governed at the organization level
(d) Quality management planning is governed at the PMO level

Question Category: Difficult
The right answer is Option (B)
The Standards for Program Management - 4th Edition - reference: Chapter (6), Program

Governance, 6.1.7 PROGRAM QUALITY GOVERNANCE, page 74
Clarification and Tips:
Quality management planning is often performed at the component level and is therefore governed at that level, so Option (B) is the right answer.
Domain: Program Governance
Phase or Element: PROGRAM GOVERNANCE PRACTICES

Q22 - The program sponsor of the program that you are managing is discussing with you the appropriate way to oversee the program. He was thinking about having three steering committees to oversee the program from different dimensions; the benefits, the financial and the strategic objectives. What is your recommendation to the program sponsor?

 (a) I will agree with his suggestion of having these three committees
 (b) I will suggest adding a fourth steering committee to oversee the program from the risk standpoint
 (c) I will recommend having only one steering committee for the program as this is more efficient
 (d) I will recommend having no steering committee as having the program sponsor should be sufficient

Question Category: Difficult
The right answer is Option (C)
The Standards for Program Management - 4th Edition - reference: Chapter (6), Program Governance, 6.2.2 PROGRAM STEERING COMMITTEE, page 82
Clarification and Tips:
Establishing a single committee that maintains and is accountable for all critical elements of program oversight within an organization is considered to be the most efficient means for providing effective and adaptive governance oversight, so Option (C) is the right answer.
Domain: Program Governance
Phase or Element: PROGRAM GOVERNANCE PRACTICES

Q23 - Ravi is appointed to manage a running program after the program manager left. Ravi started to gather information to understand the program details by reviewing the program documentation and meeting the key stakeholders. During his review for the resource management plan, Ravi found that the sum of human resources needed to successfully complete each component is less than the total quantity of human resources needed to complete the program. What is the most probable reason for this difference?

 (a) The sum of human resources needed to successfully complete each component is less than the total quantity of human resources needed to complete the program because

Exam 1 - Questions and Answers

the resources can be reallocated between components as the components are completed
(b) The sum of human resources needed to successfully complete each component is less than the total quantity of human resources needed to complete the program because the resources can work more than eight hours a day
(c) This difference indicates wrong human resource calculation, so Ravi should review the human resource planning in detail
(d) This difference indicates wrong human resource calculation, so Ravi should report this problem before he starts managing the program

Question Category: Difficult
The right answer is Option (A)
The Standards for Program Management - 4th Edition - reference: Chapter (8), Program Activities, 8.1.2.9 PROGRAM RESOURCE MANAGEMENT PLANNING, pages 119
Clarification and Tips:
In the case of human resources, the sum of resources needed to successfully complete each component can be less than the total quantity of resources needed to complete the program because the resources can be reallocated between components as the components are completed.
Therefore, Option (A) is the right answer.
Please note that Option (B) is overkilling for the resources and against labor laws in many countries.
Domain: Life Cycle Management
Phase or Element: Definition

Q24 - Which of the following documents include the stakeholder engagement guidelines and a detailed strategy for effective stakeholder engagement?

(a) Stakeholder map
(b) Stakeholder register
(c) Stakeholder engagement plan
(d) The power/interest grid

Question Category: Moderate
The right answer is Option (C)
The Standards for Program Management - 4th Edition - reference: Chapter (5), Program Stakeholder Engagement, 5.3 PROGRAM STAKEHOLDER ENGAGEMENT PLANNING, page 64
Clarification and Tips:
The stakeholder engagement plan includes the stakeholder engagement guidelines and a detailed strategy for effective stakeholder engagement, so Option (C) is the right answer.
Domain: Stakeholder Engagement
Phase or Element: PROGRAM STAKEHOLDER ENGAGEMENT PLANNING

Q25 - Allan worked for a week with his management team to collect important information for the program charter creation. He requested the charter approval during the steering committee meeting. Unfortunately, the charter was not approved and the program was not authorized. What should Allan do with the collected information?

(a) This information is ignored as the program charter was not approved
(b) This information is added to the rejection report
(c) This information is recorded and captured in a lessons learned repository
(d) This information is captured in the issue log

Question Category: Moderate
The right answer is Option (C)
The Standards for Program Management - 4th Edition - reference: Chapter (7), Program Life Cycle Management, 7.1.2.1 PROGRAM FORMULATION, page 92
Clarification and Tips:
If the program is not authorized, the information gathered for creating the charter should be recorded and captured in a lessons learned repository, so Option (C) is the right answer.
Domain: Life Cycle Management
Phase or Element: Definition

Q26 - The following items are shared between the stakeholders and the risks, except:

(a) They should be identified, studied, categorized, and tracked
(b) They can be managed by the program team
(c) They may be internal or external to the program
(d) They may have a positive or negative impact on the outcome of the program

Question Category: Easy
The right answer is Option (B)
The Standards for Program Management - 4th Edition - reference: Chapter (5), Program Stakeholder Engagement, General
Clarification and Tips:
Options (A), (C), and (D) have items that are shared between the stakeholders and the risks. Option (B) is valid only for the risk, and not for the stakeholders as the term used with stakeholders is "Stakeholder Engagement" or "Manage Stakeholder Expectations."
Therefore, the right answer is Option (B).
Domain: Stakeholder Engagement
Phase or Element: General

Q27 - Your program faced a hard quality audit where the auditors created a long list of non-conformances that include some quality changes.
Who is responsible for implementing all required quality changes?

- (a) The program manager
- (b) The program management office
- (c) The program component managers
- (d) The program management team

Question Category: Difficult
The right answer is Option (D)
The Standards for Program Management - 4th Edition - reference: Chapter (8), Program Activities, 8.2.6 PROGRAM QUALITY ASSURANCE AND CONTROL, page 132
Clarification and Tips:
The program management team is responsible for implementing all required quality changes. The program team includes the program manager, the component managers, the program management office and the team members. Therefore, Option (D) is the right answer.
Domain: Life Cycle Management
Phase or Element: Delivery

Q28 - The following statements may specify program charter, except:

- (a) The program charter formally expresses a chronological representation of a program's intended direction
- (b) The program charter formally expresses the organization's vision, mission, and benefits expected to be produced by the program
- (c) The program charter provides the program manager with authority for leading other subsidiary programs, projects, and related activities to be initiated
- (d) The program charter defines program-specific goals and objectives in alignment with the organization's strategic plan

Question Category: Moderate
The right answer is Option (A)
The Standards for Program Management - 4th Edition - reference: Chapter (3), Program Strategy Alignment, 3.2 PROGRAM CHARTER, page 36
Clarification and Tips:
Options (B), (C), and (D) are considered descriptions for the program charter, but Option (A) is not considered a description for the charter, it is considered for the roadmap. Therefore, Option (A) is the right answer.

Domain: Strategy Alignment
Phase or Element: PROGRAM CHARTER

Q29 - Jimmy is working in his program and is facing reluctance while driving changes in the organization. He is looking for support in driving these changes, who should provide him with the required support?

(a) The component managers
(b) The program management office
(c) The subject matter experts
(d) The program sponsor

Question Category: Moderate
The right answer is Option (D)
The Standards for Program Management - 4th Edition - reference: Chapter (6), Program Governance, 6.2.1 PROGRAM SPONSOR, page 80
Clarification and Tips:
Very often, the program sponsor is required to drive changes through the organization so that operations can accommodate capabilities delivered by the program, so Option (D) is the right answer.
Domain: Program Governance
Phase or Element: PROGRAM GOVERNANCE PRACTICES

Q30 - Adam is managing a serious program in your organization. He is an experienced program manager who closed a few programs successfully in your organization. Adam is preparing to rebaseline his program. When should the program budget be rebaselined?

(a) When a new program sponsor is assigned
(b) When a new program manager is assigned
(c) When the program is cancelled
(d) When there are changes which are approved and have significant cost impacts

Question Category: Moderate
The right answer is Option (D)
The Standards for Program Management - 4th Edition - reference: Chapter (8), Program Activities, 8.2.3 PROGRAM FINANCIAL MANAGEMENT, pages 128
Clarification and Tips:
Throughout the program as changes are approved that have significant cost impacts, the program's budget baseline is updated accordingly, and the budget is rebaselined. Therefore, the right answer is Option (D).

Assigning a new program manager or new sponsor is not a valid reason to rebaseline the budget. When the program is cancelled, the budget will not be rebaselined but will be reallocated.
Domain: Life Cycle Management
Phase or Element: Delivery

Q31 - Fatma is calculating the total cost of ownership for her starting program. She conducted few meetings with the projects managers and the subsidiary program managers to gather their input. She collected the development and implementation costs for all the program components and the program management costs. Which cost is she missing?

- (a) The risk management cost
- (b) The transition and sustainment cost
- (c) The quality management cost
- (d) The third-part cost

Question Category: Difficult
The right answer is Option (B)
The Standards for Program Management - 4th Edition - reference: Chapter (8), Program Activities, 8.1.2.3 PROGRAM COST ESTIMATION, pages 113
Clarification and Tips:
The total cost of ownership includes the full life cycle costs, transition cost and sustainment costs. The full life cycle costs include the development and implementation costs for all the program components and the program management cost.
Therefore, Option (B) is the right answer.
Please note that costs related to risk management, quality management and third-party should be distributed as part of the component cost, program management cost or transition and sustainment cost.
Domain: Life Cycle Management
Phase or Element: Definition

Q32 - As a program manager, and during the financial management planning, you identified financial risks.
Where should you document these risks?

- (a) In the financial management plan
- (b) In the risk management plan
- (c) In the program financial framework
- (d) In the program risk register

Question Category: Moderate
The right answer is Option (D)
The Standards for Program Management - 4th Edition - reference: Chapter (8), Program Activities, 8.1.2.5 PROGRAM FINANCIAL MANAGEMENT PLANNING, pages 115
Clarification and Tips:
Program financial risks that are identified as part of the financial management plan should be incorporated into the program risk register.
Therefore, Option (D) is the right answer.
Domain: Life Cycle Management
Phase or Element: Definition

Q33 - Which of the following documents may contain politically and legally sensitive information, and may have access and review restrictions placed on it by the program manager?

(a) Program roadmap
(b) Stakeholder register
(c) Program management plan
(d) Transition plan

Question Category: Moderate
The right answer is Option (B)
The Standards for Program Management - 4th Edition - reference: Chapter (5), Program Stakeholder Engagement, 5.1 PROGRAM STAKEHOLDER IDENTIFICATION, page 60
Clarification and Tips:
The stakeholder register may contain politically and legally sensitive information and may have access and review restrictions placed on it by the program manager, so the right answer is Option (B).
Domain: Stakeholder Engagement
Phase or Element: PROGRAM STAKEHOLDER IDENTIFICATION

Q34 - James is writing his first program governance plan. He asked you to provide him with some examples. Which of the following may be included in your example of the program governance plan?

(a) A schedule of anticipated program-related governance meetings
(b) The structure and composition of the group of governance participants and the definitions of the roles and responsibilities of key stakeholders
(c) List of governance key dependencies, assumptions, and constraints
(d) All the above

Question Category: Easy
The right answer is Option (D)
The Standards for Program Management - 4th Edition - reference: Chapter (6), Program Governance, 6.1.1 PROGRAM GOVERNANCE PLAN, page 70
Clarification and Tips:
Options (A), (B), and (C) are elements that may be included in the program governance plan, so Option (D) is the right answer.
Domain: Program Governance
Phase or Element: PROGRAM GOVERNANCE PRACTICES

Q35 - Chao has just finished the transition activities of his program after three years of hard working. He is currently working on getting the official program closure. Which of the following factors may he consider to obtain the formal closure?

(a) The clearance of all opened program issues
(b) The mitigation of all opened risks with high impact and high probability
(c) The judgment of the approved business case, actual program outcomes, and the current goals and strategic objectives of the organization
(d) The clearance of all the requested change requests

Question Category: Moderate
The right answer is Option (C)
The Standards for Program Management - 4th Edition - reference: Chapter (7), Program Life Cycle Management, 7.2.2.5 PROGRAM CLOSEOUT, page 102
Clarification and Tips:
Successful completion of the program is judged against the approved business case, actual program outcomes, and the current goals and strategic objectives of the organization, so Option (C) is the right answer.
Please note that Options (A), (B), and (D) have elements that are not prerequisite to obtain the formal closure.
Domain: Life Cycle Management
Phase or Element: Closing

Q36 - The Sodim organization is thinking about creating a program to manage the organization transformation. Because of the limited information, time and resources available, it is difficult to develop a highly detailed or accurate cost estimate for this program. Therefore, Sodim uses a rough order of magnitude to estimate the program cost. What is your advice to Sodim?

(a) This initial rough order-of-magnitude estimate is a good option as it allows financial decision makers in Sodim to decide if the program should be funded

(b) This initial rough order-of-magnitude estimate is misleading and should be avoided for a proper estimate
(c) Sodim should find internal resources to execute the required analysis and create an accurate estimate
(d) Sodim should recruit external resources to execute the required analysis and create an accurate estimate

Question Category: Difficult
The right answer is Option (A)
The Standards for Program Management - 4th Edition - reference: Chapter (8), Program Activities, 8.1.1.3 PROGRAM INITIAL COST ESTIMATION, pages 107
Clarification and Tips:
Because of the limited information, time and resources available, it may be difficult to develop a highly detailed or accurate cost estimate. Often the numbers will only be accurate to a rough order of magnitude. The initial rough order-of-magnitude estimate allows financial decision makers to decide if the program should be funded.
Therefore, Option (A) is the right answer.
Domain: Life Cycle Management
Phase or Element: Definition

Q37 - John is a program manager in your organization, he is creating a procurement management setup to control all the component procurements at the program level. One of the component managers was not happy with this process and wanted to control the procurement of his component on the component level. He came to you asking for advice. What is your advice to him?

(a) I will advise him to reject the procurement process imposed by the program manager on his component level
(b) I will advise him to escalate the subject to the program sponsor
(c) It is common to direct, centralize and conduct all the procurements on the program-level team rather than to individual components
(d) It is not usual that all procurements are centralized on the program level as some components may have their own procurements special requirements

Question Category: Difficult
The right answer is Option (C)
The Standards for Program Management - 4th Edition - reference: Chapter (8), Program Activities, 8.2.5 PROGRAM PROCUREMENT MANAGEMENT, pages 131
Clarification and Tips:
It is a common structure used by the program manager to direct all procurements to be centralized and conducted by a program-level team rather than assigning that responsibility to individual components.

Therefore, Option (C) is the right answer.
Domain: Life Cycle Management
Phase or Element: Delivery

Q38 - All the following activities belong to benefits sustainment, except:

(a) Monitoring the performance of the product, service, capability, or results from reliability and availability-for-use perspective
(b) Monitoring the continued suitability of the deployed product, service, capability, or results
(c) Review of applicable contractual agreements
(d) Implementing the required change efforts to ensure that the capabilities provided during the course of the program continue when the program is closed

Question Category: Moderate
The right answer is Option (C)
The Standards for Program Management - 4th Edition - reference: Chapter (4), Program Benefits Management, 4.5 BENEFITS SUSTAINMENT, page 55
Clarification and Tips:
Options (A), (B), and (D) are activities belonging to the benefits sustainment, but Option (C) includes activity belong to benefits transition. Therefore, Option (C) is the right answer.
Domain: Benefits Management
Phase or Element: BENEFITS SUSTAINMENT

Q39 - All the following are considered part of the effective program governance, except:

(a) Executing reviews and health checks of the program progress
(b) Evaluating opportunities and threats affecting benefits, including updating the benefits register for new opportunities and risks affecting benefits
(c) Facilitating the engagement of program stakeholders by establishing clear expectations for each program's interactions with key governing stakeholders throughout the program
(d) Making decisions to transition between phases, terminate, or close the program

Question Category: Moderate
The right answer is Option (B)
The Standards for Program Management - 4th Edition - reference: Chapter (6), Program Governance, page 69
Clarification and Tips:
Options (A), (C), and (D) are considered part of the effective program governance, but Option (B) is considered part of the benefits delivery.

Therefore, Option (B) is the right answer.
Domain: Program Governance
Phase or Element: General

Q40 - George is developing a document that graphically depicts dependencies between major milestones and decision points. Which document is this?

- (a) The program schedule
- (b) The milestone list
- (c) The program roadmap
- (d) The program management plan

Question Category: Moderate
The right answer is Option (C)
The Standards for Program Management - 4th Edition - reference: Chapter (3), Program Strategy Alignment, 3.3 PROGRAM ROADMAP, page 36
Clarification and Tips:
The program roadmap is a chronological representation of a program's intended direction, graphically depicting dependencies between major milestones and decision points, which reflects the linkage between the business strategy and the program work.
Therefore, Option (C) is the right answer.
Domain: Strategy Alignment
Phase or Element: PROGRAM ROADMAP

Q41 - Question Set (1/2) - Ahmed is assigned as a program PMO, and he is looking after the Ad-Val program which is a critical program in his organization. He noticed that the program team is confused about their roles and responsibilities. So, he decided to review all the program roles and responsibilities, which document should Ahmed review?

- (a) Program Communication Plan
- (b) Stakeholder Engagement Plan
- (c) Program Governance Plan
- (d) Program Organization Chart

Question Category: Moderate
The right answer is Option (C)
The Standards for Program Management - 4th Edition - reference: Chapter (6), Program Governance, 6.1.1 PROGRAM GOVERNANCE PLAN, page 72
Clarification and Tips:
Program roles and responsibilities are part of the program governance plan, so the right answer

is Option (C).
Domain: Program Governance
Phase or Element: PROGRAM GOVERNANCE PRACTICES

Q42 - Question Set (2/2) - Ahmed is assigned as a program PMO, and he is looking after the Ad-Val program which is a critical program in his organization. He noticed that the program team is confused about their roles and responsibilities. After he reviewed the roles and responsibilities, he decided to update them with the program team main players and then get the required approval.
Who should approve these roles and responsibilities?

- (a) Program steering committee
- (b) Program sponsor
- (c) Program management office
- (d) Corporate PMO

Question Category: Moderate
The right answer is Option (A)
The Standards for Program Management - 4th Edition - reference: Chapter (6), Program Governance, 6.1.8 PROGRAM CHANGE GOVERNANCE, page 74
Clarification and Tips:
The program manager assesses whether the risks associated with potential changes are acceptable or desirable, whether the proposed changes are operationally feasible and organizationally supportable, and whether the changes are significant enough to require the approval of the program steering committee. The program manager then recommends changes that require approval by program governance participants through the program steering committee.
Therefore Option (A) is the right answer.
Please note that the program steering committee is responsible for defining the types of changes that a program manager would be independently authorized to approve and those changes that would be significant enough to require further discussion prior to approval.
Domain: Program Governance
Phase or Element: General

Q43 - When is the program manager usually selected and assigned?

- (a) During the formulation subphase
- (b) During the planning subphase
- (c) During the delivery phase

(d) Before the program is initiated

Question Category: Moderate
The right answer is Option (A)
The Standards for Program Management - 4th Edition - reference: Chapter (7), Program Life Cycle Management, 7.1.2 PROGRAM DEFINITION PHASE, page 91
Clarification and Tips:
The program manager is selected and assigned during program formulation, so Option (A) is the right answer.
Domain: Life Cycle Management
Phase or Element: Definition

Q44 - You have five phase-gates in your program as follows:
Phase-gate 1 in Jan-2019, Phase-gate 2 in Apr-2019, Phase-gate 3 in Dec-2019, Phase-gate 4 in Jan-2020, and Phase-gate 5 in Feb-2020.
You have a request from the governing body in your organization to add a health check in your governance plan. Where is the best schedule to add a program health check?

(a) Between phase-gate 1 and phase-gate2
(b) Between phase-gate 2 and phase-gate3
(c) At phase-gate 4
(d) At phase-gate 5

Question Category: Difficult
The right answer is Option (B)
The Standards for Program Management - 4th Edition - reference: Chapter (6), Program Governance, 6.1.10 PROGRAM PERIODIC HEALTH CHECKS, page 76
Clarification and Tips:
Program periodic health checks, generally held between decision-point reviews, assess a program's ongoing performance and progress towards the realization and sustainment of benefits. The importance and use of these reviews increase when there is an extended period between scheduled decision-point reviews. In this question, the period between phase-gate 2 and phase-gate3 is the longest, so this is the best place to schedule a health check. Therefore, Option (B) is the right answer.
Domain: Program Governance
Phase or Element: PROGRAM GOVERNANCE PRACTICES

Q45 - Lee, the project manager, is managing a component in your program came asking you to provide him with a component contingency reserve to handle risk responses. What is your right answer to Anil?

(a) I will provide him with a reasonable contingency reserve to handle component-level risk responses
(b) I will tell him that the component-level risk responses will be handled by the contingency reserves at the program level
(c) I will tell him that he does not need to have a contingency reserve to handle risks as this should be included in the component budget
(d) I will ask him to raise a change request

Question Category: Difficult
The right answer is Option (A)
The Standards for Program Management - 4th Edition - reference: Chapter (8), Program Activities, 8.2.8.3 PROGRAM RISK RESPONSE MANAGEMENT, pages 135
Clarification and Tips:
The program manager may hold contingency reserves at the program level to support risk responses. The program contingency reserve is not a substitute for the component contingency reserve, which is held at the component level.
Therefore, Option (A) is the right answer.
Domain: Life Cycle Management
Phase or Element: Delivery

Q46 - Omar is a program manager executing a program whose main objective is to create a very competitive thermal camera. During the program phase-gate review, the program steering committee found that the program is not likely to deliver its expected benefits due to rapid technology change in the competitive market of the thermal cameras. What decision should be taken by the steering committee?

(a) The steering committee should request the program manage to activate the change management process
(b) The steering committee should request a business case review
(c) The steering committee should take the hard decision to terminate the program
(d) The steering committee should request the program manager to create a recovery plan for the situation

Question Category: Difficult
The right answer is Option (C)
The Standards for Program Management - 4th Edition - reference: Chapter (6), Program Governance, 6.1.9 PROGRAM GOVERNANCE REVIEWS, page 76
Clarification and Tips:
When the program is no longer expected to fulfill the planned benefits, it is recommended to terminate the program. Therefore, the right answer is Option (C).

Option (A) is wrong as the change management process has no value at this stage.
Option (B) is wrong as the business case review may be required when there is a change in the organization strategical objectives, and will not be helpful when the program is not going to achieve its benefits.
Option (D) is wrong as the recovery plan may be required whenever there is a large deviation in expected quality, schedule or defined scope and will not be helpful when the program is not going to achieve its benefits.
Domain: Program Governance
Phase or Element: PROGRAM GOVERNANCE PRACTICES

Q47 - Lee is working in the program schedule management planning where he just created the initial program master time schedule.
What is usually expected in the initial program master time schedule?

(a) The order and start/end dates of components and their key interdependencies with other components
(b) The detailed component benefits realization
(c) The program transition plan details
(d) The initial component schedules including the component deliverables

Question Category: Moderate
The right answer is Option (A)
The Standards for Program Management - 4th Edition - reference: Chapter (8), Program Activities, 8.1.2.11 PROGRAM SCHEDULE MANAGEMENT PLANNING, pages 122
Clarification and Tips:
The first draft of a program master schedule often only identifies the order and start/end dates of components and their key interdependencies with other components. Later, it may be enriched with more intermediate component results as the component schedules are developed.
Therefore, Option (A) is the right answer.
Domain: Life Cycle Management
Phase or Element: Definition

Q48 - Miguel is managing a program that is related to public works in order to create roads between three major cities. The benefits to be realized by this program are examples of:

(a) Benefits to be realized at the end of the program
(b) Benefits to be realized incrementally during the program life cycle
(c) Benefits to be realized after the program is closed

(d) Benefits to be realized at the beginning of the program

Question Category: Difficult
The right answer is Option (A)
The Standards for Program Management - 4th Edition - reference: Chapter (4), Program Benefits Management, page 45
Clarification and Tips:
Examples of programs that deliver the intended benefits at the end of the program include public works programs such as roads, so Option (A) is the right answer.
Please note that Option (D) is wrong, in principle, as benefits cannot be realized at the beginning of the program.
Domain: Benefits Management
Phase or Element: General

Q49 - You are appointed to manage a program which is a joint effort between the Happy organization and its competitor Driving organization. It was agreed between the two organizations that Happy will fund 60% of the required funding and Driving will fund 40%. You are defining the governance plan and working with the senior management in both organizations to establish steering committee(s) for the program. What is your best recommendation?

(a) I will recommend having one joint steering committee for both Happy and Driving organizations
(b) I will recommend having one steering committee for the Happy organization as it is funding 60% of the program funding
(c) I will recommend having three steering committees; one for the Happy organization, another for the Driving organization, and the third as a joint steering committee for both Happy and Driving organizations
(d) I will recommend having only one steering committee for the program as this is more efficient

Question Category: Difficult
The right answer is Option (C)
The Standards for Program Management - 4th Edition - reference: Chapter (6), Program Governance, 6.2.2 PROGRAM STEERING COMMITTEE, page 82
Clarification and Tips:
Some programs may need to report to multiple steering committees; for example, programs managed as collaborations between private but otherwise competitive organizations.
Option (C) is the only options that support multiple steering committees, so Option (C) is the right answer.

Domain: Program Governance
Phase or Element: PROGRAM GOVERNANCE PRACTICES

Q50 - Which of the following documents is approved first?

(a) The program charter
(b) The program management plan
(c) The program roadmap
(d) The program business case

Question Category: Moderate
The right answer is Option (D)
The Standards for Program Management - 4th Edition - reference: Chapter (3), Program Strategy Alignment, 3.2 PROGRAM CHARTER, page 36
Clarification and Tips:
The usual right order is: The program business case, the program charter, the program roadmap, then the program management plan.
Therefore, Option (D) is the right answer.
Domain: Strategy Alignment
Phase or Element: PROGRAM CHARTER

Q51 - Who should evaluate the fitness for use of the benefits delivered by the program?

(a) The program manager
(b) The testing team
(c) The staff who receive it
(d) The PMO

Question Category: Moderate
The right answer is Option (C)
The Standards for Program Management - 4th Edition - reference: Chapter (8), Program Activities, 8.2.6.1 PROGRAM QUALITY CONTROL, pages 132
Clarification and Tips:
The fitness for use of the benefits, product, or service delivered by the program is best evaluated by those who receive it, so Option (C) is the right answer.
Domain: Life Cycle Management
Phase or Element: Delivery

Q52 - Ahmed was one of the executives who had high interest in your program and high level of

power. During the last organization change, Ahmed was promoted to the board level role where he became less interested in your program.
According to the stakeholder map, how should you interact with Ahmed?

(a) Manage closely
(b) Keep satisfied
(c) Keep informed
(d) Monitor

Question Category: Moderate
The right answer is Option (B)
The Standards for Program Management - 4th Edition - reference: Chapter (5), Program Stakeholder Engagement, 5.2 PROGRAM STAKEHOLDER ANALYSIS, page 63
Clarification and Tips:
The current situation is that Ahmed has low interest and high level of power. So, the interaction strategy with Ahmed should be "Keep satisfied" as per the Power/Interest Grid.
Therefore, the right answer is Option (B)
Domain: Stakeholder Engagement
Phase or Element: PROGRAM STAKEHOLDER ANALYSIS

Q53 - Assume that your organization is specialized in producing and exporting specific goods and services efficiently and at a lower opportunity cost than other companies. This is an example of:

(a) Opportunity cost
(b) Comparative advantage
(c) Positive risk
(d) Negative risk

Question Category: Difficult
The right answer is Option (B)
The Standards for Program Management - 4th Edition - reference: Chapter (3), Program Strategy Alignment, 3.4.2.1 COMPARATIVE ADVANTAGE ANALYSIS, page 39
Clarification and Tips:
This is an example of comparative advantage.
The opportunity cost is the lost opportunity, of the best alternate way to spend your budget.
The positive risk is the risk with positive impact.
The negative risk is the risk with negative impact.
Therefore, the right answer is Option (B).
Domain: Strategy Alignment
Phase or Element: ENVIRONMENTAL ASSESSMENTS

Q54 - All the following tools may help in environmental analysis while managing a program, except:

(a) SWOT analysis
(b) Document analysis
(c) Assumptions analysis
(d) Historical information analysis

Question Category: Moderate
The right answer is Option (B)
The Standards for Program Management - 4th Edition - reference: Chapter (3), Program Strategy Alignment, 3.4.1 ENTERPRISE ENVIRONMENTAL FACTORS, page 38
Clarification and Tips:
Options (A), (C), and (D) are tools that may help in environmental analysis while managing a program. However, Option (B) contains the document analysis which does not help in environmental analysis, it is mainly used to review and assess any relevant documented information. Therefore, Option (B) is the right answer.
Domain: Strategy Alignment
Phase or Element: ENVIRONMENTAL ASSESSMENTS

Q55 - Richard got the program management plan completed and approved. He started the delivery phase of his program and while going into planning details related to one of the program components, he discovered some conflicting priorities, assumptions and constraints that will influence the approved program management plan. What should he do?

(a) He should not update the program management plan as it was approved by the steering committee
(b) He should not update the program management plan as he already started the delivery phase
(c) He should not update the program management plan as he closed the planning subphase where he developed the program management plan
(d) He should apply the required updates and revisions to the program management plan and its subsidiary plans, then request approval through the Program Governance Performance Domain

Question Category: Difficult
The right answer is Option (D)
The Standards for Program Management - 4th Edition - reference: Chapter (7), Program Life Cycle Management, 7.1.2.2 PROGRAM PLANNING, page 95
Clarification and Tips:

It is important to remember that development of the program management plan is an iterative activity since it is prepared early in the program life cycle and conflicting priorities, assumptions and constraints may arise due to changes in critical factors, such as business goals, deliverables, benefits, time and cost. To address these factors, updates and revisions to the program management plan and its subsidiary plans are approved or rejected through the Program Governance Performance Domain.
Therefore, Option (D) is the right answer.
Domain: Life Cycle Management
Phase or Element: Definition

Q56 - Myra, the program manager in your organization, confuses the program payment schedules with the component payment schedules. How can you help her?

- (a) The component payment schedules identify the schedules and milestones where funding is received, but the program payment schedules indicate how and when contractors are paid
- (b) The program payment schedules identify the schedules and milestones where funding is received, but the component payment schedules indicate how and when contractors are paid
- (c) The program payment schedules are related to the payments on the program level, but the component payment schedules are related to the payments on the component level
- (d) There is no difference between the program payment schedules and the component payment schedules

Question Category: Moderate
The right answer is Option (B)
The Standards for Program Management - 4th Edition - reference: Chapter (8), Program Activities, 8.2.3.1 PROGRAM COST BUDGETING, pages 129
Clarification and Tips:
The program payment schedules identify the schedules and milestones where funding is received by the funding organization.
The component payment schedules indicate how and when contractors are paid in accordance with the contract provisions.
Therefore, Option (B) is the right answer.
Domain: Life Cycle Management
Phase or Element: Delivery

Q57 - Sam, an experienced program manager, joined a new organization. He was assigned a few months ago to his first program in the new organization, but he is not happy about his granted degree of autonomy for oversight of his program's components. He requested your advice, which of the following will be your best advice?

(a) I will advise him to escalate the subject to the program sponsor and ask him to review the given responsibilities to the program manager role
(b) I will advise him to escalate the subject to the program governance participants and ask them to review the given responsibilities to the program manager role
(c) I will advise him to wait until he better understood the organization culture and the rationale behind the given authority as the degree of autonomy given to the program manager for oversight of his program's components are different among organizations
(d) I will advise him to assume the responsibility that he deserves and behave accordingly

Question Category: Difficult
The right answer is Option (C)
The Standards for Program Management - 4th Edition - reference: Chapter (6), Program Governance, 6.3 PROGRAM GOVERNANCE DESIGN AND IMPLEMENTATION, page 86
Clarification and Tips:
The more reasonable answer is Option (C) as the degree of autonomy given to the program manager for oversight of his program's components are different among organizations and it is better for Sam to understand his organization culture, especially since he joined the organization only a few months ago.
Domain: Program Governance
Phase or Element: PROGRAM GOVERNANCE DESIGN AND IMPLEMENTATION

Q58 - James is very concerned about the accuracy of the information distributed within the program, so he has many meetings with his management team stressing on the accuracy of the information. What is the impact of distributing incorrect information within a program?

(a) Incorrect information has no effect as it will be filtered by the recipient
(b) Incorrect information has a negative impact on the program manager reputation
(c) Incorrect information may lead to errors and incorrect decisions
(d) Incorrect information will not lead to incorrect decisions

Question Category: Moderate
The right answer is Option (C)
The Standards for Program Management - 4th Edition - reference: Chapter (8), Program Activities, 8.2.3.2 COMPONENT COST ESTIMATION, pages 129
Clarification and Tips:
Attention should be paid to the accuracy and timeliness of the information to avoid errors and incorrect decisions.

Therefore, Option (C) is the right answer.
Domain: Life Cycle Management
Phase or Element: Delivery

Q59 - All the following are established as part of the program change management principles and procedures, except:

- (a) Evaluating each requested change
- (b) The approach for capturing requested changes
- (c) Identify the source of change
- (d) Determining the disposition of each requested change

Question Category: Moderate
The right answer is Option (C)
The Standards for Program Management - 4th Edition - reference: Chapter (8), Program Activities, 8.1.2.1 PROGRAM CHANGE MANAGEMENT PLANNING, pages 112
Clarification and Tips:
Options (A), (B), and (D) are established as part of the program change management principles and procedures, but Option (C) is part of the program change assessment. Therefore, Option (C) is the right answer.
Domain: Life Cycle Management
Phase or Element: Definition

Q60 - Alberto is a new program manager. He is currently preparing the program cost estimates and he needs to know how the program cost is attributed. How can you respond to his query?

- (a) The majority of the program's cost is attributable to managing the program itself and not to the individual components within the program
- (b) The majority of the program's cost is attributable to the individual components within the program and not to manage the program itself
- (c) The majority of the program's cost is attributable to both the individual components within the program and to managing the program itself
- (d) The program's cost is attributable to the program sponsor needs as he is responsible for the program funding

Question Category: Difficult
The right answer is Option (B)
The Standards for Program Management - 4th Edition - reference: Chapter (8), Program Activities, 8.2.3.1 PROGRAM COST BUDGETING, pages 129
Clarification and Tips:

The majority of the program's cost is attributable to the individual components within the program and not to manage the program itself.
Therefore, Option (B) is the right answer, the rest of the options are just to create confusion.
Domain: Life Cycle Management
Phase or Element: Delivery

Q61 - When there is a significant change in the program master schedule, which of the following program artifacts should be assessed for potential revision?

- (a) The program mandate
- (b) The program roadmap
- (c) The program charter
- (d) The program management plan

Question Category: Moderate
The right answer is Option (B)
The Standards for Program Management - 4th Edition - reference: Chapter (8), Program Activities, 8.2.9 PROGRAM SCHEDULE MONITORING AND CONTROLLING, page 136
Clarification and Tips:
The program roadmap should be assessed for potential revision when there is a significant change in the program master schedule in order to assure synchronization. So, Option (B) is the right answer.
Domain: Life Cycle Management
Phase or Element: Delivery

Q62 - While you are executing your program delivery phase, you noticed that there is a minor overrun in the financial. What is expected to happen in your program?

- (a) This overrun is minor, so it will be neglected
- (b) This overrun is subject to audit and management oversight and should be justified
- (c) You will be requested to decrease the expenses to overcome this overrun
- (d) Your program will be subject to cancellation

Question Category: Difficult
The right answer is Option (B)
The Standards for Program Management - 4th Edition - reference: Chapter (8), Program Activities, 8.2.3 PROGRAM FINANCIAL MANAGEMENT, pages 127
Clarification and Tips:
A program whose costs exceed the planned budget may no longer satisfy the business case used

to justify it and may be subject to cancellation. Even minor overruns are subject to audit and management oversight and should be justified.
Therefore, Option (B) is the right answer.
Domain: Life Cycle Management
Phase or Element: Delivery

Q63 - Which of the following statements describes precisely the difference between component-level risks and program risks?

- (a) Component-level risks should be dealt with within a relatively long time frame, while program risks may be applicable to short time frame
- (b) Component-level risks should be dealt with within a relatively short time frame, while program risks may be applicable at a point in the potentially distant future
- (c) Component-level risks and program risks usually have a similar time frame
- (d) The time scale is not a factor when comparing Component-level risks and program risks

Question Category: Difficult
The right answer is Option (B)
The Standards for Program Management - 4th Edition - reference: Chapter (8), Program Activities, 8.2.8.2 PROGRAM RISK ANALYSIS, pages 135
Clarification and Tips:
One essential difference between programs and components is the time scale; component-level risks should be dealt with within a relatively short time frame (i.e., at the end of a phase or a component), while program risks may be applicable at a point in the potentially distant future.
Therefore, Option (B) is the right answer.
Domain: Life Cycle Management
Phase or Element: Delivery

Q64 - Sam, the program manager, is preparing an announcement for the past and future customers who will be watching intently to see how well the program delivers the stated benefits. What are these customers called?

- (a) Important customers
- (b) New customers
- (c) Old customers
- (d) Potential customers

Question Category: Easy
The right answer is Option (D)
The Standards for Program Management - 4th Edition - reference: Chapter (5), Program

Stakeholder Engagement, 5.1 PROGRAM STAKEHOLDER IDENTIFICATION, page 61
Clarification and Tips:
The past and future customers who will be watching intently to see how well the program delivers the stated benefits are called potential customers, so Option (D) is the right answer.
Domain: Stakeholder Engagement
Phase or Element: PROGRAM STAKEHOLDER IDENTIFICATION

Q65 - Halinka has a financial review from the organization on the program payments. She was asked by the review team how did she make the program payments, what is the right answer of Halinka?

(a) In accordance with the achieved benefits
(b) In accordance with the contracts
(c) In accordance with the invoices
(d) In accordance with the progress

Question Category: Moderate
The right answer is Option (B)
The Standards for Program Management - 4th Edition - reference: Chapter (8), Program Activities, 8.2.3 PROGRAM FINANCIAL MANAGEMENT, pages 128
Clarification and Tips:
As part of this activity, payments are made in accordance with the contracts, with the financial infrastructure of the program, and with the status of the contract deliverables.
Therefore, Option (B) is the right answer.
Domain: Life Cycle Management
Phase or Element: Delivery

Q66 - Which of the following elements are expected to appear in the financial management plan?

(a) Funding schedules and milestones
(b) Financial reporting activities and mechanisms
(c) Financial metrics
(d) All the above

Question Category: Easy
The right answer is Option (D)
The Standards for Program Management - 4th Edition - reference: Chapter (8), Program Activities, 8.1.2.5 PROGRAM FINANCIAL MANAGEMENT PLANNING, pages 115
Clarification and Tips:

Options (A), (B), and (C) are elements expected to appear in the financial management plan, so Option (D) is the right answer.
Domain: Life Cycle Management
Phase or Element: Definition

Q67 - The FLX program is very crucial to the Good Day organization. During the program kick-off meeting, some stakeholders stressed that they need to assess the overall health of the program and take appropriate action to ensure successful benefits delivery. What is the most important action that should be done by the program manger to fulfil this request?

(a) The program manager should refine program benefits risks
(b) The program manager should ensure having a strong communication management plan
(c) The program manager should send the new status of the benefits register to the key stakeholders
(d) The program manager should consistently monitor and report on benefits metrics to the stakeholders

Question Category: Difficult
The right answer is Option (D)
The Standards for Program Management - 4th Edition - reference: Chapter (4), Program Benefits Management, 4.3 BENEFITS DELIVERY, page 51
Clarification and Tips:
The most important action that should be done by the program manger to fulfil the stakeholders request is to consistently monitor and report on benefits metrics to the stakeholders, so Option (D) is the right answer.
Options (A) and (C) are not related to the stakeholders' request, so they are wrong answers. Option (B) may help in fulfilling the stakeholders request, but Option (A) is much better as it is direct and clear driving to achieve the stakeholders request.
Domain: Benefits Management
Phase or Element: BENEFITS DELIVERY

Q68 - Kristin is writing a document that contains the explanation defining the processes for creating, maximizing, and sustaining the program benefits. What document is Kristin writing?

(a) The benefits register
(b) The benefits management plan
(c) The benefits delivery schedule
(d) The program transition plan

Question Category: Moderate
The right answer is Option (B)
The Standards for Program Management - 4th Edition - reference: Chapter (4), Program Benefits Management, 4.2.1 BENEFITS MANAGEMENT PLAN, page 50
Clarification and Tips:
The benefits management plan is a document that contains the explanation defining the processes for creating, maximizing, and sustaining the program benefits, so Option (B) is the right answer.
Option (A) is wrong as the benefits register collects and lists the planned benefits for the program and is used to measure and communicate the delivery of benefits throughout the duration of the program.
Option (C) is wrong as there is no program artifact in PMI standards called benefits delivery schedule.
Option (D) is wrong as the transition plan is related to transition preparations.
Domain: Benefits Management
Phase or Element: BENEFITS ANALYSIS AND PLANNING

Q69 - Omar is managing an Organization transformation program in the Zenon organization, one of the IT leading organizations in Silicon Valley. While working on the benefits register, Omar found one benefit which is related to consolidation of positions in the operation division, which may have a negative impact on the division staff. What should Omar do as a program manager?

(a) Omar should neglect the negative impact of the benefits as the benefits are related to the program objectives
(b) Omar should minimize the negative impact of the benefits and he should manage, measure, and properly communicate the negative impact to the organization's leadership
(c) Omar should escalate the negative impact to the program sponsor
(d) Omar should protect this information of negative impact from reaching the impacted staff

Question Category: Difficult
The right answer is Option (B)
The Standards for Program Management - 4th Edition - reference: Chapter (4), Program Benefits Management, page 44
Clarification and Tips:
The right answer is that Omar should minimize the negative impact of the benefits and he should manage measure, and properly communicate the negative impact to the organization's leadership, which is Option (B).
Options (A) and (C) are wrong as the program manager should minimize the negative impacts as important as realizing the benefits.

Option (D) is wrong as it is unethical.
Domain: Benefits Management
Phase or Element: General

Q70 - Jason was estimating the costs of his program components. He has high uncertainty for one program component. Therefore, he calculated the component estimate as close to the beginning of a work effort as possible. A few months later, he found that the cost of the output of this component is lower than originally planned. What is the best action he can do?

- (a) He should wait until he closes this component and then he can ask for a reward for the saved budget
- (b) He can present an opportunity to the program sponsor for additional products that would be acquired later in the program
- (c) He should open an opportunity on the risk register for the extra money
- (d) He should wait until he closes this component and then he can use the budget to help the other components with budget deficiency

Question Category: Difficult
The right answer is Option (B)
The Standards for Program Management - 4th Edition - reference: Chapter (8), Program Activities, 8.2.3.2 COMPONENT COST ESTIMATION, pages 129
Clarification and Tips:
It is a generally accepted good practice to calculate an estimate as close to the beginning of a work effort as possible. This way, if the cost of the output is lower than originally planned, the program manager may present an opportunity to the program sponsor for additional products that would be acquired later in the program.
Therefore, Option (B) is the right answer.
Please note that Option (C) is wrong as it is too late to open a positive risk.
Domain: Life Cycle Management
Phase or Element: Delivery

Q71 - Jimmy is confused about how the resources and program costs are managed on both the program level and component level, what is your advice to Jimmy?

- (a) The majority of resources and program costs are managed at the program level
- (b) The majority of resources and program costs are managed at the component level instead of the program level
- (c) All the resources and program costs are managed at the program level

(d) All the resources and program costs are managed at the component level instead of the program level

Question Category: Difficult
The right answer is Option (B)
The Standards for Program Management - 4th Edition - reference: Chapter (7), Program Life Cycle Management, 7.2.2.1 PROGRAM INFRASTRUCTURE DEVELOPMENT, pages 101
Clarification and Tips:
The majority of resources and program costs are managed at the component level instead of the program level, so Option (B) is the right answer.
Domain: Life Cycle Management
Phase or Element: Definition

Q72 - During your work to manage the ABC program, you noticed one stakeholder did not participate in any activity although there are three benefits that are going to affect his department. Your project manager dealing with this department assumed that he is a satisfied stakeholder and he did not participate in the program activities as he is confident about the program progress.
Incorrect assumptions about stakeholder behaviour may lead to all the following, except:

(a) Satisfied stakeholder
(b) Unanticipated issues
(c) Poor program management decisions
(d) Unhappy stakeholder

Question Category: Moderate
The right answer is Option (A)
The Standards for Program Management - 4th Edition - reference: Chapter (5), Program Stakeholder Engagement, 5.4 PROGRAM STAKEHOLDER ENGAGEMENT, page 65
Clarification and Tips:
Incorrect assumptions about stakeholder behaviour may lead to an unhappy stakeholder, unanticipated issues or poor program management decisions, but most probably will not lead to a satisfied customer.
Therefore, Option (A) is the right answer.
Domain: Stakeholder Engagement
Phase or Element: PROGRAM STAKEHOLDER ENGAGEMENT

Q73 - Peter is in the definition phase of his program, he started to gather the communication requirements in order to create his communication plan. He got advice from a more experienced program manager to ensure that the communications requirements are clearly defined. What is the best reason for this advice?

(a) To create a strong communication plan
(b) To create a strong stakeholder engagement plan
(c) To facilitate the transfer of information from the program to the proper stakeholders with the proper content and delivery methods
(d) To ensure alignment between the program roadmap and the program charter

Question Category: Difficult
The right answer is Option (C)
The Standards for Program Management - 4th Edition - reference: Chapter (8), Program Activities, Program Management Supporting Processes, 8.1.2.2 PROGRAM COMMUNICATIONS MANAGEMENT PLANNING, page 112
Clarification and Tips:
Communication requirements should be clearly defined to facilitate the transfer of information between the program and its components and from the program to the appropriate stakeholders with the appropriate content and delivery methods.
Crafting the communication plan or engagement plan is not the objective by itself, but they are tools to reach the objective of having clear communication or satisfying stakeholder engagement.
Therefore, the right answer is Option (C).
Domain: Life Cycle Management
Phase or Element: Definition

Q74 - Per is a program manager who has just created his stakeholder engagement plan including the stakeholder metrics. When should Per review the stakeholder engagement metrics?

(a) Regularly
(b) During the program closure to record the lessons learned
(c) At the time of accepting a benefit delivery
(d) In the Transition and Closure subphase

Question Category: Moderate
The right answer is Option (A)
The Standards for Program Management - 4th Edition - reference: Chapter (5), Program Stakeholder Engagement, 5.4 PROGRAM STAKEHOLDER ENGAGEMENT, page 65
Clarification and Tips:
The program manager should review the stakeholder metrics regularly to identify potential risks caused by a lack of participation from stakeholders. Thus, the right answer is Option (A).
Domain: Stakeholder Engagement
Phase or Element: PROGRAM STAKEHOLDER ENGAGEMENT

Q75 - During the last steering meeting, a decision was made to cancel the Mody program in your organization. The program manager was very disappointed as he exerted big effort to work towards achieving the program objectives. Which of the following may be the reason to cancel the Mody program?

(a) The change in technology made the product, which is delivered by one of the program components, has an obsolete architecture
(b) The change in technology made the program business case incorrect with wrong targets
(c) The program is suffering a high number of change requests
(d) The program has many open issues with high impact

Question Category: Moderate
The right answer is Option (B)
The Standards for Program Management - 4th Edition - reference: Chapter (6), Program Governance, 6.1.9 PROGRAM GOVERNANCE REVIEWS, page 76
Clarification and Tips:
The program may be terminated when it is determined that the business case becomes incorrect and its targets are wrong, so Option (B) is the right answer.
Having many change requests or open issues are not good reasons to terminate the program. Having obsolete product architecture for one of the program components may affect the component highly, but not necessarily the program.
Domain: Program Governance
Phase or Element: PROGRAM GOVERNANCE PRACTICES

Q76 - Kim is working as a program manager to the X-Tel program. He has five components which are managed by contractors. How is the baseline budget created in this case of contractors' involvement?

(a) The details of the budget come from the contracts, then the program overhead is added to the initial budget figure before a baseline budget can be prepared.
(b) The contracts constructed the baseline budget
(c) The program manager prepared his bottom-up cost regardless of the contracts
(d) The program sponsor is consulted to agree on the best approach to defining the baseline budget

Question Category: Difficult
The right answer is Option (A)
The Standards for Program Management - 4th Edition - reference: Chapter (8), Program Activities, 8.2.3.1 PROGRAM COST BUDGETING, page 129

Clarification and Tips:
When contractors are involved, the details of the budget come from the contracts. Option (A) has the complete right answer, the rest of the options are just to create confusion.
Domain: Life Cycle Management
Phase or Element: Delivery

Q77 - John is conducting a risk identification session in his program where he invited the program team, subject matter experts from outside the program team, and component managers. Who else should he invite?

(a) No need to invite more people, the current group is enough
(b) He should invite the program sponsor, customers, end users, stakeholders and risk management experts
(c) He should invite the program sponsor and risk management experts
(d) He has more staff than required, so he should remove the invitation for the subject matter experts from outside the program team

Question Category: Moderate
The right answer is Option (B)
The Standards for Program Management - 4th Edition - reference: Chapter (8), Program Activities, 8.2.8.1 PROGRAM RISK IDENTIFICATION, pages 134
Clarification and Tips:
Participants in risk identification activities may include the program manager, program sponsor, program team members, risk management team, subject matter experts from outside the program team, customers, end users, component managers, managers of other program components, stakeholders, risk management experts and external reviewers, as required. Therefore, Option (B) is the right answer.
Domain: Life Cycle Management
Phase or Element: Delivery

Q78 - Which of the following plans may have updates to reflect the needs of the program sponsor and the funding organizations' representatives with regard to financial arrangements?

(a) The program communications management plan
(b) The stakeholder engagement plan
(c) The quality management plan
(d) Options (A) and (B)

Question Category: Difficult
The right answer is Option (D)

The Standards for Program Management - 4th Edition - reference: Chapter (8), Program Activities, 8.1.2.4 PROGRAM FINANCIAL FRAMEWORK ESTABLISHMENT, pages 114
Clarification and Tips:
It is important to understand the specific and unique needs of the program sponsor and the funding organizations' representatives with regard to financial arrangements. The program communications management and stakeholder engagement plans may need updates to reflect these needs.
Therefore, Option (C) is the right answer.
Domain: Life Cycle Management
Phase or Element: Definition

Q79 - _____ is the measure of the degree of acceptable variation around a program objective that reflects the risk appetite of the organization and program stakeholders.

- (a) Risk appetite
- (b) Risk exposure
- (c) Risk register
- (d) Risk threshold

Question Category: Moderate
The right answer is Option (D)
The Standards for Program Management - 4th Edition - reference: Chapter (3), Program Strategy Alignment, 3.5.2 PROGRAM RISK THRESHOLDS, page 41
Clarification and Tips:
Risk appetite is an assessment of the organization's willingness to accept and deal with risks.
Risk exposure is an aggregate measure of the potential impact of all risks at any given point in time in a project, program, or portfolio.
The risk register is a repository in which outputs of risk management processes are recorded.
Risk threshold is the measure of the degree of acceptable variation around a program objective that reflects the risk appetite of the organization and program stakeholders.
Therefore, the right answer is Option (D).
Domain: Strategy Alignment
Phase or Element: PROGRAM RISK MANAGEMENT STRATEGY

Q80 - Milan has multiple change requests in the program that he is managing. One change request has multiple ways to implement the change, what should Milan do to select the best way?

- (a) Milan should assess the costs, risks, and other aspects of each option to enable selection of the approach most likely to deliver the program's intended benefits

(b) Milan should assess the costs of each option to enable selection of the best way to execute the change
(c) Milan should assess the schedule impact of each option to enable selection of the best way to execute the change
(d) Milan should call the organization change management team to assess the different ways and provide advice

Question Category: Difficult
The right answer is Option (A)
The Standards for Program Management - 4th Edition - reference: Chapter (6), Program Governance, 8.2.1 PROGRAM CHANGE MONITORING AND CONTROLLING, page 125
Clarification and Tips:
When there are multiple ways to implement the change, costs, risks, and other aspects of each option should be assessed to enable selection of the approach most likely to deliver the program's intended benefits, so Option (A) is the right answer.
Domain: Program Governance
Phase or Element: PROGRAM GOVERNANCE PRACTICES

Q81 - Sam is managing a program in a Y5 organization. During his work in the delivery phase, he started to review more details regarding the program components with his team. Unfortunately, he discovered that one of the program components has more scope than planned which will affect the integration with two other components. He was angry with the component manager and came to you asking for advice, what is your best advice to him?

(a) I will advise him to go back to the planning subphase to review all the component planning activities before continuing in the delivery phase
(b) I will tell him that he needs to continually oversee the components throughout the delivery phase and when necessary, replan for their proper integration or realign to accommodate changes
(c) I will tell him that he needs to continually oversee the components throughout the delivery phase and collect the pitfalls to be escalated to the steering committee
(d) I will advise him to ignore this change as it is the mistake of the component manager

Question Category: Difficult
The right answer is Option (B)
The Standards for Program Management - 4th Edition - reference: Chapter (7), Program Life Cycle Management, 7.1.3 PROGRAM DELIVERY PHASE, pages 95
Clarification and Tips:
The program manager needs to continually oversee the components throughout the delivery phase and when necessary, replan for their proper integration or realign to accommodate changes in program direction through adaptive change.
Therefore, Option (B) is the right answer.

Please note the following:
Option (A) is wrong as this change is expected due to program uncertainty, so he should continually oversee the components throughout the delivery phase.
Option (C) is wrong as the escalation is not the right action, he should expect such change due to program uncertainty.
Option (D) is wrong as ignoring the change will be worse.
Domain: Life Cycle Management
Phase or Element: Delivery

Q82 - Ahmed is preparing for a program review in which a decision will be made to end one of the program components. What is the name of the review that Ahmed is preparing?

   (a) Independent Review
   (b) Peer review
   (c) Phase-gate review
   (d) Walkthrough

Question Category: Moderate
The right answer is Option (C)
The Standards for Program Management - 4th Edition - reference: Chapter (6), Program Governance, 6.1.9 PROGRAM GOVERNANCE REVIEWS, page 75
Clarification and Tips:
Phase-gate reviews are reviews at the end of a phase in which a decision is made to continue to the next phase, to continue with modification or to end a program or program component, so Option (C) is the right answer.
Domain: Program Governance
Phase or Element: PROGRAM GOVERNANCE PRACTICES

Q83 - Sam is working on the program planning activity with his program management team. He started to plan for the resource management, so he conducted a meeting with the concerned stakeholders including the program quality manager.
What is the role of the program quality manager in developing the resources management plan?

   (a) The program quality manager has no role in developing the resources management plan
   (b) The program quality manager participates in the planning activity of the program resource management plan to verify that quality activities and controls are applied and flow down to all the components
   (c) The program quality manager participates in the planning activity of the program resource management plan to verify that the quality assurance and control added to the quality plan comply with the resource management plan

(d) The program quality manager participates in the planning activity of the program resource management plan to define the changes required in the quality management plan to be aligned with the resource management plan

Question Category: Difficult
The right answer is Option (B)
The Standards for Program Management - 4th Edition - reference: Chapter (8), Program Activities, 8.1.2.8 PROGRAM QUALITY MANAGEMENT PLANNING, pages 118
Clarification and Tips:
Quality management should be considered when defining all program management activity as well as for every deliverable and service.
When developing a program resource management plan, it is recommended that a program quality manager participates in the planning activity to verify that quality activities and controls are applied and flow down to all the components, including those performed by subcontractors. Therefore, Option (B) is the right answer.
Domain: Life Cycle Management
Phase or Element: Definition

Q84 - Jack is a program manager in the First company. He manages an IT program to be delivered to the Healthy, which is a leading pharmaceutical organization. He is currently in the program transition phase. All preparation processes and activities within the Healthy organization that are related to ensuring that the service is received and incorporated as planned, are still not finished. Who should be responsible for completing them?

(a) Jack, the program manager
(b) Healthy organization team
(c) First company team
(d) Program steering committee

Question Category: Moderate
The right answer is Option (B)
The Standards for Program Management - 4th Edition - reference: Chapter (4), Program Benefits Management, 4.4 BENEFITS TRANSITION, page 53
Clarification and Tips:
The receiving organization or function is responsible for all preparation processes and activities within their domain to ensure that the product, service or capability is received and incorporated into their domain, so Option (B) is the right answer.
Domain: Benefits Management
Phase or Element: BENEFITS TRANSITION

Q85 - Anil is managing his first program in your organization. He is suffering from the changes requested by some stakeholders that may affect the program schedule. Which of the following bounds the changes authorized for a program?

(a) The program scope
(b) Organizational strategy
(c) The organization risk exposure
(d) The program schedule

Question Category: Difficult
The right answer is Option (B)
The Standards for Program Management - 4th Edition - reference: Chapter (6), Program Governance, 6.1.8 PROGRAM CHANGE GOVERNANCE, page 74
Clarification and Tips:
The extent to which a change can be authorized by program governance is bounded by the program business case and organizational strategy, so Option (B) is the right answer.
Please remember that programs are managed in a manner that accepts and adapts to change as necessary to optimize the delivery of benefits.
Domain: Program Governance
Phase or Element: PROGRAM GOVERNANCE PRACTICES

Q86 - Which of the following dimensions may the organization consider during the feasibility study process to decide on the proposed program?

(a) The organization's sourcing
(b) The organization's complexity
(c) The organization's financial
(d) All the above

Question Category: Easy
The right answer is Option (D)
The Standards for Program Management - 4th Edition - reference: Chapter (3), Program Strategy Alignment, 3.4.2.2 FEASIBILITY STUDIES, page 40
Clarification and Tips:
Options (A), (B), and (C) are dimensions that the organization may consider during the feasibility study process to decide on the proposed program. So the right answer is Option (D).
Domain: Strategy Alignment
Phase or Element: ENVIRONMENTAL ASSESSMENTS

Q87 - Michelle is working in the program closure activities in the MeanWel organization. She

found some risks that are still open and may affect the realized benefits during the sustainment period which is covered by another organization; the Mena organization.
What should Michelle do to these opened risks?

(a) She should ignore them as the program activities are closed
(b) She should transfer them to the operation team of the Mena organization
(c) She should transfer these risks, along with any supporting analysis and response information, to the Mena organizational risk register
(d) She should keep them as part of the MeanWel organization risk register even if the project is closed

Question Category: Difficult
The right answer is Option (C)
The Standards for Program Management - 4th Edition - reference: Chapter (8), Program Activities, 8.3.5 PROGRAM RISK MANAGEMENT TRANSITION, page 140
Clarification and Tips:
Option (C) is the right answer as adding the risks with the available analysis and response information to the Mena organizational risk register will keep the risk monitored by the performing organization during the sustainment period.
Options (A) and (D) are wrong.
Option (B) is not as good as the operation team is not usually qualified to deal with risks.
Domain: Life Cycle Management
Phase or Element: Closing

Q88 - While managing his program in the ABC organization, John is looking for the assessment of the ABC organization's willingness to accept and deal with risks. Which of the following is John looking for?

(a) Risk threshold
(b) Risk appetite
(c) Risk exposure
(d) Risk audit

Question Category: Moderate
The right answer is Option (B)
The Standards for Program Management - 4th Edition - reference: Chapter (3), Program Strategy Alignment, 3.5.1 RISK MANAGEMENT FOR STRATEGY ALIGNMENT, page 41
Clarification and Tips:
Risk threshold is the measure of the degree of acceptable variation around a program objective that reflects the risk appetite of the organization and program stakeholders.
Risk appetite is an assessment of the organization's willingness to accept and deal with risks.

Risk exposure is an aggregate measure of the potential impact of all risks at any given point in time in a project, program, or portfolio.
Risk Audit is a type of audit used to consider the effectiveness of the risk management process. Therefore, the right answer is Option (B).
Domain: Strategy Alignment
Phase or Element: PROGRAM RISK MANAGEMENT STRATEGY

Q89 - Which of the following areas of expertise may help the program manager in stakeholder engagement?

(a) Enterprise resource management (ERP)
(b) Customer relationship management (CRM)
(c) Knowledge management system (KMS)
(d) Information management system

Question Category: Moderate
The right answer is Option (B)
The Standards for Program Management - 4th Edition - reference: Chapter (5), Program Stakeholder Engagement, General
Clarification and Tips:
Customer relationship management (CRM) is the most suitable area of expertise within the given options that may help the program manager in stakeholder engagement. So, the right answer is Option (B).
Option (A) is wrong as ERP is mainly to manage the company resources; HR, financial and logistics.
Option (C) and (D) may be helpful, but option (B) is much better.
Domain: Stakeholder Engagement
Phase or Element: General

Q90 - VK is a program manager who detected some changes in his program. He started to update the benefits management plan, what is the other important document that he should update with the benefits management plan update?

(a) Program Roadmap
(b) Benefits register
(c) Program governance
(d) Business case

Question Category: Moderate
The right answer is Option (A)

The Standards for Program Management - 4th Edition - reference: Chapter (4), Program Benefits Management, 4.3.1 BENEFITS AND PROGRAM COMPONENTS, page 52

Clarification and Tips:
When there are updates to be applied to the benefits management plan due to program changes, the program roadmap should also be modified to reflect the changes in the relationship between program major milestones and expected benefits. Changes may also be applied to the benefits register, but the changes to the roadmap are obligatory and more important. Therefore, the right answer is Option (A).

Domain: Benefits Management
Phase or Element: General

Q91 - The following items are included in the program business case, except:

(a) Financial analysis
(b) Stakeholders influence
(c) Intrinsic and extrinsic benefits
(d) Market demands or barriers

Question Category: Moderate
The right answer is Option (B)
The Standards for Program Management - 4th Edition - reference: Chapter (3), Program Strategy Alignment, 3.1 PROGRAM BUSINESS CASE, page 35

Clarification and Tips:
The business case may include details about the program outcomes, approved concept, issues, high-level risk and opportunity assessment, key assumptions, business and operational impact, cost benefit analysis, alternative solutions, financial analysis, intrinsic and extrinsic benefits, market demands or barriers, potential profits, social needs, environmental influences, legal implications, time to market, constraints, and the extent to which the program aligns with the organization's strategic plan.
Option (B) is not expected to appear in the business case, so Option (B) is the right answer.

Domain: Strategy Alignment
Phase or Element: PROGRAM BUSINESS CASE

Q92 - Santiago is the program manager assigned to manage one program in your organization that has three projects and one subsidiary program. He executed the program planning subphase and now he wants to initiate his first program component, which is the Leen project. He is seeking your help to advise him about the proper action. What is your advice?

(a) Wait until all the components are ready, then request their authorization from the steering committee

(b) Wait until he has all the components ready, then request their authorization from the program management office
(c) Request the authorization for the new program component from the steering committee
(d) Request the authorization for the new program component from the program management office

Question Category: Difficult
The right answer is Option (C)
The Standards for Program Management - 4th Edition - reference: Chapter (6), Program Governance, 6.1.11 PROGRAM COMPONENT INITIATION AND TRANSITION, page 76
Clarification and Tips:
Program steering committee approval is usually required prior to the initiation of individual components of the program, because the authorization of a component requires resource commitment from the organization and introduction of additional governance structures handling the new component. Therefore, Option (C) is the right answer.
Please note that:
The program management office is usually reporting to the program manager, so the program manager will not ask the office for authorization.
It is wrong to wait until initiating all components together as components are initiated according to the roadmap, in some cases a component will be initiated after another is completed.
Domain: Program Governance
Phase or Element: PROGRAM GOVERNANCE PRACTICES

Q93 - When are the program benefits expected to exceed program costs?

(a) Program benefits are expected to exceed program costs at the project completion
(b) Program benefits are expected to exceed program costs at the project completion if the program is successful
(c) Program benefits are expected to exceed program costs over the time, as specified in the business case
(d) Program benefits are expected to exceed program costs over the time, as specified in the transition plan

Question Category: Difficult
The right answer is Option (C)
The Standards for Program Management - 4th Edition - reference: Chapter (4), Program Benefits Management, 4.2 BENEFITS ANALYSIS AND PLANNING, page 48
Clarification and Tips:
Program benefits are expected to exceed program costs over the time, as specified in the business case, so Option (C) is the right answer.

Options (A) and (B) are wrong in principle, while Option (D) is wrong as the benefits information is not expected in the transition plan.
Domain: Benefits Management
Phase or Element: BENEFITS ANALYSIS AND PLANNING

Q94 - After you approve the program change request, which of the following activities should be executed?

- (a) Communicate the change request to appropriate stakeholders
- (b) Record the change request in the program change log
- (c) Reflect in updates to component plans
- (d) All the above

Question Category: Easy
The right answer is Option (D)
The Standards for Program Management - 4th Edition - reference: Chapter (6), Program Governance, 8.2.1 PROGRAM CHANGE MONITORING AND CONTROLLING, page 125
Clarification and Tips:
Options (A), (B), and (C) are activities that should be executed after the change request is approved, so Option (D) is the right answer.
Domain: Program Governance
Phase or Element: PROGRAM GOVERNANCE PRACTICES

Q95 - Ahmed is working on his program closure. He has three components which are officially closed. He is transferring the responsibility of the operation and maintenance or the program benefits to the operation team who lack the skills of the new technology used in one of the program components. If Ahmed needs to release the resources of the program components as part of the program closure. What is the best choice that he should do for these resources?

- (a) He should try to transfer some of the resources who have the skills of the new technology to the operation team
- (b) He will release the resources from the program components regardless of their next move
- (c) He will release the resources from the program components and transfer their allocation responsibility to the program sponsor
- (d) He will release the resources from the program components and transfer their allocation responsibility to the operation team

Question Category: Moderate
The right answer is Option (A)

The Standards for Program Management - 4th Edition - reference: Chapter (8), Program Activities, 8.3.4 PROGRAM RESOURCE TRANSITION, page 140

Clarification and Tips:
Reassignment of resources at the component level could include transitioning resources to another component already in execution or another program within the organization that requires a similar skill set.
Therefore, Option (A) is the best choice and the right answer.
Please note that:
Option (B) is not bad, but Option (A) is much better.
Options (C) and (D) are wrong as it is not the responsibility of the program sponsor or operation team to reassign the released resources.
Domain: Life Cycle Management
Phase or Element: Closing

Q96 - Prior to program closure, Fatma, the program manager, is developing a document to identify the program risks, processes, measures, metrics, and tools necessary to ensure the continued realization of the benefits delivered. Which document is this?

(a) Benefits register
(b) Benefits management plan
(c) Benefits sustainment plan
(d) Benefits transition plan

Question Category: Moderate
The right answer is Option (C)
The Standards for Program Management - 4th Edition - reference: Chapter (4), Program Benefits Management, 4.5 BENEFITS SUSTAINMENT, page 55

Clarification and Tips:
A benefits sustainment plan should be developed prior to program closure to identify the risks, processes, measures, metrics, and tools necessary to ensure the continued realization of the benefits delivered, so Option (C) is the right answer.
Domain: Benefits Management
Phase or Element: BENEFITS SUSTAINMENT

Q97 - Mustafa is assigned to manage the Yen program after the previous program manager was promoted to another position in your organization. Mustafa is looking for the list of planned benefits for the Yen program. Which document should Mustafa refer to?

(a) The benefits management plan
(b) The program management plan

(c) The benefits register
(d) The program charter

Question Category: Moderate
The right answer is Option (C)
The Standards for Program Management - 4th Edition - reference: Chapter (4), Program Benefits Management, 4.1.1 BENEFITS REGISTER, page 47
Clarification and Tips:
The benefits register collects and lists the planned benefits for the program, so Option (C) is the right answer.
Domain: Benefits Management
Phase or Element: BENEFITS IDENTIFICATION

Q98 - Aisa is writing the program governance and is adding some elements related to the program success criteria. Which of the following is the best description of these criteria?

(a) The criteria describe the definition of success consistent with the expectations and needs of key program stakeholders
(b) The criteria describe the definition of success consistent with the program objectives
(c) The criteria describe the definition of success consistent with the needs of key program stakeholders
(d) The criteria describe the definition of success consistent with the expectations and needs of key program stakeholders, and reinforce the program alignment to deliver the maximum attainable benefits

Question Category: Moderate
The right answer is Option (D)
The Standards for Program Management - 4th Edition - reference: Chapter (6), Program Governance, 6.1.4 PROGRAM SUCCESS CRITERIA, page 72
Clarification and Tips:
The criteria describe the definition of success consistent with the expectations and needs of key program stakeholders, and reinforce the program alignment to deliver the maximum attainable benefits, so Option (D) is the right answer.
Options (A) and (C) are partially good, but Option (D) is the complete answer.
Domain: Program Governance
Phase or Element: PROGRAM GOVERNANCE PRACTICES

Q99 - Per is working with a stakeholder analysis tool that groups the stakeholders based on their level of authority and their level of concern regarding the project outcomes. Which tools is this?

Exam 1 - Questions and Answers

(a) The stakeholder map
(b) The stakeholder register
(c) The power/interest grid
(d) The stakeholder cube

Question Category: Moderate
The right answer is Option (C)
The Standards for Program Management - 4th Edition - reference: Chapter (5), Program Stakeholder Engagement, 5.2 PROGRAM STAKEHOLDER ANALYSIS, page 62
Clarification and Tips:
The stakeholder map visually represents the interaction of all stakeholders' current and desired support and influence. The map serves as a tool to assess the impact of a change on the program community.
The stakeholder register lists the stakeholders and categorizes their relationship to the program, their ability to influence the program outcome and their degree of support for the program.
The power/interest grid groups stakeholders based on their level of authority power and their level of concern interest regarding the project outcomes.
The stakeholder cube combines the grid elements into a three-dimensional model that can be useful in identifying and engaging their stakeholder community.
Therefore, the right answer is Option (C).
Domain: Stakeholder Engagement
Phase or Element: PROGRAM STAKEHOLDER ANALYSIS

Q100 - Oscar is working on a component of the program management plan that includes the information management policies and distribution lists, which subsidiary plan is this?

(a) The program communication management plan
(b) The program information management plan
(c) The program change management plan
(d) The program schedule management plan

Question Category: Moderate
The right answer is Option (B)
The Standards for Program Management - 4th Edition - reference: Chapter (8), Program Activities, 8.1.2.6 PROGRAM INFORMATION MANAGEMENT PLANNING, pages 116
Clarification and Tips:
The program communications management plan is the component of the program management plan that describes how, when and by whom information will be administered and disseminated.
The program information management plan is a component of the program management plan that describes how the program's information assets will be prepared, collected, organized, and

secured. It includes information management policies, distribution lists, appropriate tools, templates, and reporting formats.

The program change management plan is a component of the program management plan that establishes program change management principles and procedures, including the approach for capturing requested changes, evaluating each requested change, determining the disposition of each requested change, communicating a decision to impacted stakeholders, documenting the change request and supporting detail, and authorizing funding and work.

The program schedule management plan is a component of the program management plan that establishes the criteria and the activities for developing, monitoring, and controlling the schedule.

Therefore, Option (B) is the right answer.

Domain: Life Cycle Management
Phase or Element: Definition

Q101 - Ahmed is managing his first program in the Uni-Corn organization. His program is the only program managed as stand-alone outside the existing two organization portfolio structures. Ahmed started to develop his program governance plan. He wants to align the program governance with the governance of the organization governing body, but he got an advice from an older program manager to align the program governance with one of the existing two portfolios governance.

What should Ahmed do?

(a) Ahmed should align his program governance with any of the existing portfolio governance
(b) Ahmed should align his program governance with the more complicated existing portfolio governance
(c) Ahmed can align his program governance with any of the existing portfolio governance or with the governance of the organization governing body
(d) Ahmed should align his program governance with the governance of the organization governing body

Question Category: Difficult
The right answer is Option (D)
The Standards for Program Management - 4th Edition - reference: Chapter (6), Program Governance, page 68

Clarification and Tips:
For stand-alone programs that are outside of a portfolio structure, a governing body provides governance-supporting functions and processes to programs, including governance policies, oversight, control, integration and decision-making functions and processes, so Option (D) is the right answer.

Please note that for a program within a portfolio structure, the program governance should be aligned with the portfolio governance.
Domain: Program Governance
Phase or Element: General

Q102 - Ahmed started to review and evaluate the acceptance criteria applicable to delivered components, review operational and program process documentation, and review training and maintenance materials. Which phase of the benefits delivery is he working on?

- (a) Benefits identification
- (b) Benefits transition
- (c) Benefits delivery
- (d) Benefits sustainment

Question Category: Difficult
The right answer is Option (B)
The Standards for Program Management - 4th Edition - reference: Chapter (4), Program Benefits Management, 4.4 BENEFITS TRANSITION, page 54
Clarification and Tips:
Review and evaluation of the acceptance criteria applicable to delivered components, review of operational and program process documentation, and review of training and maintenance materials are activities related to the benefits transition, so Option (B) is the right answer.
Domain: Benefits Management
Phase or Element: BENEFITS TRANSITION

Q103 - How should the program manager deal with resources which are no longer necessary for the program?

- (a) The program manager should create work for these resources to make their work necessary for the program
- (b) The program manager should seek consultation or advice from the program sponsor
- (c) The program manager should keep the resources until the program ends even if they are no longer necessary for the program
- (d) The program manager ensures resources are released for other programs when they are no longer necessary for the current program

Question Category: Difficult
The right answer is Option (D)
The Standards for Program Management - 4th Edition - reference: Chapter (8), Program Activities, 8.2.7 PROGRAM RESOURCE MANAGEMENT, pages 133

Exam 1 - Questions and Answers

Clarification and Tips:
The program manager ensures resources are released for other programs when they are no longer necessary for the current program.
Therefore, Option (D) is the right answer.
Domain: Life Cycle Management
Phase or Element: Delivery

Q104 - Linda is working on a program activity that creates the program change thresholds, which activity is this?

(a) Program change management planning
(b) Program change assessment
(c) Program change monitoring and controlling
(d) Program scope assessment

Question Category: Difficult
The right answer is Option (A)
The Standards for Program Management - 4th Edition - reference: Chapter (8), Program Activities, 8.1.2.1 PROGRAM CHANGE MANAGEMENT PLANNING, pages 112
Clarification and Tips:
The outputs of the program change management planning activity include a program change management plan and program change thresholds.
Therefore, Option (C) is the right answer.
Domain: Life Cycle Management
Phase or Element: Definition

Q105 - Governance of programs in the diverse fields may have remarkably different needs based on the unique political, regulatory, legal, technical, and competitive environments in which they operate. In such cases, what is the most important common rule of governance between the different fields?

(a) The risk management
(b) A sponsor organization seeks to implement governance practices that enable the organization to monitor the program's support of the organizational strategy
(c) A sponsor organization seeks to implement governance practices that enable the organization to manage the risks properly
(d) The benefits realization to be assured

Question Category: Moderate
The right answer is Option (B)

The Standards for Program Management - 4th Edition - reference: Chapter (6), Program Governance, 6.3 PROGRAM GOVERNANCE DESIGN AND IMPLEMENTATION, page 85
Clarification and Tips:
Governance of programs in the diverse fields may have remarkably different needs based on the unique political, regulatory, legal, technical, and competitive environments in which they operate. In each case, a sponsor organization seeks to implement governance practices that enable the organization to monitor the program's support of the organizational strategy. Therefore, Option (B) is the right answer.
Domain: Program Governance
Phase or Element: PROGRAM GOVERNANCE DESIGN AND IMPLEMENTATION

Q106 - How do usually the program stakeholders view the program benefits?

(a) As a positive risk
(b) As a change
(c) As an opportunity
(d) As an issue to be resolved

Question Category: Difficult
The right answer is Option (B)
The Standards for Program Management - 4th Edition - reference: Chapter (5), Program Stakeholder Engagement, page 59
Clarification and Tips:
Stakeholders view the program benefits as change and stakeholder engagement at the program level can be challenging as people are usually reluctant to change. Therefore, the right answer is Option (B).
Domain: Stakeholder Engagement
Phase or Element: General

Q107 - What of the following are valid program funding models?

(a) Supported by internal and external sources of funding
(b) Funded entirely within a single organization
(c) Managed within a single organization but funded separately
(d) All the above

Question Category: Easy
The right answer is Option (D)
The Standards for Program Management - 4th Edition - reference: Chapter (8), Program Activities, 8.1.2.4 PROGRAM FINANCIAL FRAMEWORK ESTABLISHMENT, pages 114

Clarification and Tips:
Options (A), (B), and (C) are valid program funding models, so Option (D) is the right answer.
Domain: Life Cycle Management
Phase or Element: Definition

Q108 - How often does the program management deal with the program resources?

(a) Resources are often shared among different components within a program
(b) Resources are often fully dedicated to one component
(c) Resources are often dedicated to a maximum of two components
(d) Resources are often shared between maximum two components within the program

Question Category: Moderate
The right answer is Option (A)
The Standards for Program Management - 4th Edition - reference: Chapter (8), Program Activities, 8.2.7 PROGRAM RESOURCE MANAGEMENT, pages 133
Clarification and Tips:
Resources are often shared among different components within a program. The program manager should work to ensure that the interdependencies do not cause a delay in benefits delivery.
Therefore, Option (A) is the right answer.
Domain: Life Cycle Management
Phase or Element: Delivery

Q109 - How do the organizations consider their resources?

(a) Organization assets to execute the programs, projects, and operation
(b) One of the organization limiting factors
(c) Organization constraint
(d) All the above

Question Category: Difficult
The right answer is Option (D)
The Standards for Program Management - 4th Edition - reference: Chapter (3), Program Strategy Alignment, page 33
Clarification and Tips:
Organizations consider their resources as limited assets to be used for the projects and programs. Usually, they are considered as a constraint for the organization that limits the organization desire to execute projects and programs. In specific organizations, the resources are considered unlimited as they extend their resources from the market. So, the right answer

is Option (D).
Domain: Strategy Alignment
Phase or Element: General

Q110 - Who is responsible to ensure alignment of the individual component plans with the program's goals and intended benefits in support of the achievement of the organization's strategy?

- (a) The program manager
- (b) The component manager
- (c) The program sponsor
- (d) The whole program team

Question Category: Difficult
The right answer is Option (A)
The Standards for Program Management - 4th Edition - reference: Chapter (1), INTRODUCTION, 1.3 WHAT IS PROGRAM MANAGEMENT, page 9

Clarification and Tips:
The program manager is responsible for ensuring alignment of the individual component plans with the program's goals and intended benefits in support of the achievement of the organization's strategy.
The component manager (project manager or subsidiary program manager) is responsible for managing the component within the program.
The program sponsor champions the program and is responsible for providing program resources.
So the right answer is Option (A).
Domain: Strategy Alignment
Phase or Element: General

Q111 - Anil is writing the program charter for his first time and needs some help. Which of the following items can you suggest to Anil to include in the charter?

- (a) High-level benefits
- (b) Assumptions and constraints
- (c) Key stakeholders
- (d) All the above

Question Category: Easy
The right answer is Option (D)
The Standards for Program Management - 4th Edition - reference: Chapter (3), Program

Strategy Alignment, 3.2 PROGRAM CHARTER, page 36
Clarification and Tips:
Options (A), (B), and (C) are elements that may appear in the program charters, so Option (D) is the right answer.
Domain: Strategy Alignment
Phase or Element: PROGRAM CHARTER

Q112 - Anil is part of the strategy board in your organization. He is working with his board members to define the organization's strategic plan. Which of the following factors may influence the strategic plan?

(a) Shareholders
(b) Competitor plans and actions
(c) Customer and partner requests
(d) All the above

Question Category: Easy
The right answer is Option (D)
The Standards for Program Management - 4th Edition - reference: Chapter (3), Program Strategy Alignment, 3.1 PROGRAM BUSINESS CASE, page 35
Clarification and Tips:
The organization's strategic plan is subdivided into a set of organizational initiatives that are influenced in part by market dynamics, customer and partner requests, shareholders, government regulations, organization's strengths and weaknesses, risk exposure, and competitor plans and actions.
Therefore, Option (D) is the right answer.
Domain: Strategy Alignment
Phase or Element: PROGRAM BUSINESS CASE

Q113 - All the following information is expected to appear in the stakeholder register, except:

(a) Stakeholder's name and role in the program
(b) Stakeholder's degree of support for the program
(c) Stakeholder's span of control
(d) Stakeholder's ability to influence the program outcome

Question Category: Moderate
The right answer is Option (C)
The Standards for Program Management - 4th Edition - reference: Chapter (5), Program Stakeholder Engagement, 5.1 PROGRAM STAKEHOLDER IDENTIFICATION, page 60

Clarification and Tips:
Options (A), (B), and (D) are contents expected to appear in the stakeholder register, but Option (C) is not as it refers to the number of subordinates a supervisor has.
Therefore, Option (C) is the right answer.
Domain: Stakeholder Engagement
Phase or Element: PROGRAM STAKEHOLDER IDENTIFICATION

Q114 - Omar is working as a program manager to manage a program that consists of four projects and one subsidiary program. During the execution of this program, some changes were applied to the industry regulations that mandates changes to three components.
What is your best choice to have an optimal contract(s) that supports your program to comply with these regulations?

(a) It is good to have three different contracts with three different companies for the three different components to implement the required changes
(b) It is optimal to have three different contracts with one company for the three different components to implement the required change
(c) It will be optimal to award one complete contract to implement the required changes in the three components
(d) I will check with the program sponsor to get his advice to have one contract or three contracts

Question Category: Difficult
The right answer is Option (C)
The Standards for Program Management - 4th Edition - reference: Chapter (8), Program Activities, 8.1.2.7 PROGRAM PROCUREMENT MANAGEMENT PLANNING, pages 117
Clarification and Tips:
The best program-wide approach to balancing specific external regulatory mandates; for example, rather than setting aside a certain percentage of each contract in the program to meet a small-business mandate, it may be optimal to award one complete contract to achieve the same mandate.
Therefore, Option (C) is the right answer.
Domain: Life Cycle Management
Phase or Element: Definition

Q115 - Santiago is a program manager in your organization, he created a strong procurement management to control all the component procurements at the program level. He decided to administer all the program contracts at the program level. What will be the role of the component managers in contract administration?

(a) Component managers have no role in the contract administration if the program contracts are administered at the program level
(b) Component managers accept invoices for component contract payments
(c) Component managers report deliverable acceptance and contract changes
(d) Component managers pay for the contract changes

Question Category: Moderate
The right answer is Option (C)
The Standards for Program Management - 4th Edition - reference: Chapter (8), Program Activities, 8.2.5.1 PROGRAM CONTRACT ADMINISTRATION, pages 131
Clarification and Tips:
Where contracts are administered at the program level, however, component managers coordinate or report deliverable acceptance, contract changes and other contract issues with the program staff.
Therefore, Option (C) is the right answer.
Domain: Life Cycle Management
Phase or Element: Delivery

Q116 - Miguel is expecting turbulences in his program coming from the anticipated regulation changes that will lead to major changes in two of his program components. He arranged a meeting with the two component managers and the EPMO to discuss the subject and agree on a decision. Which of the following is the best decision that they can make?

(a) Ignore the anticipated change as it is still not happening
(b) Take the anticipated change into account to continue alignment with the organization's strategic goals and objectives
(c) Register this expected change as a risk in the relevant program component
(d) Escalate the problem to the next program steering committee

Question Category: Difficult
The right answer is Option (B)
The Standards for Program Management - 4th Edition - reference: Chapter (3), Program Strategy Alignment, 3.4 ENVIRONMENTAL ASSESSMENTS, page 38
Clarification and Tips:
Program managers should identify these influences and take them into account when managing the program, in order to ensure ongoing stakeholder alignment, the program's continued alignment with the organization's strategic goals and objectives, and overall program success.
Therefore, Option (B) is the right answer.
Domain: Strategy Alignment
Phase or Element: ENVIRONMENTAL ASSESSMENTS

Q117 - What is the primary objective of stakeholders' engagement?

(a) Gain and maintain stakeholder buy-in for the program's objectives, benefits, and outcomes
(b) Involve stakeholders in quality analysis reviews
(c) Involve stakeholders in goal setting
(d) Establish direct and indirect communication among the stakeholder and the program's leaders and team

Question Category: Moderate
The right answer is Option (A)
The Standards for Program Management - 4th Edition - reference: Chapter (5), Program Stakeholder Engagement, page 57
Clarification and Tips:
The primary objective of stakeholders' engagement is to gain and maintain stakeholder buy-in for the program's objectives, benefits, and outcomes, so Option (A) is the right answer.
Domain: Stakeholder Engagement
Phase or Element: General

Q118 - You are currently creating your program stakeholder engagement plan, which of the following aspects should be considered for each stakeholder?

(a) His culture to deal with his subordinates
(b) Attitudes about the program and its sponsor
(c) His span of control
(d) All the above

Question Category: Moderate
The right answer is Option (B)
The Standards for Program Management - 4th Edition - reference: Chapter (5), Program Stakeholder Engagement, 5.3 PROGRAM STAKEHOLDER ENGAGEMENT PLANNING, page 64
Clarification and Tips:
Only Option (B) can be considered for each stakeholder as part of the engagement plan. Options (A) and (C) contents are irrelevant.
Therefore, the right answer is Option (B).
Domain: Stakeholder Engagement
Phase or Element: PROGRAM STAKEHOLDER ENGAGEMENT PLANNING

Q119 - After being assigned as program manager for X-Tel program, Per is reviewing the program major artifacts and started to document factors that, for planning purposes, are considered true, real, or certain. What are these factors?

(a) They are the program assumptions
(b) They are the enterprise environmental factors
(c) They are the program constraints
(d) They are the program risks

Question Category: Difficult
The right answer is Option (A)
The Standards for Program Management - 4th Edition - reference: Chapter (3), Program Strategy Alignment, 3.4.2.4 ASSUMPTIONS ANALYSIS, page 40
Clarification and Tips:
Assumptions are factors that, for planning purposes, are considered true, real, or certain.
Enterprise environmental factors refer to conditions, not under the immediate control of the team, that influence, constrain, or direct the program.
The constraint is a limiting factor that affects the execution of a project, program, portfolio, or process.
Program Risk is an uncertain event or condition that, if it occurs, has a positive or negative effect on the program.
Therefore, Option (A) is the right answer.
Domain: Strategy Alignment
Phase or Element: ENVIRONMENTAL ASSESSMENTS

Q120 - The program sponsor is writing a document to authorize the program management team to use organizational resources, in order to execute the program. Which document is this?

(a) The program mandate
(b) The program business case
(c) The program charter
(d) The program roadmap

Question Category: Moderate
The right answer is Option (C)
The Standards for Program Management - 4th Edition - reference: Chapter (3), Program Strategy Alignment, page 33
Clarification and Tips:
The program mandate is not used or referenced in the new program management standards; the 4th edition.

The program business case is a documented economic feasibility study used to establish the validity of the benefits to be delivered by a program.

The program charter is a document issued by a sponsor that authorizes the program management team to use organizational resources to execute the program and links the program to the organization's strategic objectives.

The program roadmap is a chronological representation of a program's intended direction, graphically depicting dependencies between major milestones and decision points, which reflects the linkage between the business strategy and the program work.

Therefore, Option (C) is the right answer.

Domain: Strategy Alignment
Phase or Element: General

Q121 - Sam is writing a risk to the risk register that arises as a direct outcome of implementing the risk response. What is the name of this risk?

(a) Secondary risk
(b) Residual risk
(c) Positive risk
(d) Black swan risk

Question Category: Moderate
The right answer is Option (A)
The Standards for Program Management - 4th Edition - reference: Chapter (8), Program Activities, 8.2.8.3 PROGRAM RISK RESPONSE MANAGEMENT, pages 135

Clarification and Tips:
Secondary risks arise as a direct outcome of implementing the risk response.
Residual risks are expected to remain after planned responses have been taken, as well as those that have been deliberately accepted.
Positive risk is the opportunity; the risk with positive impact.
A black swan risk is a risk that is related to a few low probable events that will impact the portfolio dramatically when all of them happen together.
Therefore, Option (A) is the right answer.

Domain: Life Cycle Management
Phase or Element: Delivery

Q122 - Simon defined his components cost estimation during the program Definition phase. Now during the Benefits Delivery phase, Simon discovered that his estimation is not accurate enough for one of his components and he found that the budget for this component is more than required. What is the best choice for Simon?

(a) Simon will discuss the subject with the component manager to get a solution
(b) Simon may present an opportunity to the sponsor for additional products that would be acquired later in the program
(c) Simon should create a positive risk in the risk register
(d) Simon may use this extra budget to reward the good performance program team

Question Category: Difficult
The right answer is Option (B)
The Standards for Program Management - 4th Edition - reference: Chapter (8), Program Activities, 8.2.3.2 COMPONENT COST ESTIMATION, pages 129
Clarification and Tips:
The best choice for Simon in the given options is to present an opportunity to the sponsor for additional products that would be acquired later in the program. Discussing the subject with the component manager or creating a positive risk in the risk register are not good choices as they are not helping to resolve the situation. Using this extra budget to reward the good performance program team is not a decision to be taken by Simon. Thus, the right answer is Option (B).
Domain: Life Cycle Management
Phase or Element: Delivery

Q123 - Jack is managing a program in the Hola organization. During his planning activities, he found some of the services required for his program are offered by the Hola organization. He came asking you for advice on how to acquire this service, what is your best reply?

(a) I will advise him to follow the program procurement management plan
(b) I will advise him to follow the organization procurement management plan
(c) I will advise him to contact the service owner in Hola and agree with him on how to acquire the services as per the policies and procedures within the Hola organization
(d) I will advise him not to acquire service from within the organization

Question Category: Difficult
The right answer is Option (C)
The Standards for Program Management - 4th Edition - reference: Chapter (8), Program Activities, 8.1.2.7 PROGRAM PROCUREMENT MANAGEMENT PLANNING, pages 116
Clarification and Tips:
The program procurement management plan describes how the program will acquire goods and services from outside of the performing organization.
The organization procurement management plan if exists, helps the organization to acquire goods and services from outside of the organization.

Therefore, the best answer is Option (C) to deal with and agree with the service owner.
Domain: Life Cycle Management
Phase or Element: Definition

Q124 - A program is closed either because the program charter is fulfilled or internal/external conditions arise that bring the program to an early end. Which of the following may be one of these conditions?

(a) Open issues that need to be contained during the sustainment phase
(b) Missed milestones that were rescheduled after the transition to production
(c) Changes in the business case that no longer make the program necessary
(d) Some major risks that cannot be mitigated and the program management decided to accept them

Question Category: Difficult
The right answer is Option (C)
The Standards for Program Management - 4th Edition - reference: Chapter (7), Program Life Cycle Management, 7.2.2.5 PROGRAM CLOSEOUT, page 102
Clarification and Tips:
A program is closed either because the program charter is fulfilled or internal/external conditions arise that bring the program to an early end. These conditions may include changes in the business case that no longer make the program necessary or a determination that the expected benefits cannot be achieved. Therefore, Option (C) is the right answer.
Options (A), (B), and (D) are not conditions that may lead to program termination.
Domain: Life Cycle Management
Phase or Element: Closing

Q125 - Sylwia is a program manager who managed many programs during her experience. She noticed that the timing of funding has a direct impact on a program's ability to perform, but she did not grasp the objective of financing in program development. What is your explanation to Sylwia?

(a) The objective of financing in program development is to minimize the risk if the program fails
(b) The objective of financing in program development is to share the risk of failure with another entity
(c) The objective of financing in program development is to share the profit with another entity
(d) The objective of financing in program development is to obtain funds to bridge the gap between paying out monies for development and obtaining the benefits of the

programs

Question Category: Difficult
The right answer is Option (D)
The Standards for Program Management - 4th Edition - reference: Chapter (8), Program Activities, 8.1.2.4 PROGRAM FINANCIAL FRAMEWORK ESTABLISHMENT, pages 114
Clarification and Tips:
The timing of funding has a direct impact on a program's ability to perform. To a much greater extent than for projects, program costs occur earlier (often years earlier) than their related benefits. The objective of financing in program development is to obtain funds to bridge the gap between paying out monies for development and obtaining the benefits of the programs. Therefore, Option (D) is the right answer.
Domain: Life Cycle Management
Phase or Element: Definition

Q126 - Aisa is working to establish common high-level expectations for the program stakeholders regarding the delivery of the program's benefits. Which of the following actions is the best to be done by Aisa?

(a) Provide stakeholders with detailed program status on a regular basis
(b) Provide stakeholders with summary information from the program charter and program business case
(c) Provide stakeholders with appropriate information contained in the program charter and program business case, and provide an accompanying executive brief to summarize the details of the risks, dependencies, and benefits
(d) Provide the stakeholders with the details of the benefits register

Question Category: Difficult
The right answer is Option (C)
The Standards for Program Management - 4th Edition - reference: Chapter (5), Program Stakeholder Engagement, 5.4 PROGRAM STAKEHOLDER ENGAGEMENT, page 65
Clarification and Tips:
To help stakeholders establish common high-level expectations for the delivery of the program's benefits, the program manager provides stakeholders with appropriate information contained in the program charter and program business case, which can include an accompanying executive brief to summarize the details of the risks, dependencies, and benefits. Therefore, Option (C) is the right answer.
Option (A) has more details than what is required and is missing important summaries in Option (C).
Option (B) is good, but Option (C) is better.

Option (D) is missing much important information mentioned in Option (C).
Domain: Stakeholder Engagement
Phase or Element: PROGRAM STAKEHOLDER ENGAGEMENT

Q127 - Harish started to establish the benefits management plan, define and prioritize program components, and define the key performance indicators required to monitor the delivery of program benefits. Which stage or phase of the benefits management is he executing?

- (a) Benefits delivery
- (b) Benefits identification
- (c) Benefits analysis and planning
- (d) Benefits transition

Question Category: Easy
The right answer is Option (C)
The Standards for Program Management - 4th Edition - reference: Chapter (4), Program Benefits Management, 4.2 BENEFITS ANALYSIS AND PLANNING, page 48
Clarification and Tips:
The question includes activities related to the benefits analysis and planning, so Option (C) is the right answer.
Domain: Benefits Management
Phase or Element: BENEFITS ANALYSIS AND PLANNING

Q128 - Pierre is a new appointed program manager. He is managing his first program in the X-Com organization. Pierre started to meet the program stakeholders to gather their expectations. He was confused and came to you asking how to manage the stakeholders. What is your advice to him?

- (a) My advice to Pierre is to create a strong stakeholder management plan
- (b) My advice to Pierre is to create a stakeholder engagement plan
- (c) My advice to Pierre first is to categorize the stakeholders before developing the stakeholder management plan
- (d) My advice to Pierre is that he should manage the stakeholder expectations rather than the stakeholders themselves

Question Category: Moderate
The right answer is Option (D)
The Standards for Program Management - 4th Edition - reference: Chapter (5), Program Stakeholder Engagement, General
Clarification and Tips:

"Stakeholder Engagement" is the right term, "stakeholder management" is an old term that is not used in the PMI standards anymore. Stakeholder expectations should be managed by the program manager.
Therefore, the right answer is Option (D).
Domain: Stakeholder Engagement
Phase or Element: General

Q129 - When is usually the stakeholder engagement active during the different phases of the program life cycle?

   (a) Stakeholder engagement is active during the planning phase of the program
   (b) Stakeholder engagement is a continuous program activity, so it is running during the whole program life cycle
   (c) Stakeholder engagement is active during the program planning subphase
   (d) Stakeholder engagement is active during the stakeholder engagement planning

Question Category: Difficult
The right answer is Option (B)
The Standards for Program Management - 4th Edition - reference: Chapter (5), Program Stakeholder Engagement, 5.4 PROGRAM STAKEHOLDER ENGAGEMENT, page 64
Clarification and Tips:
Stakeholder engagement is a continuous program activity, so it should not be limited to one phase of the program life cycle. It should be running during the whole program life cycle. So, the right answer is Option (B).
Domain: Stakeholder Engagement
Phase or Element: PROGRAM STAKEHOLDER ENGAGEMENT

Q130 - Chao is working in the program planning activities with his program team. He is creating the program work breakdown structure with the help of the component managers and technical leads. He went deep in the WBS decomposition even to the fifth level of the components. What is your advice to Chao?

   (a) I will advise him to stop decomposition as level five of the components is good enough
   (b) I will advise him to stop decomposition at the first two levels of the components
   (c) I will advise him to continue decomposition to level ten of the components
   (d) I will advise him to review the subject with the component managers and agree on the decomposition level

Question Category: Moderate
The right answer is Option (B)

The Standards for Program Management - 4th Edition - reference: Chapter (8), Program Activities, 8.1.2.12 PROGRAM SCOPE MANAGEMENT PLANNING, pages 123

Clarification and Tips:
The program WBS provides an overview of the program and shows how each component contributes to the objectives of the program. Decomposition stops at the level of control required by the program manager (typically to the first one or two levels of a component). Therefore, Option (B) is the right answer.

Domain: Life Cycle Management
Phase or Element: Definition

Q131 - During the benefits realization, there may be a window of opportunity for the realization of a planned benefit and for that benefit to generate real value.
Who may determine if the window of opportunity was met or compromised by actual events in the program or component?

- (a) The program manager
- (b) The program steering committee
- (c) The key stakeholders
- (d) All the above

Question Category: Moderate
The right answer is Option (D)
The Standards for Program Management - 4th Edition - reference: Chapter (4), Program Benefits Management, 4.3.2 BENEFITS AND PROGRAM GOVERNANCE, page 52

Clarification and Tips:
The program manager, program steering committee, and key stakeholders may determine if the window of opportunity for the realization of a planned benefit was met or compromised by actual events in the program or components, so Option (D) is the right answer.

Domain: Benefits Management
Phase or Element: BENEFITS DELIVERY

Q132 - You are managing the O3 program in your organization. During the regular team meeting, you were informed that the purchasing department manager is reluctant to send his team for the training session as per the agreed upon schedule. The subsidiary program manager added that this is not the first time that this manager represents a negative contribution to the O3 program. What should be your right action?

- (a) I should meet the purchasing department manager and put some pressure on him to recover the missed training session

(b) I should meet the purchasing department manager, work to minimize any negative impact on him as a result of the O3 program and work to mitigate the effect of his negative contribution

(c) I should meet the purchasing department manager and threaten him to escalate the subject to the steering committee

(d) I should escalate the subject to the steering committee and use the committee power to enforce this stakeholder to respect the program schedule activities

Question Category: Difficult
The right answer is Option (B)
The Standards for Program Management - 4th Edition - reference: Chapter (5), Program Stakeholder Engagement, Page 57
Clarification and Tips:
Stakeholders might not realize a benefit from the program and may be subject to negative impacts, the program manager should minimize the negative impact on the stakeholders and should balance between activities related to mitigating the effect of stakeholders who view the program negatively and encouraging the active support of stakeholders who see the program as a positive contribution.
Therefore, Option (B) is the right answer.
Option (A) and (C) are negative attitudes from the program manager that shouldn't exist.
Option (D) should not happen until the program manager does his job first and works with the stakeholders to mitigate his negative contribution, to explain the benefits of the training session and to clear any confusion.
Domain: Stakeholder Engagement
Phase or Element: General

Q133 - Marcie is managing the REF program in her organization. She has a meeting with a group of participants representing various program-related interests with the purpose of supporting the program under its authority by providing guidance, endorsements, and approvals through the governance practices. Which group is this?

(a) Change control board
(b) Board of director
(c) Program steering committee
(d) Regulatory agencies

Question Category: Moderate
The right answer is Option (C)
The Standards for Program Management - 4th Edition - reference: Chapter (5), Program Stakeholder Engagement, 5.1 PROGRAM STAKEHOLDER IDENTIFICATION, page 61
Clarification and Tips:

Program steering committee is a group of participants representing various program-related interests with the purpose of supporting the program under its authority by providing guidance, endorsements, and approvals through the governance practices.

The regulatory agency is a public authority or government agency responsible for setting and managing the regulatory and legal boundaries of their local and national sovereign governments. Typically, these organizations will set mandatory standards or requirements. Therefore, Option (C) is the right answer.

Domain: Stakeholder Engagement
Phase or Element: PROGRAM STAKEHOLDER IDENTIFICATION

Q134 - The program manager should deal with the stakeholders using all the following options, except:

(a) Be aware of the stakeholders' impact
(b) Understand the stakeholders' level of influence
(c) Manage the stakeholders' expectation
(d) Manage the stakeholders

Question Category: Easy
The right answer is Option (D)
The Standards for Program Management - 4th Edition - reference: Chapter (5), Program Stakeholder Engagement, page 57
Clarification and Tips:
Unlike program resources, not all stakeholders can be managed directly, but their expectations can be. Stakeholders may be more senior in the organization than the program manager. Therefore, Option (D) is the right answer.
Domain: Stakeholder Engagement
Phase or Element: General

Q135 - You are assigned to execute a critical program in your organization, the program infrastructure includes a risk manager who was appointed by the governing body. When you started to apply major program scope change, the risk manager requested to repeat the risk management planning in order to accommodate this change. What is your reply to him?

(a) I will tell him that risk management planning is executed once during the program definition phase and there is no need to repeat it again
(b) I will escalate the subject to the governing board to get their feedback
(c) I will let him repeat the program risk planning to accommodate the major change introduced to the program

(d) I will involve the PMO to judge if there is a need to repeat the risk management planning again

Question Category: Difficult
The right answer is Option (C)
The Standards for Program Management - 4th Edition - reference: Chapter (8), Program Activities, 8.1.2.10 PROGRAM RISK MANAGEMENT PLANNING, pages 120
Clarification and Tips:
The program risk management planning activity should be conducted early in the program definition phase and it will be repeated whenever major changes occur in the program. Therefore, the right answer is Option (C).
Domain: Life Cycle Management
Phase or Element: Definition

Q136 - Ahmed is working in the risk management activities of Program JEK. He executed the risk identification for the third time in the program and added the identified risks to the risk register. Which of the following statements describes the iteration of the risk identification correctly?

(a) Risk identification is an iterative activity where the frequency of iteration is ten times maximum in any program
(b) Risk identification is an iterative activity where the frequency of iteration and involvement of participants may vary
(c) Risk identification is an iterative activity where the involvement of participants is usually the same within the same program
(d) Risk identification is an iterative activity that may be repeated within the definition and delivery phases only

Question Category: Difficult
The right answer is Option (B)
The Standards for Program Management - 4th Edition - reference: Chapter (8), Program Activities, 8.2.8.1 PROGRAM RISK IDENTIFICATION, pages 134
Clarification and Tips:
Risk identification is an iterative activity. As the program progresses, new risks may evolve or become known. The frequency of iteration and involvement of participants may vary, but the format of the risk statements should be consistent.
Therefore, Option (B) is the right answer.
Domain: Life Cycle Management
Phase or Element: Delivery

Q137 - Santiago is managing an important program in your organization. He was working on the program scope monitoring and controlling where he went down to the program level to see the impact of the suggested change on the component scope. What is your advice to Santiago?

(a) I will advise Santiago to manage the scope of the components as well as he manages the scope of the program to ensure program benefits realization as planned
(b) I will advise Santiago to restrict his activities to managing scope only to the allocated level for components and avoid controlling component scope
(c) I will advise Santiago to restrict his activities to managing scope only to the allocated level for components and should avoid controlling component scope unless there is a major change
(d) I will advise Santiago to restrict his activities to managing scope only to the program level and not to look at the component levels as they are managed by the component managers

Question Category: Moderate
The right answer is Option (B)
The Standards for Program Management - 4th Edition - reference: Chapter (8), Program Activities, 8.2.10 PROGRAM SCOPE MONITORING AND CONTROLLING, pages 137
Clarification and Tips:
Program managers should restrict their activities to managing scope only to the allocated level for components and should avoid controlling component scope that has been further decomposed by the project manager or by subsidiary program managers.
Therefore, Option (B) is the right answer.
Please review carefully options (A), (C), and (D) as they are close to each other.
Domain: Life Cycle Management
Phase or Element: Delivery

Q138 - Simon is working in the program schedule management planning activities. He created the program high level schedule and is looking for some documents to help him with the delivery dates and major milestones. Which document(s) do you suggest to Simon?

(a) The program roadmap
(b) The program charter
(c) The program roadmap and the program charter
(d) The component schedules

Question Category: Moderate
The right answer is Option (C)
The Standards for Program Management - 4th Edition - reference: Chapter (8), Program Activities, 8.1.2.11 PROGRAM SCHEDULE MANAGEMENT PLANNING, pages 121
Clarification and Tips:
The program's delivery date and major milestones are developed using the program roadmap

and the program charter, so the program manager will refer to these two documents to get the needed information for the program high level schedule.
Therefore, Option (C) is the right answer.
Please note that:
Option (A) and (B) are partially correct, but Option (C) is a better and complete answer.
Option (D) is wrong as the detail component schedule is usually created after the high level schedule.
Domain: Life Cycle Management
Phase or Element: Definition

Q139 - Which of the following stakeholder aspects are important for the stakeholder analysis and engagement planning?

(a) Attitudes about the program and its sponsors
(b) Relevant phase(s) applicable to stakeholders' specific engagement
(c) The expectation of program benefits delivery
(d) All the above

Question Category: Easy
The right answer is Option (D)
The Standards for Program Management - 4th Edition - reference: Chapter (5), Program Stakeholder Engagement, 5.3 PROGRAM STAKEHOLDER ENGAGEMENT PLANNING, page 64
Clarification and Tips:
Options (A), (B), and (C) have stakeholder aspects that are important for the stakeholder analysis and engagement planning, so Option (D) is the right answer.
Domain: Stakeholder Engagement
Phase or Element: PROGRAM STAKEHOLDER ENGAGEMENT PLANNING

Q140 - Richard is the program manager for one critical program in his organization. Richard requested his program management team to send him the communication that they want to distribute to certain key stakeholders. Richard wants to review these communications and provide his team with his input before the distribution. Why is Richard doing that?

(a) He is doing that because an incorrect message to an audience may cause problems for the program and in some cases, lead to the stoppage of a program
(b) He is doing that because he is applying the quality assurance processes
(c) He is doing that because he is applying an autocratic leadership style
(d) He is doing that because he is not trusting his team

Question Category: Difficult
The right answer is Option (A)
The Standards for Program Management - 4th Edition - reference: Chapter (8), Program Activities, 8.2.2 PROGRAM COMMUNICATIONS MANAGEMENT, pages 126
Clarification and Tips:
Regardless of the distribution method, the information should remain in the program's control. An incorrect message to an audience may cause problems for the program and in some cases, lead to the stoppage of a program. Therefore, Option (A) is the right answer.
Please note the following:
Option (B) is wrong as these reviews may be categorized as quality control and should be categorized as quality assurance.
Options (C) and (D) are wrong as there is no evidence in the question to consolidate this view.
Domain: Life Cycle Management
Phase or Element: Delivery

Q141 - Ming is currently in the program closure phase, he found that the charter is fulfilled and operations are not necessary to continue realization of ongoing benefits. What should he do for the transition activities?

(a) Ming should review the program roadmap to see what he has to do
(b) Ming should terminate the program with no transition to operations
(c) Ming should terminate the program after executing the transition to operations
(d) Ming should consult the program management office on what he should do

Question Category: Difficult
The right answer is Option (B)
The Standards for Program Management - 4th Edition - reference: Chapter (4), Program Benefits Management, 4.4 BENEFITS TRANSITION, page 54
Clarification and Tips:
If the charter is fulfilled and operations are not necessary to continue realization of ongoing benefits, the program manager should terminate the program with no transition to operations, so Option (B) is the right answer.
Option (A) is wrong as a roadmap does not include the transition details.
Option (C) is wrong as the transition will not add value in benefits realization.
Option (D) is wrong as the program management office is usually reporting to the program manager.
Domain: Benefits Management
Phase or Element: BENEFITS TRANSITION

Q142 - Nilson is working on the Kom program which is expected to run for three years. After one year of hard working in the program, Nilson found that the initial cost estimates for the Geo project, which is one of the program components, is less than what it should be. This was discovered after practical understanding for the program current environment. What should Nilson do?

(a) Nilson should halt the program execution until he audits all the components estimated costs
(b) Nilson should update the cost estimate to reflect the current environment considerations
(c) Nilson should ask the PMO to review all the program components costs
(d) Nilson should ask the team who originally estimated the program cost to meet and review again all of their estimations

Question Category: Difficult
The right answer is Option (B)
The Standards for Program Management - 4th Edition - reference: Chapter (8), Program Activities, 8.2.3.2 COMPONENT COST ESTIMATION, pages 129
<u>**Clarification and Tips:**</u>
Given the typically long duration of a program, the initial estimates may need to be updated to reflect the current environment and cost considerations. This is expected because programs have a significant element of uncertainty, not all program components may be known when the initial order-of-magnitude estimates are calculated during the program definition phase Therefore, Option (B) is the right answer.
Domain: Life Cycle Management
Phase or Element: Delivery

Q143 - The business case of the GenWin program was developed by the portfolio organization. During the program formulation and after the program manager is assigned, more analysis was executed to determine the priority of the GenWin program and the program manager found elements to be updated in the business case. What is the right action to be done?

(a) Keep the business case as it is because it was developed by the portfolio management which is a higher authority than the program management
(b) The business case should be revised and updated according to the new information
(c) Hold the update as more updates may be collected during the planning subphase of the delivery phase
(d) The business case should not be updated, the requested update will be included in the program charter

Question Category: Difficult
The right answer is Option (B)
The Standards for Program Management - 4th Edition - reference: Chapter (7), Program Life

Cycle Management, 7.1.2.1 PROGRAM FORMULATION, page 92
Clarification and Tips:
Option (B) is the right answer as the business case can be updated based on the information collected during the program formulation if it was developed prior to program formulation.
Domain: Life Cycle Management
Phase or Element: Definition

Q144 - Fatma is performing the initial program planning with her team, during the initial program risk assessment, she identified risk related to strategy alignment. Which of the following risks may be related to strategy alignment?

(a) Program roadmap not aligned with organizational roadmap
(b) Program roadmap not supportive of portfolio roadmaps
(c) Program objectives not supportive of organizational objectives
(d) All the above

Question Category: Moderate
The right answer is Option (D)
The Standards for Program Management - 4th Edition - reference: Chapter (3), Program Strategy Alignment, 3.5.3 INITIAL PROGRAM RISK ASSESSMENT, page 42
Clarification and Tips:
Options (A), (B), and (C) are considered risk related to strategy alignment.
Therefore, Option (D) is the right answer.
Domain: Strategy Alignment
Phase or Element: General

Q145 - Chung was preparing a plan that is used as a response to a risk that has occurred and the primary response proves to be inadequate. Which plan is this?

(a) Risk management plan
(b) Fallback plan
(c) Contingency plan
(d) Financial management plan

Question Category: Moderate
The right answer is Option (B)
The Standards for Program Management - 4th Edition - reference: Chapter (8), Program Activities, 8.2.8.3 PROGRAM RISK RESPONSE MANAGEMENT, pages 135
Clarification and Tips:
The fallback plan is used as a response to a risk that has occurred and the primary response

proves to be inadequate, so Option (B) is the right answer.
Domain: Life Cycle Management
Phase or Element: Delivery

Q146 - Milan wants to measure the performance of the stakeholders' engagement. He met his project managers and subsidiary program manager to create some metrics.
What are the primary metrics for stakeholder engagement should he consider?

- (a) Stakeholder participation
- (b) Frequency or rate of communication with the program team
- (c) Positive contributions to the realization of the program's objectives and benefits,
- (d) All the above

Question Category: Easy
The right answer is Option (D)
The Standards for Program Management - 4th Edition - reference: Chapter (5), Program Stakeholder Engagement, 5.4 PROGRAM STAKEHOLDER ENGAGEMENT, page 65
Clarification and Tips:
Options (A), (B), and (C) are considered primary metrics for stakeholder engagement, so Option (D) is the right answer.
Domain: Stakeholder Engagement
Phase or Element: PROGRAM STAKEHOLDER ENGAGEMENT

Q147 - Chao has completed his first program a few months ago. That program was created to develop the benefits at one time which is at the program completion. Now, Chao is requested to manage a new program that will deliver benefits on a regular basis. Chao is planning to utilize the same governance that he applied in the first program and he is asking you for advice. What will you recommend to him?

- (a) I will advise him to change the governance of the old program before applying it to the new program as the benefits realization are coming in increments in the new program rather than one time as the old one
- (b) I will advise him to keep the governance of the old program and to apply it to the new program with minor changes if needed
- (c) I will advise him to keep the governance of the old program and to apply it to the new program as there is no expected difference in governance between the two programs because of the different benefits realization plans
- (d) I will advise him to use the governance of the old program as it was proved to be successful in the execution of the first program

Question Category: Difficult
The right answer is Option (A)
The Standards for Program Management - 4th Edition - reference: Chapter (6), Program Governance, 6.3 PROGRAM GOVERNANCE DESIGN AND IMPLEMENTATION, page 86
Clarification and Tips:
A program that regularly delivers benefits to the organization is likely to require different governance than a program delivering all or most of the benefits at the end. Regular delivery of benefits potentially requires constant change in the operations of the organization and the governance to manage this change is critical throughout the life cycle.
Therefore, Option (A) is the right answer.
Domain: Program Governance
Phase or Element: PROGRAM GOVERNANCE DESIGN AND IMPLEMENTATION

Q148 - After Kathy had created the benefits register in her program with the help of the component managers and key team members, what is the next step to be done?

(a) Review the benefits register with the program sponsor
(b) Review the benefits register with the key stakeholders to develop the appropriate performance measures
(c) Develop the benefits management plan
(d) Start the benefits delivery phase

Question Category: Difficult
The right answer is Option (B)
The Standards for Program Management - 4th Edition - reference: Chapter (4), Program Benefits Management, 4.1.1 BENEFITS REGISTER, page 47
Clarification and Tips:
After the benefits register is created, the register is then reviewed with key stakeholders to develop the appropriate performance measures for each of the benefits, so Option (B) is the right answer.
Domain: Benefits Management
Phase or Element: BENEFITS IDENTIFICATION

Q149 - Which of the following statements is describing the program benefit accurately?

(a) A benefit is the gains and assets realized by the organization only as the result of outcomes delivered by the program
(b) A benefit is the outcome of the program
(c) A benefit is the gains and assets realized by the organization and other stakeholders as the result of outcomes delivered by the program

(d) A benefit is produced by the output as a desired operational result

Question Category: Moderate
The right answer is Option (C)
The Standards for Program Management - 4th Edition - reference: Chapter (4), Program Benefits Management, page 44
Clarification and Tips:
A benefit is the gains and assets realized by the organization and other stakeholders as the result of outcomes delivered by the program. So Option (C) is the right answer.
Option (A) is partially correct, but Option (C) is a better and complete option.
Option (B) is wrong.
Option (D) is wrong as it contains the outcome definition; the outcome is produced by the output as a desired operational result.
Domain: Benefits Management
Phase or Element: General

Q150 - Which of the following artifacts serves as the framework for developing the program master schedule and defines the program manager's management control points?

(a) The program WBS
(b) The program component schedule
(c) The program charter
(d) The program benefits realization plan

Question Category: Difficult
The right answer is Option (A)
The Standards for Program Management - 4th Edition - reference: Chapter (8), Program Activities, 8.1.2.12 PROGRAM SCOPE MANAGEMENT PLANNING, pages 123
Clarification and Tips:
The program WBS serves as the framework for developing the program master schedule and defines the program manager's management control points.
Therefore, Option (A) is the right answer.
Domain: Life Cycle Management
Phase or Element: Definition

Q151 - The program manager is further defining program benefits and adding more details. Which of the following aspects is the most important for him/her to consider?

(a) The program manager should refine program benefits risks and quantify new benefits risks

(b) The program manager should review the benefits register
(c) The program manager should send the new status of the benefits register to the key stakeholders
(d) The program manager should freeze the changes to the benefits register

Question Category: Difficult
The right answer is Option (A)
The Standards for Program Management - 4th Edition - reference: Chapter (4), Program Benefits Management, 4.2 BENEFITS ANALYSIS AND PLANNING, page 49
Clarification and Tips:
While further defining program benefits and adding more details, the program manager should refine program benefits risks and quantify new benefits risks, so Option (A) is the right answer. Options (B) and (C) are good to have, but Option (A) is much better.
Option (D) is wrong as the benefits register is usually not frozen to allow adding changes and status updates to the benefits.
Domain: Benefits Management
Phase or Element: BENEFITS ANALYSIS AND PLANNING

Q152 - Adrian was assigned to one program in his organization. He created his program communication management plan and started to execute it. After he distributed his program weekly report, he got some communication from one of the program stakeholders asking for more details about one specific deliverable. In general, what should be the response of Adrian when he got communication from one or more of the stakeholders?

(a) Communication should be a one-way information flow with the stakeholder. So, Adrian should ignore the stakeholder's communication unless he has a query to be answered
(b) Adrian should review his program communication plan and respond accordingly
(c) Adrian should gather, analyze and distribute the communications received from the stakeholders back within the program as required
(d) Adrian should consult his program key influencer to reach an agreement on his probable feedback in similar cases

Question Category: Difficult
The right answer is Option (C)
The Standards for Program Management - 4th Edition - reference: Chapter (8), Program Activities, 8.2.2 PROGRAM COMMUNICATIONS MANAGEMENT, General
Clarification and Tips:
Communication should be a two-way information flow. Any communication from the customers or stakeholders regarding the program performance should be gathered by program management, analyzed and distributed back within the program as required. Thus, the right answer is Option (C).

Domain: Life Cycle Management
Phase or Element: Delivery

Q153 - Adam is preparing the program reporting to send it to the key stakeholders as per the communications management plan. One of his component managers was confused with the purpose of having the program reporting. What should Adam tell him?

(a) He should tell him that the program reporting provides the stakeholders with information about major program change requests
(b) He should tell him that the program reporting provides the stakeholders with information about milestone status
(c) He should tell him that the program reporting provides the stakeholders with information about how resources are being used to deliver program benefits
(d) He should tell him that the program reporting is part of the communications governance that should be followed

Question Category: Moderate
The right answer is Option (C)
The Standards for Program Management - 4th Edition - reference: Chapter (8), Program Activities, 8.2.2.2 PROGRAM REPORTING, pages 127
Clarification and Tips:
Program reporting is the activity of consolidating performance and reporting related data to provide stakeholders with information about how resources are being used to deliver program benefits.
Therefore, Option (C) is the right answer.
Domain: Life Cycle Management
Phase or Element: Delivery

Q154 - What do we call those risks that have been deliberately accepted?

(a) Secondary risks
(b) Negative risks
(c) Positive risks
(d) Residual risks

Question Category: Moderate
The right answer is Option (D)
The Standards for Program Management - 4th Edition - reference: Chapter (8), Program Activities, 8.2.8.3 PROGRAM RISK RESPONSE MANAGEMENT, pages 135

Clarification and Tips:
Secondary risks that arise as a direct outcome of implementing the risk response.
The negative risk is the risk with negative impact.
Positive risk is the opportunity; the risk with positive impact.
Residual risks are expected to remain after planned responses have been taken, as well as those that have been deliberately accepted.
Therefore, Option (D) is the right answer.
Domain: Life Cycle Management
Phase or Element: Delivery

Q155 - Which of the following statements describes the responsibilities of the program manager and the component manager in resource management?

(a) The program manager manages resources at the program level only
(b) Only the component managers are working in managing resources at the component level
(c) The program manager manages resources at the program level and at the component level
(d) The program manager manages resources at the program level and works with the component managers who manage resources at the component level

Question Category: Difficult
The right answer is Option (D)
The Standards for Program Management - 4th Edition - reference: Chapter (8), Program Activities, 8.2.7 PROGRAM RESOURCE MANAGEMENT, pages 133
Clarification and Tips:
The program manager manages resources at the program level and works with the component managers who manage resources at the component level to balance the needs of the program with the availability of resources.
Therefore, Option (D) is the right answer.
Domain: Life Cycle Management
Phase or Element: Delivery

Q156 - Why is the stakeholder engagement a continuous program activity?

(a) Because the change requests are affecting the program scope
(b) Because the list of stakeholders and their attitudes and opinions change as the program progresses and delivers benefits
(c) To accommodate any new requirements

(d) To deal with the changing environment around the program

Question Category: Difficult
The right answer is Option (B)
The Standards for Program Management - 4th Edition - reference: Chapter (5), Program Stakeholder Engagement, 5.4 PROGRAM STAKEHOLDER ENGAGEMENT, page 64
Clarification and Tips:
Stakeholder engagement is a continuous program activity because the list of stakeholders and their attitudes and opinions change as the program progresses and delivers benefits, so Option (B) is the right answer.
Domain: Stakeholder Engagement
Phase or Element: PROGRAM STAKEHOLDER ENGAGEMENT

Q157 - Ahmed is currently in the Benefits Delivery phase of his program where he aggregates all performance information across projects and non-project activity to provide a clear picture of the program performance as a whole. Which activity does Ahmed execute?

(a) Program information distribution activity
(b) Program reporting activity
(c) Components reporting activity
(d) Program audit

Question Category: Moderate
The right answer is Option (B)
The Standards for Program Management - 4th Edition - reference: Chapter (8), Program Activities, 8.2.2.2 PROGRAM REPORTING, pages 127
Clarification and Tips:
The description in this question is related to program reporting activity as it is the program manager who aggregates all performance information across projects and non-project activity to provide a clear picture of the program performance. It is neither for program components reporting nor for information distribution. And it is clear that it is not a program audit activity which should concentrate on the program process and aim to answer the question Are we doing it right? Therefore, the right answer is Option (B).
Domain: Life Cycle Management
Phase or Element: Delivery

Q158 - After Hong, the program manager, got the steering committee approval on the program charter, which phase or subphase should she start?

(a) She should start the component oversight and integration

(b) She should start the program delivery
(c) She should start the program formation
(d) She should start the program planning

Question Category: Moderate
The right answer is Option (D)
The Standards for Program Management - 4th Edition - reference: Chapter (7), Program Life Cycle Management, 7.1.2.2 PROGRAM PLANNING, page 94
Clarification and Tips:
Program planning commences upon formal approval of the program charter by the program steering committee, so Option (D) is the right answer.
Domain: Life Cycle Management
Phase or Element: Definition

Q159 - Mohamed started to manage his first program in the Fajr organization. He started to create a document that justifies the need for a program by defining how a program's expected outcomes would support the organization's strategic goals and objectives. Which document is Mohamed working on?

(a) Mohamed is working on the program charter
(b) Mohamed is working on the program business case
(c) Mohamed is working on the program roadmap
(d) Mohamed is working on the program management plan

Question Category: Difficult
The right answer is Option (B)
The Standards for Program Management - 4th Edition - reference: Chapter (3), Program Strategy Alignment, page 34
Clarification and Tips:
The program business case justifies the need for a program by defining how a program's expected outcomes would support the organization's strategic goals and objectives, so Option (B) is the right answer.
Domain: Strategy Alignment
Phase or Element: General

Q160 - What is the most important reason for you as a program manager to define a robust program risk management strategy?

(a) Program risk management strategy defines ways to control risks in the watch list

(b) Program risk management strategy drives consistency and effectiveness in program risk management activities throughout the program as part of program integration and supporting activities
(c) Program risk management strategy assesses the required risk categories to be used through-out the program life cycle
(d) Program risk management strategy defines the risk responses required for major risks

Question Category: Difficult
The right answer is Option (B)
The Standards for Program Management - 4th Edition - reference: Chapter (3), Program Strategy Alignment, 33.5.4 PROGRAM RISK RESPONSE STRATEGY, page 42
Clarification and Tips:
Program risk management strategy drives consistency and effectiveness in program risk management activities throughout the program as part of program integration and supporting activities, so Option (B) is the right answer.
Options (A) and (D) are wrong as they detailed level for risk management plan.
Option (C) may be an indirect reason, but Option (B) is a much better choice.
Domain: Strategy Alignment
Phase or Element: PROGRAM RISK MANAGEMENT STRATEGY

Q161 - If your program received the required budget and now begins paying expenses, what is the role of the financial activities?

(a) No need for financial activities as the budget was approved
(b) The financial effort will focus on reporting
(c) The financial effort moves into tracking, monitoring, and controlling the program's funds and expenditures
(d) The financial effort will focus on the component level

Question Category: Moderate
The right answer is Option (C)
The Standards for Program Management - 4th Edition - reference: Chapter (8), Program Activities, 8.2.3 PROGRAM FINANCIAL MANAGEMENT, pages 127
Clarification and Tips:
Once the program receives initial funding and begins paying expenses, the financial effort moves into tracking, monitoring and controlling the program's funds and expenditures.
Therefore, the right answer is Option (C).
Domain: Life Cycle Management
Phase or Element: Delivery

Q162 - Sam, the program manager, is working closely with the program sponsor and key stakeholders to develop a document that is used to assess the program's investment against the intended benefits. Which document is Sam working on?

(a) The program charter
(b) The program management plan
(c) The program business case
(d) The program stakeholder register

Question Category: Difficult
The right answer is Option (C)
The Standards for Program Management - 4th Edition - reference: Chapter (3), Program Strategy Alignment, 3.1 PROGRAM BUSINESS CASE, page 35
Clarification and Tips:
During program definition, the program manager collaborates with key sponsors and stakeholders to develop the program's business case. This business case is developed to assess the program's investment against the intended benefits.
Therefore, Option (C) is the right answer.
Domain: Strategy Alignment
Phase or Element: PROGRAM BUSINESS CASE

Q163 - Which of the following are factors to be considered when optimizing and tailoring program governance?

(a) Decision-making hierarchy
(b) Program funding structure
(c) Risk of failure
(d) All the above

Question Category: Easy
The right answer is Option (D)
The Standards for Program Management - 4th Edition - reference: Chapter (6), Program Governance, 6.3 PROGRAM GOVERNANCE DESIGN AND IMPLEMENTATION, page 85
Clarification and Tips:
Options (A), (B), and (C) are common factors to consider when optimizing and tailoring program governance. Therefore, Option (D) is the right answer.
Domain: Program Governance
Phase or Element: PROGRAM GOVERNANCE DESIGN AND IMPLEMENTATION

Q164 - Question Set (1/2) - Your organization assigned you to manage a program that is required to develop the matching engine for a stock exchange. One of your stakeholders is curious about the program and often raises many questions. You as a program manager, are preparing efficient answers to his question. As a program approach how should you deal with these communications with the very active stakeholder?

(a) These communications with the active stakeholder should be captured and published in a way that will allow multiple stakeholders to benefit from them
(b) Only the part of these communications which is reviewed and accepted by the program sponsor will be published in a way that will allow multiple stakeholders to benefit from them
(c) Only the part of these communications which is reviewed and accepted by the program governance board will be published in a way that will allow multiple stakeholders to benefit from them
(d) These communications are between specific stakeholders and the program manager and should be kept private to these stakeholders

Question Category: Difficult
The right answer is Option (A)
The Standards for Program Management - 4th Edition - reference: Chapter (5), Program Stakeholder Engagement, 5.5 PROGRAM STAKEHOLDER COMMUNICATIONS, page 66
Clarification and Tips:
Communications with the active stakeholder should be captured and published in a way that will allow multiple stakeholders to benefit from them. These communications are not private to the stakeholder nor should be approved to be communicated across the program stakeholders. Please note that in some cases part of the stakeholder communications will be kept private within a certain group of stakeholders; like financial details or some legal related communications.
Therefore, the right answer is Option (A).
Domain: Stakeholder Engagement
Phase or Element: PROGRAM STAKEHOLDER COMMUNICATIONS

Q165 - Question Set (2/2) - Your organization assigned you to manage a program that is required to develop the matching engine for a stock exchange. One of your stakeholders is curious about the program and often raises many questions. You, as a program manager, are preparing efficient answers to his question. If you decide to share these communications with other stakeholders, what is the best approach to deliver this information?

(a) These communications need to be formatted and presented in two packages; one for an internal group and another for an external group
(b) These communications need to be formatted and presented in one package for all stakeholders

(c) These communications need to be formatted and presented differently for certain stakeholder groups to keep their interest in reviewing them
(d) As stated earlier, there is no need to share this information

Question Category: Difficult
The right answer is Option (C)
The Standards for Program Management - 4th Edition - reference: Chapter (5), Program Stakeholder Engagement, 5.5 PROGRAM STAKEHOLDER COMMUNICATIONS, page 66
Clarification and Tips:
The best approach to share these communications with other stakeholders is to format and present the information differently for certain stakeholder groups to keep their interest in reviewing them. Therefore, the right answer is Option (C).
Domain: Stakeholder Engagement
Phase or Element: PROGRAM STAKEHOLDER COMMUNICATIONS

Q166 - Fatma is managing a program in the Cell organization. She is executing the program delivery phase and working on the risk management. Fatma wants to determine whether program assumptions are still valid. Which risk activity is she working on?

(a) Risk response planning
(b) Risk categorization
(c) Risk monitoring
(d) Risk identification

Question Category: Moderate
The right answer is Option (C)
The Standards for Program Management - 4th Edition - reference: Chapter (8), Program Activities, 8.2.8 PROGRAM RISK MONITORING AND CONTROLLING, pages 134
Clarification and Tips:
Risk monitoring is conducted to determine whether: 1) Program assumptions are still valid, 2) Assessed risk has changed from its prior state, 3) Proper risk management policies and procedures are being followed, and 4) Cost or schedule contingency reserves are modified in line with the risks of the program.
Therefore, Option (C) is the right answer.
Domain: Life Cycle Management
Phase or Element: Delivery

Q167 - Alex is managing a program that has five projects. He finished the definition phase and is currently working in the delivery phase. Alex noticed that projects are creating deliverables, but the associated benefits are not realized at the program level, he was trying to understand the reason behind this problem. What is the most probable reason to have this problem?

(a) The program is missing the consolidation of the integration efforts of the program components
(b) This program has no benefits to realize, but it has deliverables at the component level
(c) The program benefits are usually realized at the end of the program
(d) The program is missing the roadmap

Question Category: Difficult
The right answer is Option (A)
The Standards for Program Management - 4th Edition - reference: Chapter (7), Program Life Cycle Management, 7.1.3.2 COMPONENT OVERSIGHT AND INTEGRATION, pages 96
Clarification and Tips:
There may be cases where the program manager may initiate a new component to consolidate the integration efforts of multiple components. Without this step, individual components may produce deliverables; however, the benefits may not be realized without the coordinated delivery.
Therefore, Option (A) is the right answer.
Domain: Life Cycle Management
Phase or Element: Delivery

Q168 - Omar is in the execution of the Benefits Delivery phase, he knows that the resulting benefits review requires analysis of the planned versus actual benefits across a wide range of factors, but he doesn't know which item is most important to start with. How can you help him?

(a) Value delivery
(b) CPI and SPI values for the program components
(c) Program Change request status
(d) Program performance status

Question Category: Difficult
The right answer is Option (A)
The Standards for Program Management - 4th Edition - reference: Chapter (4), Program Benefits Management, 4.3 BENEFITS DELIVERY, page 52
Clarification and Tips:
The resulting benefits review requires analysis of the planned versus actual benefits across a wide range of factors. The most important aspects to be analyzed and assessed in this manner are the strategic alignment and the value delivery, which focuses on ensuring that the program delivers the promised benefits.

Therefore, the right answer is Option (A).
Domain: Benefits Management
Phase or Element: BENEFITS DELIVERY

Q169 - Zia is executing his first program ABC in Q-Lon company. He is executing the program strategy alignment process and became confident that the charter, business case, and roadmap are all aligned together. He asked you when to end the program strategy alignment process, what is your right answer?

- (a) As the charter, business case and roadmap are all aligned together, Zia can end the program strategy alignment process immediately
- (b) The program strategy alignment process should run until the end of the program life cycle
- (c) The program strategy alignment process is performed during the formulation subphase, then it can be terminated
- (d) Zia should wait until the program management plan is created to ensure that no updates are required which could affect the strategy alignment

Question Category: Difficult
The right answer is Option (B)
The Standards for Program Management - 4th Edition - reference: Chapter (3), Program Strategy Alignment, page 34
Clarification and Tips:
During the execution of the program formulation subphase, the program strategy alignment process is initiated and runs until the end of the program life cycle. Therefore, Option (B) is the right answer.
Domain: Strategy Alignment
Phase or Element: General

Q170 - Jacob presented one of his program components to the steering committee in order to approve the component initiation. After reviewing the details of the component authorization, the steering committee approved the component authorization. After the meeting, Jacob started to redefine the priorities of existing program components. Why did Jacob start this redefinition?

- (a) To ensure optimal resource allocation and management of interdependencies
- (b) To review the dependencies between the new component and the other existing components
- (c) To ensure that none of the existing components should be closed

(d) To review the progress of the existing components and select the right timing to present the new component

Question Category: Moderate
The right answer is Option (A)
The Standards for Program Management - 4th Edition - reference: Chapter (7), Program Life Cycle Management, 7.2.2.2 PROGRAM DELIVERY MANAGEMENT, pages 100
Clarification and Tips:
A decision is made utilizing the governance function on whether the component should be initiated. If the component is approved, the program manager may need to redefine the priorities of existing program components to ensure optimal resource allocation and management of interdependencies.
Therefore, the right answer is Option (A).
Please note:
Option (B) is partially correct, but Option (A) is a complete answer.
Domain: Life Cycle Management
Phase or Element: Delivery

1. Exam 2 - Questions

Q1 - Linda is working on a document which is considered a formal declaration of the value that the program is expected to deliver and a justification for the resources that will be expended to deliver it. Which document is Linda developing?

(a) The program business case
(b) The program charter
(c) The program benefits management plan
(d) The benefits register

Q2 - The following items are key elements of the program charter, except:

(a) Program scope
(b) Program components issues and risks
(c) Program assumptions and constraints
(d) Program success factors

Q3 - Mohamed is managing a program for his first time. He is working in the procurement planning and he needs to optimize program procurement management and the requirements to adhere to all legal and financial obligations. What is the best action that should he do?

(a) He should manage all the procurements requests from the program component himself
(b) He should establish procurement audit process to apply on any procurement activities in the program and its components
(c) He should involve the program management office in all procurements' activities
(d) He should drive all personnel responsible for procurement at the component level to work closely together, especially during the planning phase

Q4 - You are managing a program which is a joint effort between the Wings organization that you are working in and the Ministry of labors. You are defining the governance plan and working with the senior management in Wings organization and the prime minister of the Ministry of labors to establish steering committee(s) for the program. Which of the following is your best recommendation?

(a) I will recommend having only one steering committee for the program as this is more efficient
(b) I will recommend having three steering committees; one for Wings organization, another for the Ministry of labors, and the third as a joint steering committee for the Wings organization and the Ministry of labors

(c) I will recommend having a steering committee for Wings organization, and another for the Ministry of labors
(d) I will recommend having one steering committee only for the Wings organization

Q5 - Question Set (1/3) - Antonin is the program manager of the Telcom program. His program consists of four projects and one subsidiary program. One of the four projects is about to be transitioned to production.
Who should collaborate with Antonin to agree and secure resources to undertake the component transition activities?

(a) The customer
(b) The program sponsor
(c) The customer or the program sponsor
(d) The end user

Q6 - Question Set (2/3) - Antonin is the program manager of the Telcom program. His program consists of four projects and one subsidiary program. One of the four projects is about to be transitioned to production.
Who should approve the request to transition this project?

(a) The program sponsor
(b) The customer program manager
(c) The steering committee
(d) The customer and the program sponsor

Q7 - Question Set (3/3) - Antonin is the program manager of the Telcom program. His program consists of four projects and one subsidiary program. One of the four projects is about to be transitioned to production.
During the project transition, there might be some updates reflected on the program roadmap. Which of the following updates may be included at this time?

(a) Updates reflect both go/no-go decisions
(b) Approved change requests that affect the high-level milestones
(c) Approved change requests that affect the timing of major stages scheduled throughout the program
(d) All of the above

Q8 - What is the key skill differentiating between the program manager and the project manager?

    (a) Planning skills to align program goals with the long-term goals of the organization
    (b) Skills in issue resolution
    (c) Time management
    (d) Business knowledge

Q9 - In which of the following cases the lessons learned are critical assets to be reviewed?

    (a) When updating the program risk register
    (b) When updating the program stakeholder register
    (c) When updating the program communications management register
    (d) All of the above

Q10 - Jacob the program manager, is working with his component managers to review the program risks and the component-level risks. At the end of the revision, they are expecting to have changes to the risk register.
What is the main difference between program risks and component-level risks?

    (a) Program risks should be dealt with within a relatively short time frame, but component-level risks may be applicable at a point in the potentially distant future
    (b) Program risks and component-level risks are different in the risk categorization
    (c) Program risks and component-level risks are different in the risk identification process
    (d) Program risks may be applicable at a point in the potentially distant future, but component-level risks should be dealt with within a relatively short time frame

Q11 - Which of the following roles can participate in the risk identification activities?

    (a) Risk management team
    (b) Managers of other program components
    (c) External reviewers
    (d) All of the above

Q12 - Anil is a project manager executing a project which is a component of the X-Trail program. Anil needs to initiate his project and he is looking for the best organization role to approve the project authorization. How can you advise Anil?

    (a) I will advise him to go to the corporate PMO

(b) I will advise him to contact the program sponsor as he is the one who is responsible for authorizing the program components
(c) I will advise him to go to the steering committee
(d) I will advise him to contact the program manager as he acts as the proposer when seeking authorization for program components

Q13 - While you were executing a regular revision on the benefits register with your program team, you found one of the program benefits has a negative impact on the team working in the manufacturing department. What is the best action that you should do?

(a) I will hide the information of the negative impact from reaching the manufacturing department
(b) I will escalate the negative impact to the program sponsor
(c) I will neglect the negative impact of the benefit
(d) I will work to minimize the negative impact of the benefits and I will manage, measure, and properly communicate the negative impact to the organization's leadership

Q14 - Ming is the program manager assigned to the Z-Tech program in his organization. He was working with his component managers to review a document that represents an effective way to communicate the overarching plan and benefits to stakeholders. Which document were Ming and his team reviewing?

(a) The benefits management plan
(b) The benefits register
(c) The stakeholder engagement plan
(d) The program roadmap

Q15 - Chung is working to establish a governance structure, define the initial program organization and assemble a team to develop the program management plan. Which subphase is he working in?

(a) The component transition and closure subphase
(b) The component authorization and planning subphase
(c) The program planning subphase
(d) The program transition subphase

Q16 - Simon is working in the program delivery phase in the financial management activities. Which of the following may appear in the output of the program financial management activities?

(a) Program financial management plan
(b) Program operational costs
(c) Program funding schedules
(d) Program budget baseline updates

Q17 - Chao is a new program manager working in the Hunting organization. After he was appointed to manage a starting program, he spent some time with the program sponsor to understand how the funding will be for his program. The program sponsor informed him that the Hunting organization uses a tiered funding process with a series of go/no-go decisions at each major stage of the program. Chao was not happy with this information as he thought that the budget would be allocated according to the program total cost of ownership. What is your advice to Chao?

(a) I will advise Chao to ask the sponsor to allocate the total funds at the program startup
(b) I will advise Chao to struggle to allocate the total funds at the program startup to increase its success probability
(c) I will advise Chao to avoid using a tiered funding for his program
(d) I will advise Chao to accept a tiered funding principle in his program and to get management agreement on an overall financial management plan

Q18 - All the following artifacts are expected in the program work breakdown structure (WBS), except:

(a) Program management plans, procedures, standards, and processes
(b) Out of scope items
(c) Program management deliverables
(d) Program management office (PMO) support deliverables

Q19 - On your new program, you started to fill-in your stakeholder register. Which of the following is not considered an Internal Stakeholder?

(a) Portfolio governance body
(b) Program team
(c) Investors
(d) Departments Managers

Q20 - What is the difference between program payment schedules and component payment schedules?

(a) The component payment schedules and the program payment schedules indicate how and when contractors are paid in accordance with the contract provisions
(b) No difference, they are the same
(c) The component payment schedules identify the schedules and milestone points where funding is received by the funding organization. The program payment schedules indicate how and when contractors are paid in accordance with the contract provisions.
(d) The program payment schedules identify the schedules and milestone points where funding is received by the funding organization. The component payment schedules indicate how and when contractors are paid in accordance with the contract provisions.

Q21 - What is the risk Watch List?

(a) Risk Watch List contains the list of all Black Swan risks
(b) Risk Watch List contains all the important and high probable risks to be monitored
(c) Risk Watch List contains the risks with obviously low ratings of probability and impact and they are not retained for additional work
(d) Risk Watch List contains all risks that were emerged as a result of executing risk responses

Q22 - Mustafa is managing a program in his organization, which is progressing well as planned. But, due to recent changes in a few environmental factors, the strategic objectives changed. Which of the following statement describes the most probable action that will be taken regarding this program?

(a) The program may be changed, put on hold, or canceled
(b) The program will not be canceled as it is well performed, but change management will be applied
(c) The program manager will call the steering committee as a second level of escalation to discuss how to absorb the change
(d) The change manager will call the change board to discuss the impact of the change

Q23 - Ian defined his components cost estimation during the program Definition phase. Now during the Benefits delivery phase, Ian discovered that his estimation is not accurate enough for one of his components and he had to request more budget for this component. What is the best choice for Ian?

(a) Ian will create a change request to get the required additional budget
(b) Ian will record this issue in the log

(c) Ian should lower the scope of this component to accommodate the allocated budget
(d) Ian will communicate the subject to the component manager to find a solution

Q24 - The following risks are all related to the strategy alignment, except:

(a) Program objective not supportive of portfolio objectives
(b) Program resource requirements include scarce resources
(c) Program objectives not supportive of organizational objectives
(d) Program resource requirements out of sync with organizational capacity and capability

Q25 - An organization whose personnel are the most directly involved in doing the work of the program is called:

(a) Receiving organization
(b) Performing organization
(c) External organization
(d) Internal organization

Q26 - When a stakeholder has not been actively participating in your program activities, it may be that the stakeholder is confident in the program's direction or has lost interest in the program. What should you do to know the right reason for a non-participating stakeholder?

(a) I should call him in front of the program sponsor and ask him directly for the reason behind his reduced participation
(b) I should call him for a one-to-one meeting and ask him directly for the reason behind his reduced participation
(c) I should perform a thorough analysis to avoid incorrect assumptions about stakeholder behavior
(d) I should review the Power/Interest Grid to know his power and interest position

Q27 - All the following are considered intangible benefits, except:

(a) Goodwill
(b) Revenue increased
(c) Improved morale
(d) Perception of the organization

Q28 - As a part of program governance plan development, Mohamed is creating effective risk and issue management processes and procedures.
How do you think the effective risk and issue management practices are important to the program?

(a) They ensure that all risks are mitigated and all issues are resolved
(b) They ensure that key risks and issues are escalated appropriately and resolved in a timely manner
(c) They ensure that all risks and issues are recorded in the respected log
(d) They ensure that all risks and issues have response plans

Q29 - Which of the following will be included in the review to initiate a program component?

(a) Ensuring appropriate program-level communications of the component's closure to key stakeholders
(b) Confirming that the business case for the component has been sufficiently satisfied
(c) Assessing lessons learned of the component
(d) Authorizing the governance structure to track the component's progress against its goals

Q30 - Lee is managing a program in his organization where he created a strong quality management plan and is performing on Quality control throughout the duration of the program. He was about to request an evaluation for fitness for use of the delivered products.
Who should evaluate the fitness for use of the products delivered by the program?

(a) The team who received these products
(b) The team who tested these products
(c) The team who developed these products
(d) The program managers in the same organization

Q31 - Which of the following are not considered factors the organization should assume when defining the degree of autonomy given to the program manager for oversight of his program's components?

(a) The complexity and sensitivity of the program to the organization
(b) The experience level of the program manager
(c) The number of the program milestones
(d) The relation of this program to the different organization units

Exam 2 - Questions

Q32 - Which of the following actions should be taken first when a change occurs on the schedule of a program component?

(a) The program master schedule will be reviewed to assess the impact of component-level changes on other components and on the program itself
(b) The other component schedules will be reviewed to define the changes
(c) The program manager will call the steering committee to meet and discuss this change
(d) The component manager will raise a change request

Q33 - Mustafa is evaluating the program component performance against applicable acceptance criteria, reviewing the operational and program process documentation, and reviewing the readiness assessment by receiving organization. In which program benefits management phase is Mustafa working?

(a) Benefits transition phase
(b) Benefits identification phase
(c) Benefits sustainment phase
(d) Benefits delivery

Q34 - Brada is managing a program with ten components. He is currently planning for the program quality and is discussing with his team how to reduce the quality cost across the different program components. What is your advice to Brada?

(a) I will advise him to build quality plans only for the important components
(b) I will advise him to use the program quality management plan and apply it to all the components to reduce cost
(c) I will advise him to analyze program quality in order to evaluate it across the program with the goal of combining quality tests and inspections where feasible
(d) I will advise him to decrease the number of quality management staff to reduce cost

Q35 - You are working as a program manager to manage a program that consists of five projects and two subsidiary programs. Three of the five projects created contracts with a service company called Jika, which is one of the leading service companies in this industry. You have similar procurement requests from the other two projects, what is your best choice to balance your risks?

(a) I will use the same company, Jika, for the required recruitment of the other two projects
(b) I will use the same company, Jika, for the required recruitment of the other two projects, but I will ensure that they are using different resources to minimize risks

(c) I will encourage open competition in the procurement requirements for the other two projects
(d) I will extend the contract with Jika of the three projects to include the other two projects

Q36 - Who in the following roles is responsible for securing funding for the program, ensuring program goals and objectives are aligned with the strategic vision and enabling the delivery of benefits?

(a) The program sponsor
(b) The component manager
(c) The program manager
(d) The program management office

Q37 - Anne-Marie is working in the risk management activities of one program in her organization. She repeated the risk identification three times while she was working in the program delivery phase. In the risk identification session, the participants attended are different. Which of the following statements describes the involvement of the participants in the risk identification correctly?

(a) Risk identification is an iterative activity where the involvement of the participants or their variations has no influence on the sessions
(b) Risk identification is an iterative activity where the involvement of the participants will be the same group in all sessions to keep consistency
(c) Risk identification is an iterative activity where the involvement of participants may vary from one session to another
(d) Risk identification is an iterative activity where the involvement of the participants has already identified as per the risk management plan

Q38 - Who should plan the ongoing sustainment of program benefits?

(a) The receiving organization
(b) The program manager
(c) The component project managers
(d) The program manager and the component project managers

Q39 - Program D-Com is executed in your organization where its main scope is to implement an ERP solution which is a product of the Nivada company.

Exam 2 - Questions

Which of the following roles is not considered one of the common program management roles?

(a) Program Governance Board Members
(b) Nivada Account Manager
(c) Program Team Members
(d) Component Project Manager

Q40 - You started to write the program communication management plan with the help of the program management office. You are defining the requirements clearly to facilitate the transfer of information between the program and its components and from the program to the appropriate stakeholders. Where should you record the communication requirements specific to particular stakeholders?

(a) In the stakeholder register
(b) In the information management plan
(c) In the change management plan
(d) In the stakeholder engagement plan

Q41 - Which of the following tools can help the program manager to remind his team of which stakeholders need to be engaged at various times in the program life cycle?

(a) The power/interest grid
(b) The stakeholder register
(c) The stakeholder map
(d) The salience model

Q42 - All the following are considered description for the program roadmap, except:

(a) The program roadmap is an effective way to communicate the overarching plan and benefits to stakeholders to build and maintain advocacy.
(b) The program roadmap is a chronological representation of a program's intended direction
(c) The program roadmap defines program specific goals and objectives in alignment with the organization's strategic plan
(d) The program roadmap is graphically depicting dependencies between major milestones and decision points

Q43 - The following elements are included in the benefits register, except:

(a) List of planned benefits
(b) Person or group who will sustain the benefits
(c) Establishment of processes for measuring progress against the benefits plan
(d) Key performance indicators for evaluating benefits achievement

Q44 - Why should the program manager ensure resources are released for other programs when they are no longer necessary for the current program?

(a) To save cost in the current program
(b) To make these resources available for other programs
(c) To increase the morale of the other resources within the current program
(d) All of the above

Q45 - Which of the following statements are related to program benefit attributes?

(a) Benefits may be shared among multiple stakeholders
(b) Benefits are often defined in the context of the intended beneficiary
(c) Benefits are the gains and assets realized by the organization and other stakeholders as the result of outcomes delivered by the program
(d) All the above

Q46 - While you were managing one program in your organization, you noticed that the funding organization, which is different from your organization, is trying to impose some skills in the program management team and suggested specific monitoring and controlling tools. What should be your best response to the funding organization?

(a) Neglect the request of the funding organization as their role is only to fund the program
(b) Establish an interactive communication with the funding organization to inform them that program management is out of their scope
(c) Establish an interactive communication with the funding organization and work hard to manage their expectations on the program management team
(d) Escalate the subject to the program sponsor and get his advice

Q47 - Mohamed, the program manager in your organization, is suffering from the time consumed in the communications with the different stakeholders; within the program and outside the program. The size of the program which has seven components and the number of identified key stakeholders took a lot of his program management time. He is looking for a solution and asked you for advice, what is your advice to Mohamed?

(a) I will advise him to minimize the communications and use the time in the rest of the other program activities
(b) I will advise him to assign a full-time manager to hold the communication responsibilities
(c) I will advise him to delegate some of his program management responsibilities to one of the component managers
(d) I will advise him to delegate some of the program management responsibilities to the sponsor

Q48 - Which of the following is the best approach to engage the stakeholders to address the change that the program will bring?

(a) Sending regular reports to the stakeholders
(b) Engaging stakeholders to assess their readiness for change, planning for the change, providing program resources and support for the change
(c) Involving the key stakeholders in the steering meetings
(d) Sending the change requests status regularly to the stakeholders

Q49 - Kristin is the program manager in your organization. She was appointed to manage a critical program a few months ago. She is very keen on avoiding incorrect messages to the stakeholders, so she requested her program management team to review the communication that they will distribute to the key stakeholders with her first. What is the impact of an incorrect message to a stakeholder?

(a) An incorrect message to a stakeholder may make the stakeholder unhappy
(b) An incorrect message to a stakeholder may cause problems for the program and in some cases, lead to the stoppage of a program
(c) An incorrect message to a stakeholder will be reclaimed by another correct message
(d) An incorrect message to a stakeholder will be reclaimed by an apology from the program manager

Q50 - After Simon developed the program financial framework as part of the program planning activities, he found some changes that impact the original business case justifying the program. What should be done?

(a) The business case is created and approved, so there is no need to modify it
(b) The business case should not be updated after it is approved by the senior management
(c) The business case should be revised with full involvement of the decision makers
(d) The business case should be revised with the sponsor approval

Q51 - Chun is working in the program schedule management planning activities. She created the program high level schedule and is requesting the component managers to create their schedules as well. During these activities, she got a comment from the PMO asking her to create the program schedule first and then the component detail schedule. What is your advice to Chun?

(a) The initial program master schedule and the detailed schedules of the program components are created in parallel, so I will advise her to reject the PMO request
(b) The initial program master schedule is often created before the detailed schedules of the program components so it is better to keep this order
(c) The initial program master schedule is often created after the detailed schedules of the program components so it is better to keep this order
(d) Ask the PMO not to be involved with the program management role and responsibilities and concentrate on that of the PMO

Q52 - Kim has finished his financial estimation of his Absolute program and he is waiting for the sponsoring organization to approve the program financial.
Which of the following will drive the funding decision?

(a) Program benefits to be realized
(b) Program budget versus the benefits to be realized
(c) The total cost of ownership relative to the expected benefit of the program
(d) The total of used resources relative to the expected program benefits

Q53 - All the following are part of the program business case, except:

(a) The program milestones
(b) Cost benefit analysis,
(c) Time to market
(d) The extent to which the program aligns with the organization's strategic plan

Q54 - Which document is considered the baseline document that guides the delivery of benefits during the program's performance?

(a) The business case
(b) The benefits register
(c) The benefits management plan
(d) The program roadmap

Q55 - Kyra the program manager of the G5 program is reviewing one of the program agreements. She ensured that all deliverables have been satisfactorily completed, that all payments have been made and that there are no outstanding contractual issues. What is the next step to do with this agreement?

  (a) Request an audit for the agreement
  (b) Close out the agreement
  (c) Financially close the agreement
  (d) Ask the program sponsor for advice

Q56 - Which of the following items are different in handling between the stakeholders and the risks?

  (a) The impact may be positive or negative
  (b) They should be identified, studied, categorized, and tracked
  (c) They can be managed by the program team
  (d) They may generate an issue

Q57 - Santiago is creating a document that answers the following questions: Why is the program important and what does it achieve? What is the end state and how will it benefit the organization? and What are the key outcomes required to achieve the program vision and benefits?
Which document is this?

  (a) The program roadmap
  (b) The program business case
  (c) The program charter
  (d) The program benefits realization plan

Q58 - You are requested to estimate the required resources to prepare the program business case and the program charter. Which of the following are not considered a program resource?

  (a) Software
  (b) Key stakeholders
  (c) Office supplies and office space
  (d) Data centers

Q59 - Simon and Jack are discussing the program roadmap. Simon says it is a chronological representation in a graphical form of a program's intended direction. But Jack says that it is graphically depicting dependencies between major milestones and decision points, which reflects the linkage between the business strategy and the program work. What is the right description of the program roadmap?

(a) Simon's description is right
(b) Jack's description is right
(c) The program roadmap is both a chronological representation in a graphical form of a program's intended direction and is graphically depicting dependencies between major milestones and decision points, which reflects the linkage between the business strategy and the program work.
(d) Both are wrong, the program roadmap is chronologically representing the program major delivery

Q60 - During the formulation subphase, who will work to develop an initial risk assessment?

(a) The sponsor
(b) The sponsoring organization
(c) The program manager
(d) The sponsor, sponsoring organization, and the program manager work closely together

Q61 - Simon is working on developing the program change management plan for his first time. He was not sure about the main focus of the change plan and asked you to help him. What will be your best answer?

(a) The plan should focus on how to evaluate the impact of a change on the program time, cost and quality
(b) The plan should focus on how to evaluate the impact of a change on the components time, cost and quality
(c) The plan should focus on how to evaluate the impact of a change on the time, cost and quality of both the program and its components
(d) The plan should focus on how to evaluate the impact of a change to the program outcomes and therefore on the benefits expected by the stakeholders

Q62 - Cindy is appointed as a program manager and she started to create her first draft of the stakeholder engagement plan, which of the following should not be part of this stakeholder engagement plan?

(a) The strategy for effective stakeholder engagement
(b) The metrics used to measure the performance of stakeholder engagement activities
(c) Name and position of each stakeholder
(d) The guidelines for project-level stakeholder engagement

Q63 - The program manager interacts with stakeholders in the following ways, except:

(a) Includes stakeholders in program activities
(b) Engages stakeholders by assessing their attitudes and interests toward the program and their change readiness
(c) Hides the news of negative impacts that are expected by the program from reaching them
(d) Uses communications targeted to their needs, interests, requirements, expectations, and wants

Q64 - Adam is writing his program governance and is adding some elements related to the program funding. To which degree should the program governance facilitate program funding?

(a) Program governance facilitates program funding to the degree of the program scope
(b) Program governance facilitates program funding to the degree of the program scope and the approved change requests
(c) Program governance facilitates program funding to the degree necessary to support the approved business case
(d) Program governance facilitates program funding to the degree of the program budget

Q65 - George is working in the risk management planning. He is creating a document which is a living document that is updated as program risks and risk responses change during program delivery. Which document is this?

(a) The risk response plan
(b) The program roadmap
(c) The risk management plan
(d) The risk register

Q66 - You requested your program team to collect and log stakeholder issues and concerns, and then manage them to closure. If the number of stakeholders in your program is small, what is the suitable tool to be used by your team to document, prioritize, and track issues relevant to the stakeholders?

(a) A simple spreadsheet may be an adequate tracking tool
(b) A table in MS words may be more than sufficient
(c) A sophisticated tracking and prioritization mechanism using a developed application
(d) No tool is required

Q67 - Ahmed the program manager for the Falcon program used to review the stakeholder metrics with the project managers and subsidiary program managers on a weekly basis. Why should the program manager review stakeholder metrics regularly?

(a) To ensure that there are no missing stakeholders
(b) To identify potential risks caused by a lack of participation from stakeholders
(c) To ensure that new stakeholders are considered in the engagement plan
(d) To deal with the changing environment around the program

Q68 - You want to initiate your first program component in the Geely program. You have prepared two slides to represent the request to initiate the program component to the steering committee in order to get their approval. Why do you need the steering committee approval?

(a) Because the new component includes benefits to be realized
(b) To assure that the program component has still required benefits and do not become obsolete
(c) Because the new component has the introduction of additional governance structures that are responsible for monitoring and managing the component
(d) Because the new component status will be presented regularly during the steering committee

Q69 - Omar is working in the program delivery phase in the financial activities. Which of the following activities are considered part of the financial management activities?

(a) Identify any critical assumptions upon which the estimates are made
(b) Monitoring contract expenditures to ensure funds are disbursed in accordance with the contracts
(c) Identify the program's financial sources
(d) Integrate the budgets of the program components

Q70 - What is the primary objective of the stakeholder engagement?

(a) The primary objective is to gain and maintain stakeholder register for future use

(b) The primary objective is to ensure the alignment with the organization strategic objectives
(c) The primary objective is to gain and maintain stakeholder buy-in for the program's objectives and benefits
(d) The primary objective is to communicate the program status and get their feedback

Q71 - Your organization is preparing for a large program that will enhance the two major products with respect to your organization revenue. The funding organization, which is a government entity, requested to share in the decision of appointing the program manager. How should your organization decision makers deal with this request?

(a) They should accept this request from the funding organization and ask them to interview the candidate program manager as part of the approval process
(b) They should reject this request from the funding organization as they are the responsible organization in executing the program
(c) They should limit their involvement in the program only to the funding and financial issues
(d) They should raise this request as an issue in the steering meeting with the government senior management

Q72 - How is the program selected and prioritized within the organization?

(a) The program is selected and prioritized according to how well it supports the strategic goals of the organization
(b) The program is selected and prioritized according to the benefits to be realized
(c) The program is selected and prioritized according to the resource requirements
(d) The program is selected and prioritized according to the completion schedule date

Q73 - Mustafa is a program manager executing a program whose main objective is to develop a car that can be driven on the roads and on the sea. During the program phase-gate review, the program steering meeting found that the program benefits deviate from the original plan. What decision should be taken by the steering meeting?

(a) The steering meeting should take the hard decision to terminate the program
(b) The steering meeting should initiate recommendations for adaptive changes to the program's plan to improve the program's ability to pursue and deliver its intended benefits
(c) The steering meeting should ensure that this deviation is registered in the issue register
(d) The steering meeting should initiate a program health check

Q74 - Sam is a new program manager who is asking himself why he had spent all of these long hours working with the stakeholder to obtain key information. Why do you think these hours spent with stakeholders are valuable to the program?

(a) For better understanding the organizational culture and politics concerning the program
(b) For better understanding, the concerns related to the program
(c) For better understanding the overall impact of the program
(d) All the above

Q75 - Aisa is writing a document in her program that records all of the program's financial aspects; including funding schedules and milestones, initial budget, contract payments and schedules, and the financial metrics.
Which document is this?

(a) The program financial framework
(b) The financial management plan
(c) The stakeholder engagement plan
(d) The cost management plan

Q76 - James is managing a program where no transition to operation is included. How could this happen?

(a) When the chartered program is no longer of value to the organization
(b) When the charter has been fulfilled and operations are not necessary to continue realization of ongoing benefits
(c) When the program is completed earlier than planned
(d) Options (A) and (B)

Q77 - The past and future customers who will be watching intently to see how well the program delivers the stated benefits are called _____

(a) New customers
(b) Old customers
(c) Potential customers
(d) Senior customers

Q78 - In the program management environment, which entity holds the responsibilities to provide governance support for the program, ensure program goals and planned benefits align with organizational strategic and operational goals, and endorse or approve program recommendations and changes?

(a) The program management office
(b) The project management office
(c) The steering committee
(d) The group of component managers

Q79 - Sam is a program manager assigned to a New-Tech program after the first program manager left the New-Tech program due to personal reasons.
Sam found in the benefits register an item regarding the employee moral improvement. Sam felt uncomfortable about this uncertain benefit and he thinks about removing it out of the benefits register. What is your advice for Sam?

(a) I will advise Sam to work on removing it out of the benefits register as it is an uncertain outcome
(b) I will tell Sam that some benefits may be less easily quantifiable and may produce an uncertain outcome, and I will advise him to keep this benefit
(c) I will advise Sam to investigate first how this benefit was added to the register
(d) I will advise Sam to escalate the subject to the steering committee and get their advice

Q80 - Anne-Marie is at a critical stage in the program where she will have a phase-gate review and a decision is going to be made at this decision point to move forward and continue with the program or to terminate the program. Which of the following cases may lead to program termination?

(a) The program is not likely to deliver its expected benefits
(b) The program has many open issues with high impact
(c) The program has many open risks with high impact and high probability
(d) The program is suffering a high number of change requests

Q81 - Omar is a program manager for the Z-Tech program. He noticed that one of the key stakeholders is not supporting the program. What should Omar do?

(a) Omar should escalate the subject in the next steering committee
(b) Omar should escalate the subject to the program sponsor
(c) Omar should spend extensive time and energy with this stakeholder to ensure all points of view have been considered and addressed and get his interest in the program
(d) Omar should review the program governance plan and react accordingly

Q82 - Adron was a good project manager who proven himself through many completed successful projects. A month ago, he was promoted to be a program manager and appointed to manage one program in your organization. Adron thinks that the communication in program management is similar to the that in project management. He came asking you for advice in this regard, what you will tell him?

   (a) Program communications management is similar to project communications management
   (b) Program communications management requires more dedication than project communication as the number of stakeholders is higher
   (c) Program communications management is more complicated than project communications management as it affects a wider array of stakeholders with widely varying communication needs and different communication approaches
   (d) Project Communications management is more complicated than program communications management

Q83 - How should the program management work with the resource interdependencies?

   (a) The program manager should neglect the interdependencies and work with the resources according to the resource management plan
   (b) The program manager should work to ensure that the interdependencies do not cause a delay in benefits delivery
   (c) The program manager should work to ensure that his program is free from resource interdependencies
   (d) The program manager should work to ensure that the interdependencies do not cause a delay in any of the component activities

Q84 - Which of the following may be considered a key aspect of conducting a program level procurement?

   (a) To save budget that can be utilized for other program activities
   (b) To set standards for the components like; qualified seller lists, pre-negotiated contracts, blanket purchase agreements and formalized proposal evaluation criteria
   (c) To increase quality
   (d) To avoid the unethical use of budget

Q85 - To which level should the program manager control the scope of the program?

   (a) To the program level only and not look for components

(b) To the program level and to the allocated level for components
(c) To the program level and going down to control the component scope
(d) To the program level and going down to update the WBS levels of the program components

Q86 - You are managing your first program in the Fing organization. You joined this organization recently and you do not know yet the different stakeholders and the right way to deal with them. It comes to your knowledge that you will have many stakeholders in this program with different communication requirements. What should you do to assess the stakeholder's communication requirements?

(a) Survey program stakeholders to identify their expectations for program outcome and their interests in staying informed and involved during the program delivery
(b) Meet with a sample of the different stakeholders and identify their expectations for program outcome and their interests in the program communication
(c) Get an old program communication assessment that was performed earlier in the organization and then use it as a guide in my new program
(d) Apply the PMI best practices and my best experience when dealing with different stakeholders with different opinions

Q87 - Yung wonders what the meaning of stakeholder risk tolerance is, how can you help him?

(a) It is the risk which was accepted by the stakeholder as part of the response planning
(b) It is the threshold or attitude of the stakeholder towards the positive effects of risks on the program or generally on the organization
(c) It is the threshold or attitude of the stakeholder towards the positive or negative effects of risks on the program or generally on the organization
(d) It is the threshold or attitude of the stakeholder towards the negative effects of risks on the program or generally on the organization

Q88 - The following organizational factors are considered when performing a program feasibility study, except:

(a) The organization's constraint profile
(b) The organization's sourcing
(c) The organization's culture
(d) The organization's complexity

Q89 - Sam qualifies the incremental delivery of the program benefits to measure the planned benefits during the performance of the program. Why is this measurement important?

(a) Measuring the incremental delivery of the program benefits helps in establishing the benefits management plan
(b) Measuring the incremental delivery of the program benefits helps the program manager define risks as early as possible
(c) Measuring the incremental delivery of the program benefits helps the program manager determine whether benefits are delivered in a timely manner
(d) Measuring the incremental delivery of the program benefits helps the program manager and stakeholders determine whether benefits exceed their control thresholds and whether they are delivered in a timely manner

Q90 - When does the budget become the primary financial target that the program is measured against?

(a) When the program charter is created
(b) When the budget is allocated
(c) When the budget is baselined
(d) When there is no change request on the baseline budget

Q91 - Ming is managing the GUME program in one of the leading companies in the Oil and Gas industry. Ming is facing conflicting stakeholders' expectations regarding the new explored gas field in the north of the country. He found that the expectations of the office group are close to the program benefits, but the expectation of the field engineers are contradicting. What is the best action that Ming should do?

(a) Ming should encourage the office group expectations
(b) Ming should facilitate negotiation sessions among stakeholder groups to work on the expectations conflict
(c) Ming should request a meeting with the steering committee to describe the conflict and ask them to take a decision
(d) Ming should discourage the field engineering expectations

Q92 - You may create all the following elements as part of program financial management planning, except:

(a) Component payment schedules,
(b) Program financial metrics
(c) Program funding schedules

(d) Program cost management plan

Q93 - What is the main goal of linking the program to the organization's strategic plan?

(a) To ensure that the program goals and objectives are not contradicting with the organization strategy
(b) To help in creating the program business case and program charter
(c) To satisfy the stakeholders need
(d) To help the organization achieve its strategic goals and objectives

Q94 - Amy is looking for a document that should help to get the list of the stakeholders who should be engaged and communicated with during the program's life cycle and governance activities. Which document should Amy look for?

(a) The stakeholders list
(b) The stakeholder map
(c) The benefits realization plan
(d) The program governance plan

Q95 - Which is the most important element with which the program manager should provide the decision-making stakeholders to help him in making the right decisions at the right time necessary to move the program forward?

(a) The company strategic objectives
(b) The program business case
(c) The program status in a timely manner
(d) The adequate information

Q96 - You are assigned to execute a critical program in your organization, the program infrastructure includes a quality manager who was appointed by the governing body. When you started your meeting to develop a program resource plan, the quality manager requested to attend to verify that quality activities and controls are applied in the planning phase. What is your reply to him?

(a) I will welcome the quality manager to attend and to do his job in the program planning activities
(b) I will ask the quality manager to concentrate on the deliverables and services and not on the program management activities

(c) I will speak to the governing body to let the quality manager concentrating on his job only
(d) I will escalate the subject to his department manager in the organization to let him concentrate on his job only

Q97 - During the Benefits Delivery phase, the resulting benefits review require analysis of the planned versus actual benefits across a wide range of factors. Which of the following aspect is the most important to be analyzed and assessed?

(a) Program components performance status
(b) Program schedule variance
(c) Change management status
(d) Strategic alignment

Q98 - Where is the information, regarding the roles and responsibilities required to manage the program benefits, recorded?

(a) In the benefits register
(b) In the business case
(c) In the benefits management plan
(d) In the program roadmap

Q99 - George is creating the program stakeholder engagement plan, which of the following attributes will not be considered for each stakeholder?

(a) Attitudes about the program and its sponsor
(b) The degree of support or opposition to the program benefits
(c) His culture to deal with his subordinates
(d) Organizational culture and acceptance of change

Q100 - You are managing a program in your organization which has five projects. The definition phase is completed and you are currently working in the delivery phase. When the component detailed planning started, one project surprised you, the ERP project, it has more scope than required and it is going to affect one more project because of the integration. What is the best action should you do?

(a) I should ask the ERP project manager to work closely with the project manager of the other affected project to close this issue

(b) I should stop the delivery phase execution and go back to the definition phase to complete the planning properly
(c) I should replan for the proper integration with the ERP project and realign to accommodate changes in program direction through adaptive change
(d) I should escalate the problem to the program sponsor and ask him for advice

Q101 - Marcie is a program manager who is managing a program with four projects. The first project, which is managed by Anil, is currently in the planning phase. Marcie asked Anil to conduct a feasibility study. Why did Marcie request a feasibility study from Anil?

(a) She wants to understand why this project should be authorized
(b) She wants to verify that the project properly supports the program's outcomes and aligns with the strategy and ongoing work of the organization prior to authorization
(c) She wants to present the feasibility study in the coming steering committee
(d) She wants to verify that Anil can write a feasibility study for his project

Q102 - In which of the following does the program financial management plan expand upon the program financial framework?

(a) It includes more quality controls
(b) It describes the cost of items
(c) It describes the management of items
(d) Nothing, both are the same

Q103 - Khadija, the program manager of Aqsa program, is reviewing with her PMO the factors that, for planning purposes, are considered true, real, or certain to validate them and to ensure that they have not been invalidated by events or other program activities.
What analysis does Khadija execute?

(a) She executes historical information analysis
(b) She executes trend analysis
(c) She executes assumptions analysis
(d) She executes comparative advantage analysis

Q104 - What do you call the group of participants representing various program-related interests with the purpose of supporting the program under its authority by providing guidance, endorsements, and approvals through the governance practices?

(a) Program steering committee

(b) Change control board
(c) Legal agencies
(d) Board of director

Q105 - All the following are considered risks of implementing the program benefits, except:

(a) New market entrants
(b) The amount of change being absorbed by the organization
(c) Realization of unexpected outcomes
(d) Stakeholder acceptance

Q106 - If your program is part of the portfolio structure, which of the following entities should provide your program with a governance-supporting function?

(a) The governing body
(b) The portfolio
(c) The steering committee
(d) The PMO

Q107 - Anne-Marie is expecting some changes to the environmental factors in which her program is executed. She discussed the subject with the program sponsor and ensured that some of these factors would affect the organization's strategic objectives. What should she do?

(a) She should monitor the environmental factors to ensure the program remains aligned with the environmental factors
(b) She should monitor the environmental factors to ensure the program remains aligned with the organization's strategic objectives
(c) She should ignore the environmental factors as their effect on the strategy did not happen yet
(d) She should ask the sponsor for advice

Q108 - Which of the following is not important to be considered by the program manager before starting the program transition?

(a) Confirm that the stakeholders have the latest program updates
(b) Confirm that all transition work was performed within the component transition
(c) Determine whether there is another program or sustaining activity that will oversee the ongoing benefits for which this program was chartered

(d) Ensure that the program has met all of the desired benefits

Q109 - You are managing a critical program in your organization. You spent many interviews and focus group sessions with the stakeholders to analyze the stakeholders and then to create the stakeholders' engagement plan that includes guidelines. With whom should you share these guidelines?

(a) The guidelines should be shared with the component projects only
(b) The guidelines should be shared with the component subsidiary programs only
(c) The guidelines should be shared with the component projects, subsidiary programs, and other program activities under the program
(d) The guidelines should be kept with the program management team only

Q110 - What is the difference between the contingency reserves at the program level and the component contingency reserve held at the component level?

(a) The program manager holds contingency reserves at the program level to support risk responses and uses this contingency as a substitute for the component contingency reserve
(b) The program manager holds contingency reserves at the program level to support risk responses, while the component contingency reserve is held at the component level
(c) There are no differences as in programs, contingency reserve is allowed only on the program level
(d) The component contingency reserve is calculated as part of the contingency reserve at the program level

Q111 - Cindy, the program manager in Hopton organization, started to quantify all the benefits added to the benefits register. Why are benefits quantified?

(a) Benefits are quantified so sponsor approval can be obtained
(b) Benefits are quantified so customer approval can be obtained
(c) Benefits are quantified so risks can be mitigated
(d) Benefits are quantified so that their realization can be measured over time

Q112 - After assigned as a program manager, Richard started to develop the program roadmap and the program management plan as part of the program Definition phase. Richard has uncertainty regarding the full suite of program components, he thinks that some of them may not be known in the program definition phase.

How should Richard accommodate this uncertainty?

(a) Richard needs to continually oversee the components throughout the benefits delivery phase and when necessary, re-plan for their proper integration or changes in program direction
(b) Richard needs to create a program issue regarding this subject in the issue log
(c) Richard will transfer his uncertainty to his component managers to share the responsibility
(d) Richard should not start the program delivery phase until he cleared this uncertainty

Q113 - Tom is working in the risk management activities in his ORA program. He is creating a fallback plan and getting some help from the industry subject matter experts in his program. What is the purpose of using the fallback plan?

(a) The fallback plan is for the risks that have been deliberately accepted
(b) The fallback plan is for the risks that are expected to remain after planned responses have been taken
(c) The fallback plan is used as a response to a risk that has occurred and the primary response proves to be inadequate
(d) The fallback plan is for addressing the positive risks

Q114 - Which of the following is not part of the historical information?

(a) Program risks
(b) Estimations from previous programs that may be relevant to the current program
(c) Portfolio capacity and capability management
(d) Program artifacts

Q115 - On your new program, you started to fill-in your stakeholder register.
Which of the following is not considered an External Stakeholder?

(a) Business partners
(b) Customers
(c) Government and legal
(d) Business operational team

Q116 - James is working in the program closure. He provides the new supporting organization with documentation of operation and user guides, and he prepared a training session for some employees of the new supporting organization. Which activity in the program closure is he executing?

- (a) Program Procurement Closure
- (b) Program Financial Closure
- (c) Program Information Archiving and Transition
- (d) Program Resource Transition

Q117 - Which of the following can be used as a quality control measurement?

- (a) Quality control completed checklists
- (b) Customer satisfaction surveys
- (c) Quality control inspection reports
- (d) Quality audits

Q118 - The limiting factors that affect the execution of a project, program, portfolio, or process are called:

- (a) Assumption
- (b) Constraint
- (c) Risk
- (d) Issue

Q119 - Antonin is reviewing his funding sources in the program that he was assigned to manage. He was surprised when he found that the program is funded by the government, and the program components are funded by a consortium of companies in the private sector. What is your advice to Antonin regarding the funding sources?

- (a) There is no issue in funding sources as the program itself may be funded by one or more sources, and the program components may be funded by altogether different sources
- (b) There is no issue in funding sources as the program itself is funded by the government which has the upper hand with respect to the component funding source
- (c) There is a funding issue that Antonin should address to the program sponsor
- (d) There is a funding issue that Antonin should address to the program steering committee

Q120 - You are in the delivery phase of your critical program. You noticed that the program costs exceed the budget. What is expected to happen in your program?

- (a) The program sponsor will need to increase the budget
- (b) The program will continue after changing the program manager

(c) The program will have a hard steering meeting
(d) The program may no longer satisfy the business case used to justify it and may be subject to cancellation

Q121 - Mustafa is the program manager who has confirmed with his team that the program charter is fulfilled. Which of the following statements describes the benefits status after the charter is fulfilled?

(a) When a program has fulfilled its charter, its benefits may have been fully realized or benefits may continue to be realized and managed as part of organizational operations
(b) When a program fulfills its charter, its benefits will be fully realized
(c) When the program charter is fulfilled, the program benefits will be either realized or canceled
(d) There is no relation between the benefits realization and the charter. The benefits are realized according to the benefits management plan

Q122 - Richard is a program manager, he is currently monitoring the organizational environment, program objectives, and benefits realization to ensure that the program remains aligned with the organization's strategic objectives. He is also initiating, performing, transitioning, closing components, and managing the interdependencies among them. With respect to the benefits management domain, which phase is Richard executing?

(a) Benefits Identification phase
(b) Benefits Delivery phase
(c) Benefits Transition phase
(d) Benefits Sustainment

Q123 - Which of the following may be considered part of the stakeholders' engagement metrics?

(a) Stakeholder level of power
(b) Positive contribution to the realization of the program's objectives and benefits
(c) Stakeholder level of interest
(d) Stakeholder level of influence

Q124 - Pari is managing a long running program with six components. One of the components is managed by the project manager Chao. Pari noticed that Chao monitors the project schedule to identify the slippage and does not pay attention to the probable opportunity in the schedule.

Exam 2 - Questions

What should Pari do?

(a) Pari should ask Chao to identify not only schedule slippages but also opportunities to accelerate the component schedule
(b) Pari should ask Chao to continue his good job
(c) Pari should ask Chao to come to him for consultancy on how to control the component schedule
(d) Pari should ask Chao to do a better job and ask for schedule review by the PMO

Q125 - Question Set (1/2) - Mohamed focuses on having a complete and accurate program information repository, although it took a good amount of time from him and his program team. What is the importance of the program information repository?

(a) It can be an invaluable aid to other program activities
(b) It will help when there is a need to refer to past decisions
(c) It will help when there is a need to prepare analyses based on trends
(d) All of the above

Q126 - Question Set (2/2) - Mohamed focuses on having a complete and accurate program information repository, even though it took a good amount of time from him and his program team. When should the program team make the program information available to support program communications and management?

(a) It should be made available at the program closure for archiving
(b) It should be made available in the planning subphase to build accurate program plans
(c) It should be made available throughout the program life cycle
(d) It should be made available in the definition phase to have correct program startup

Q127 - Jacob is managing a project as part of the program. He has analyzed his project risks, but the program manager asked him to do further analysis. What is the most probable reason behind the program manager request?

(a) To determine if they will have impacts outside of the component that may influence the program
(b) To make sure that the impact and probability are correct
(c) To use more qualitative and quantitative technique in risk analysis
(d) To consult more SME in risk analysis

Q128 - You are pleased to be promoted to manage your first program in your organization. You started to execute the environmental assessment and you need to convince your team why the environmental assessments are conducted, which of the following options will help you?

(a) The environmental assessments are conducted to ensure ongoing stakeholder alignment
(b) The environmental assessments are conducted to ensure the program's continued alignment with the organization's strategic goals and objectives
(c) The environmental assessments are conducted to ensure overall program success
(d) The environmental assessments are conducted to ensure ongoing stakeholder alignment, the program's continued alignment with the organization's strategic goals and objectives, and overall program success

Q129 - Peter is a newly assigned program manager in your organization, he has created the stakeholder register and he was about to grant access to all the stakeholders listed in the register.
What is your advice to Peter?

(a) Peter should restrict the access to the register as the stakeholder register may contain politically and legally sensitive information.
(b) Peter should be transparent and provide access to all the stakeholders mentioned in the register
(c) Peter should grant access only to the high-power stakeholders
(d) Peter should not grant access to any of the stakeholders in the register

Q130 - Which of the following can be described as the program governance?

(a) Program Governance is the performance domain that enables and performs program decision making, establishes practices to support the program and maintains program oversight
(b) Program governance comprises the framework, functions and processes by which a program is monitored, managed and supported in order to meet organizational strategic and operational goals
(c) Program Governance refers to the systems and methods by which a program and its strategy are defined, authorized, monitored, and supported by its sponsoring organization
(d) All the above

Q131 - Which of the following options describe the stakeholders in a more precise statement?

(a) Stakeholders represent all those who will interact with the program as well as those who will be affected by the implementation of the program
(b) Stakeholders represent all organization key staff who will interact with the program as well as those who will be affected by the implementation of the program
(c) Stakeholders represent all internal who will interact with the program, as well as external who will be affected by the implementation of the program
(d) Stakeholders represent all internal or external who will interact with the program

Q132 - Which of the following assessments can be executed in the decision-point review?

(a) Strategic alignment of the program and its components with the intended goals of both the program and the organization
(b) Program resource needs and organizational commitments in addition to capabilities for fulfilling them
(c) Program compliance with organizational quality or process standards
(d) All the above

Q133 - Mustafa is executing a process that assesses the feasibility of his program within the organization's financial, sourcing, complexity, and constraint profile. Which environmental analysis is he performing?

(a) Assumptions analysis
(b) SWOT analysis
(c) Feasibility studies
(d) Comparative advantage analysis

Q134 - Mohamed is currently in the program closure phase, he is executing the benefits transition activities. He realized three opened risks that may affect the transitioned benefit, how should he deal with these risks?

(a) He should ignore these risks as the program is closing
(b) He should add these risks to the lessons learned
(c) He should transfer these risks to the receiving organization
(d) He should report these risks to the steering committee

Q135 - Which of the following are confirmed during the program transition?

(a) Program charter development is completed

(b) The program has met all of the desired benefits and that all transition work has been performed within the component transition
(c) Program charter and business case are aligned
(d) Alignment of the program roadmap with the benefits management plan

Q136 - Which of the following statements has the most important reason to have programs?

(a) Programs are designed to realize a group of agreed upon benefits
(b) Programs are designed to align with the organizational strategy and to facilitate the realization of organizational benefits
(c) Programs are designed to manage its components in a coordinated manner to obtain benefits not available from managing them individually
(d) Programs are designed to achieve specific objectives

Q137 - Jacob started to audit the Zaro program just after it was completed and he noticed that the cost is continued even after the program is closed. Which of the following cases may be a valid reason to have cost incurred for a closed program?

(a) Program costs may continue after program closeout to complete the opened change requests
(b) Program costs may continue after program closeout as operational costs to sustain the benefits
(c) Program costs may continue after program closeout to reward the program team
(d) Program costs may continue after program closeout as operational costs to resolve the opened issues

Q138 - Which of the following activities will have the focus of the financial effort after the program receives initial funding and begins paying expenses?

(a) Tracking, monitoring and controlling the program's funds and expenditures
(b) Preparing for financial change requests
(c) Recording financial issues and assumptions in the issue log
(d) Checking the financial impact if the industry standards are changed in the future

Q139 - What is the relation between the program funding and the program components funding?

(a) The program itself may be funded by one or more sources, and the program components may be funded by altogether different sources

(b) The program and program components must be funded by the same sources whatever internal or external to the performing organization
(c) The program may be funded by one or more sources internal or external to the performing organization, but the program components must be funded from internal sources
(d) The program funding and the program components funding must be different

Q140 - How is the program budget usually created?

(a) Program budgets should include the costs for each individual component as well as costs for the resources to manage the program itself
(b) Top-down cost aggregation is used to create the program budget
(c) Bottom-up cost aggregation is used to estimate the program budget, then the top-down cost estimation is used to validate it
(d) All the above

Q141 - Cindy is working with her team to adapt to the multiple changes affecting her program as a result of recent unexpected regulation changes. Cindy is asking you about elements that may bound the changes authorized for a program. What should be your answer?

(a) Organizational strategy
(b) The business case
(c) The components scope
(d) Options (A) and (B)

Q142 - Mohamed is writing a risk to the risk register that is expected to remain after planned responses have been taken. What is the name of this risk?

(a) Black swan risks
(b) Residual risks
(c) Secondary risks
(d) Negative risks

Q143 - Who issues the program charter?

(a) The program manager
(b) The program sponsor
(c) The program management office

(d) The EPMO

Q144 - As per the last steering committee actions, the program manager, Anil, will include the program forecast in the steering committee's presentation.
What does the program forecast mean?

(a) It means to assess the likelihood of the final product success
(b) It means to assess the likelihood of achieving the planned program financial
(c) It means to assess the likelihood of achieving planned outcomes of the program
(d) It means to assess the likelihood of achieving the stakeholders' expectations

Q145 - Zenon is a new program established between the Ministry of Housing and a private company called Elite to develop 10,000 housing units.
The newly assigned program manager Luis was confused to which steering committee he should report; the Ministry of Housing steering committee, or the Elite company steering committee.
What is your advice to Luis?

(a) He should report to the Elite company steering committee
(b) He should report to the two steering committees; the Ministry of Housing steering committee and the Elite company steering committee
(c) He should report to the Ministry of Housing steering committee
(d) He should assume the responsibility of the steering committee to avoid this conflict

Q146 - As part of the program change assessment activity, you started to identify the sources of change in your environment to help develop the program's business case and the program's charter.
What should you do with the identified sources of change?

(a) Estimate the likelihood of the changes that could arise from these sources
(b) Estimate the possible impacts of the changes that could arise from these sources
(c) Propose measures that could be taken to enable the program to respond to such changes in a positive way
(d) All the above

Q147 - Which of the following bounds the changes authorized for a program?

(a) The program scope
(b) The components scope
(c) The business case

(d) The organization risk appetite

Q148 - Many organizations have programs with specific objectives to achieve, and planned benefits to realize. On what basis did the organizations evaluate, select, and authorize the programs?

(a) Organizations evaluated, selected, and authorized the programs based on value added by the programs to the community
(b) Organizations evaluated, selected, and authorized the programs based on organization's limiting factors
(c) Organizations evaluated, selected, and authorized the programs based on their alignment and support to achieve the organization's strategic plan
(d) Organizations evaluated, selected, and authorized the programs based on required resources

Q149 - James is working on tools that are used to collect, integrate and communicate information critical to the effective management of one or more organizational programs. Which tools are these?

(a) Visual management tools
(b) Program information management tools
(c) The program management information system (PMIS)
(d) Internet-based group communication tools

Q150 - James is working with the program risk manager to define the minimum level of risk exposure for a risk to be included in the risk register. What does James define?

(a) The program risk exposure
(b) The program risk threshold
(c) The program risk appetite
(d) Risk category

Q151 - The benefits transition activities include all the following except:

(a) Evaluating opportunities and threats affecting benefits
(b) Verifying that the integration of the program and its components meet or exceed the benefit realization criteria
(c) Verifying that the transition and closure of the program and its components meet or exceed the benefit realization criteria

(d) Developing a transition plan

Q152 - Anil was assigned to a three year program for building a Dam. After the first year passed. Once he joined the program, he reviewed the program benefits register and found that the benefits are realized only at the program closure, what should Anil do?

(a) Anil should call for a meeting with the program sponsor to review the whole benefits register
(b) Anil should call for a meeting with the program team to review the whole benefits register
(c) It is regular for large public work programs to realize the benefits at the end of the program. So, Anil should continue without stopping at this point
(d) Anil should call for a meeting with the governance board to review the approved program governance plan

Q153 - Which of the following statements is not correct to describe the program roadmap?

(a) The roadmap outlines major program events for the purposes of planning
(b) The program roadmap summarizes the program status in a chronological order
(c) The roadmap outlines major program events for the purposes of developing more detailed schedules
(d) The program roadmap provides a high-level view of key milestones and decision points

Q154 - Amy is working on the preparation for the program reporting to send to the stakeholders as per the communication plan. Program reporting aggregates information from all the program components.
Amy needs to communicate this information to a group in order to provide them with general and background information about the program. Which group is this?

(a) The program management office
(b) The program steering committee
(c) The program team members and its constituent components
(d) The program managers in the same organization

Q155 - What is your best approach as a program manager, in handling the stakeholder register, when you have changes in your program scope that may involve the crafting department, as a new stakeholder?

(a) I should review the stakeholder register only when any required scope change is approved
(b) I should have the stakeholder register fixed during the program life cycle
(c) I should review the stakeholder register regularly and update it as the work of the program progresses and more stakeholders are engaged
(d) I should have the stakeholder register fixed during the Benefits Delivery phase

Q156 - How should the program team deal with the stakeholders' issues and concerns?

(a) The program team should select the important issues and concerns only to record
(b) The program team should review the stakeholders' issues and concerns with the program manager before logging them
(c) The program team should accept and log the stakeholders' issues and concerns and should manage them to closure
(d) The program team should neglect the less important issues and concerns to save time for the project

Q157 - Sam is working with his program team to initiate his first program, he was discussing with the team the enterprise environmental factors and how they may affect the program. Which of the following program aspects may be influenced by the enterprise environmental factors?

(a) Program funding
(b) Program selection
(c) Program design
(d) All the above

Q158 - All the following are elements of the program governance plan, except:

(a) A schedule of anticipated program-related governance meetings
(b) The pace at which benefits are realized and serves as a basis for transition and integration of new capabilities
(c) A guidance for the scheduling of additional governance meetings or activities by defining criteria for their scheduling
(d) A definition of who will have accountability and authority with respect to key decision-making categories and responsibility boundaries

Q159 - Rao had a long experience as a program manager in the local government where he executed more than five programs. Today, Rao was assigned as a program manager for a pharmaceutical development program called Pharma-1. When developing a program governance plan for Pharma-1, what should Rao do with his existing program governance plan that he developed and enhanced during the last period?

(a) Rao should use the old existing program governance plan as it is
(b) Rao should use the old governance plan as a template and start writing a new governance plan
(c) Rao should neglect his old program governance plan and he should start from scratch creating his new program governance plan
(d) Rao should apply the changes related to the pharmaceutical business needs, political, regulatory, technical and competitive environments to the existing program governance plan before using it for the Pharma-1 program

Q160 - Michelle is a program manager in your organization, she controls all the component procurements at the program level. She came asking you for advice regarding the role of the component manager in contract administration in case the contract is controlled at the program level, what is your right advice?

(a) Component manager coordinates or reports contract issues
(b) Component manager reports contract changes
(c) Component manager reports deliverable acceptance
(d) All of the above

Q161 - Question Set (1/2) - You are the program manager in the Focus organization. You started to analyze the program stakeholders, but you have a large number of stakeholders; some with positive attitudes towards your program contribution and others with negative attitudes. Which of the following tools is the best to help you to solicit feedback from a large number of stakeholders?

(a) Questionnaires and surveys
(b) Interviews
(c) Focus groups
(d) Virtual meetings

Q162 - Question Set (2/2) - You are the program manager in the Focus organization. You started to analyze the program stakeholders, but you have a large number of stakeholders; some have positive attitudes towards your program contribution and others have negative attitudes. How should you deal with the positive stakeholders and the negative stakeholders?

(a) I should focus on activities related to mitigating the effect of negative stakeholders

(b) I should establish a balance between activities related to mitigating the effect of negative stakeholders and encouraging the active support of positive stakeholders
(c) I should focus on encouraging the active support of positive stakeholders and ignore the negative stakeholders
(d) I should focus on encouraging the active support of positive stakeholders

Q163 - Matias is a program manager in your organization. He writes the information management plan. He determined the program's information management system, what is the next step he should do?

(a) Determine the program information distribution methods
(b) Determine the program information collection details
(c) Determine the program information retrieval details
(d) Options (B) and (C)

Q164 - Who is responsible for ensuring alignment of individual project management plans with the program's goals and intended benefits?

(a) The project manager
(b) The PMO
(c) The project sponsor
(d) The program manager

Q165 - Omar is the program manager who has five components in his project. Omar is asking the component managers for many details regarding component procurements to maintain visibility. What is the best reason for Omar to maintain visibility in the component procurements?

(a) To ensure the program budget is being expended properly to obtain program benefits
(b) To ensure the procurement is complying with the organization standards
(c) To verify that procurement activities are executed as per the procurement management plan
(d) To include the procurement progress in his regular reporting

Q166 - Khadija is managing the R3 program and she is currently writing the program governance with the program management office. Her aim is to create effective program governance. In which of the following cases is the effective program governance especially important?

(a) When the program environment is easy to manage and it is necessary to respond rapidly to outcomes and information that becomes available during the course of the program
(b) When the program environment is easy to manage and it is not necessary to respond rapidly to outcomes and information that becomes available during the course of the program
(c) When the program environment is highly complex or uncertain and it is necessary to respond rapidly to outcomes and information that becomes available during the course of the program
(d) When the program environment is highly complex or uncertain and it is not necessary to respond rapidly to outcomes and information that becomes available during the course of the program

Q167 - All the following options result from the approval of the program charter, except:

(a) Providing the program manager with authority to apply organizational resources to program activities
(b) Approving the program roadmap
(c) Connecting the program to the organization's ongoing work and strategic priorities
(d) Authorizing the commencement of the program

Q168 - Chao is managing a program in Bisco organization. He works in the program risk management and wants to determine whether proper risk management policies and procedures are being followed. Which risk activity does he work on?

(a) Risk planning
(b) Risk assessment
(c) Risk identification
(d) Risk monitoring

Q169 - Jack is assigned to manage the program Yen after it was running for six months and at the time it reached its delivery phase. Jack was reviewing the program documents to understand the program plans and progress. One of these documents includes definitions of roles and responsibilities, schedule of anticipated program-related governance meetings and scheduled expected decision-point reviews. Which document is this?

(a) Program governance plan
(b) Program roadmap
(c) Benefits realization plan
(d) Program business case

Q170 - Once the program steering committee approved the program change request, all the following activities will be executed, except:

(a) Reflect in updates to component plans
(b) Communicate the change request to appropriate stakeholders
(c) Define the minimum quality criteria and standards to be applied to the component level
(d) Record the change request in the program change log

2. Exam 2 – Questions and Answers

Q1 - Linda is working on a document which is considered a formal declaration of the value that the program is expected to deliver and a justification for the resources that will be expended to deliver it. Which document is Linda developing?

(a) The program business case
(b) The program charter
(c) The program benefits management plan
(d) The benefits register

Question Category: Difficult
The right answer is Option (A)
The Standards for Program Management - 4th Edition - reference: Chapter (3), Program Strategy Alignment, 3.1 PROGRAM BUSINESS CASE, page 35
Clarification and Tips:
The business case also serves as a formal declaration of the value that the program is expected to deliver and a justification for the resources that will be expended to deliver it.
Therefore, Option (A) is the right answer.
Domain: Strategy Alignment
Phase or Element: PROGRAM BUSINESS CASE

Q2 - The following items are key elements of the program charter, except:

(a) Program scope
(b) Program components issues and risks
(c) Program assumptions and constraints
(d) Program success factors

Question Category: Moderate
The right answer is Option (B)
The Standards for Program Management - 4th Edition - reference: Chapter (3), Program Strategy Alignment, 3.2 PROGRAM CHARTER, page 36
Clarification and Tips:
Key elements of a program charter consist of the program scope, assumptions, constraints, high-level risks, high-level benefits, goals and objectives, success factors, timing, key stakeholders, and other provisions that tie the program to the business case, thereby enabling program strategy alignment.
Program components issues and risks are not part of the program charter, so Option (B) is the right answer.

Domain: Strategy Alignment
Phase or Element: PROGRAM CHARTER

Q3 - Mohamed is managing a program for his first time. He is working in the procurement planning and he needs to optimize program procurement management and the requirements to adhere to all legal and financial obligations. What is the best action that should he do?

(a) He should manage all the procurements requests from the program component himself
(b) He should establish procurement audit process to apply on any procurement activities in the program and its components
(c) He should involve the program management office in all procurements' activities
(d) He should drive all personnel responsible for procurement at the component level to work closely together, especially during the planning phase

Question Category: Difficult
The right answer is Option (D)
The Standards for Program Management - 4th Edition - reference: Chapter (8), Program Activities, 8.1.2.7 PROGRAM PROCUREMENT MANAGEMENT PLANNING, pages 117
Clarification and Tips:
Due to the inherent need to optimize program procurement management and the requirements to adhere to all legal and financial obligations, it is essential that all personnel responsible for procurement at the component level work closely together, especially during the planning phase.
Therefore, Option (D) is the right answer.
Please note that:
Option (A) is micro-management.
Option (B) is an expensive solution with an unclear return.
Option (C) does not include details about the PMO with respect to the procurement activities.
Domain: Life Cycle Management
Phase or Element: Definition

Q4 - You are managing a program which is a joint effort between the Wings organization that you are working in and the Ministry of labors. You are defining the governance plan and working with the senior management in Wings organization and the prime minister of the Ministry of labors to establish steering committee(s) for the program. Which of the following is your best recommendation?

(a) I will recommend having only one steering committee for the program as this is more efficient

(b) I will recommend having three steering committees; one for Wings organization, another for the Ministry of labors, and the third as a joint steering committee for the Wings organization and the Ministry of labors
(c) I will recommend having a steering committee for Wings organization, and another for the Ministry of labors
(d) I will recommend having one steering committee only for the Wings organization

Question Category: Difficult
The right answer is Option (B)
The Standards for Program Management - 4th Edition - reference: Chapter (6), Program Governance, 6.2.2 PROGRAM STEERING COMMITTEE, page 82
Clarification and Tips:
Some programs may need to report to multiple steering committees; for example, programs that are sponsored and overseen jointly by private and governmental organizations.
Option (B) is the only options that support multiple steering committees, so Option (B) is the right answer.
Domain: Program Governance
Phase or Element: PROGRAM GOVERNANCE PRACTICES

Q5 - Question Set (1/3) - Antonin is the program manager of the Telcom program. His program consists of four projects and one subsidiary program. One of the four projects is about to be transitioned to production.
Who should collaborate with Antonin to agree and secure resources to undertake the component transition activities?

(a) The customer
(b) The program sponsor
(c) The customer or the program sponsor
(d) The end user

Question Category: Moderate
The right answer is Option (C)
The Standards for Program Management - 4th Edition - reference: Chapter (7), Program Life Cycle Management, 7.2.2.2 PROGRAM DELIVERY MANAGEMENT, page 101
Clarification and Tips:
As the program components reach the end of their respective life cycles or as planned program-level milestones are achieved, the program manager collaborates with the customer or sponsor to present a request to close or transition the component.
Therefore, Option (C) is the right answer.
Domain: Life Cycle Management
Phase or Element: Delivery

Q6 - Question Set (2/3) - Antonin is the program manager of the Telcom program. His program consists of four projects and one subsidiary program. One of the four projects is about to be transitioned to production.
Who should approve the request to transition this project?

   (a) The program sponsor
   (b) The customer program manager
   (c) The steering committee
   (d) The customer and the program sponsor

Question Category: Moderate
The right answer is Option (C)
The Standards for Program Management - 4th Edition - reference: Chapter (7), Program Life Cycle Management, 7.2.2.2 PROGRAM DELIVERY MANAGEMENT, page 101
Clarification and Tips:

Clarification and Tips:
The formal request to transition the program component is sent to the program steering committee for review and approval. Therefore, the right answer is Option (C).
Domain: Life Cycle Management
Phase or Element: Delivery

Q7 - Question Set (3/3) - Antonin is the program manager of the Telcom program. His program consists of four projects and one subsidiary program. One of the four projects is about to be transitioned to production.
During the project transition, there might be some updates reflected on the program roadmap. Which of the following updates may be included at this time?

   (a) Updates reflect both go/no-go decisions
   (b) Approved change requests that affect the high-level milestones
   (c) Approved change requests that affect the timing of major stages scheduled throughout the program
   (d) All of the above

Question Category: Easy
The right answer is Option (D)
The Standards for Program Management - 4th Edition - reference: Chapter (7), Program Life Cycle Management, 7.2.2.2 PROGRAM DELIVERY MANAGEMENT, page 101
Clarification and Tips:

The process of component transition includes making updates to the program roadmap. These updates reflect both go/no-go decisions and approved change requests that affect the high-level milestones, scope or timing of major stages scheduled throughout the program.
Therefore, Option (D) is the right answer.
Domain: Life Cycle Management
Phase or Element: Delivery

Q8 - What is the key skill differentiating between the program manager and the project manager?

    (a) Planning skills to align program goals with the long-term goals of the organization
    (b) Skills in issue resolution
    (c) Time management
    (d) Business knowledge

Question Category: Moderate
The right answer is Option (A)
The Standards for Program Management - 4th Edition - reference: Chapter (3), Program Strategy Alignment, page 34
Clarification and Tips:
With respect to the given options, the key skill differentiating between the program manager and the project manager is the planning skills to align program goals with the long-term goals of the organization. The other options have almost the same importance for both program management and project management. So the right answer is option (A).
Domain: Strategy Alignment
Phase or Element: General

Q9 - In which of the following cases the lessons learned are critical assets to be reviewed?

    (a) When updating the program risk register
    (b) When updating the program stakeholder register
    (c) When updating the program communications management register
    (d) All of the above

Question Category: Easy
The right answer is Option (D)
The Standards for Program Management - 4th Edition - reference: Chapter (8), Program Activities, 8.2.4.1 LESSONS LEARNED DATABASE, pages 130
Clarification and Tips:
Options (A), (B) and (C) are cases where the lessons learned are critical assets to be reviewed, so

Option (D) is the right answer.
Domain: Life Cycle Management
Phase or Element: Delivery

Q10 - Jacob the program manager, is working with his component managers to review the program risks and the component-level risks. At the end of the revision, they are expecting to have changes to the risk register.
What is the main difference between program risks and component-level risks?

(a) Program risks should be dealt with within a relatively short time frame, but component-level risks may be applicable at a point in the potentially distant future
(b) Program risks and component-level risks are different in the risk categorization
(c) Program risks and component-level risks are different in the risk identification process
(d) Program risks may be applicable at a point in the potentially distant future, but component-level risks should be dealt with within a relatively short time frame

Question Category: Difficult
The right answer is Option (D)
The Standards for Program Management - 4th Edition - reference: Chapter (8), Program Activities, 8.2.8.2 PROGRAM RISK ANALYSIS, pages 135
Clarification and Tips:
One essential difference between programs and components is the time scale; component-level risks should be dealt with within a relatively short time frame (i.e., at the end of a phase or a component), while program risks may be applicable at a point in the potentially distant future. Therefore, Option (D) is the right answer.
Please note that the risk categorization and the risk identification process are the same for the program risks and the component-level risks.
Domain: Life Cycle Management
Phase or Element: Delivery

Q11 - Which of the following roles can participate in the risk identification activities?

(a) Risk management team
(b) Managers of other program components
(c) External reviewers
(d) All of the above

Question Category: Moderate
The right answer is Option (D)
The Standards for Program Management - 4th Edition - reference: Chapter (8), Program

Activities, 8.2.8.1 PROGRAM RISK IDENTIFICATION, pages 134
Clarification and Tips:
Participants in risk identification activities may include the program manager, program sponsor, program team members, risk management team, subject matter experts from outside the program team, customers, end users, component managers, managers of other program components, stakeholders, risk management experts and external reviewers, as required.
Therefore, Option (D) is the right answer.
Domain: Life Cycle Management
Phase or Element: Delivery

Q12 - Anil is a project manager executing a project which is a component of the X-Trail program. Anil needs to initiate his project and he is looking for the best organization role to approve the project authorization. How can you advise Anil?

- (a) I will advise him to go to the corporate PMO
- (b) I will advise him to contact the program sponsor as he is the one who is responsible for authorizing the program components
- (c) I will advise him to go to the steering committee
- (d) I will advise him to contact the program manager as he acts as the proposer when seeking authorization for program components

Question Category: Difficult
The right answer is Option (D)
The Standards for Program Management - 4th Edition - reference: Chapter (6), Program Governance, 6.1.11 PROGRAM COMPONENT INITIATION AND TRANSITION, page 76
Clarification and Tips:
The program manager acts as the proposer when seeking authorization for program components, then he usually gets the authorization from the steering committee to initiate the program component.
Therefore, the right answer is Option (D).
Domain: Program Governance
Phase or Element: PROGRAM GOVERNANCE PRACTICES

Q13 - While you were executing a regular revision on the benefits register with your program team, you found one of the program benefits has a negative impact on the team working in the manufacturing department. What is the best action that you should do?

- (a) I will hide the information of the negative impact from reaching the manufacturing department
- (b) I will escalate the negative impact to the program sponsor

(c) I will neglect the negative impact of the benefit
(d) I will work to minimize the negative impact of the benefits and I will manage, measure, and properly communicate the negative impact to the organization's leadership

Question Category: Difficult
The right answer is Option (D)
The Standards for Program Management - 4th Edition - reference: Chapter (4), Program Benefits Management, page 44
Clarification and Tips:
The right answer is that you should minimize the negative impact of the benefits and you should manage, measure, and properly communicate the negative impact to the organization's leadership, which is Option (D).
Options (B) and (C) are wrong as the program manager should minimize the negative impacts as importantly as realizing the benefits.
Option (A) is wrong as it is unethical.
Domain: Benefits Management
Phase or Element: General

Q14 - Ming is the program manager assigned to the Z-Tech program in his organization. He was working with his component managers to review a document that represents an effective way to communicate the overarching plan and benefits to stakeholders. Which document were Ming and his team reviewing?

(a) The benefits management plan
(b) The benefits register
(c) The stakeholder engagement plan
(d) The program roadmap

Question Category: Moderate
The right answer is Option (D)
The Standards for Program Management - 4th Edition - reference: Chapter (3), Program Strategy Alignment, 3.3 PROGRAM ROADMAP, page 37
Clarification and Tips:
A roadmap is an effective way to communicate the overarching plan and benefits to stakeholders, in order to build and maintain advocacy.
Therefore, Option (D) is the right answer.
Domain: Strategy Alignment
Phase or Element: PROGRAM ROADMAP

Q15 - Chung is working to establish a governance structure, define the initial program organization and assemble a team to develop the program management plan. Which subphase is he working in?

- (a) The component transition and closure subphase
- (b) The component authorization and planning subphase
- (c) The program planning subphase
- (d) The program transition subphase

Question Category: Moderate
The right answer is Option (C)
The Standards for Program Management - 4th Edition - reference: Chapter (7), Program Life Cycle Management, 7.1.2.2 PROGRAM PLANNING, page 94
Clarification and Tips:
In the planning subphase, a governance structure is established, the initial program organization is defined and a team is assembled to develop the program management plan. Therefore, Option (C) is the right answer.
Domain: Life Cycle Management
Phase or Element: Definition

Q16 - Simon is working in the program delivery phase in the financial management activities. Which of the following may appear in the output of the program financial management activities?

- (a) Program financial management plan
- (b) Program operational costs
- (c) Program funding schedules
- (d) Program budget baseline updates

Question Category: Moderate
The right answer is Option (D)
The Standards for Program Management - 4th Edition - reference: Chapter (8), Program Activities, 8.2.3 PROGRAM FINANCIAL MANAGEMENT, pages 128
Clarification and Tips:
Option (D) is part of the outputs of the financial management activities.
Option (A), (B), and (C) are part the outputs of the financial planning activities.
Therefore, Option (D) is the right answer.
Domain: Life Cycle Management
Phase or Element: Delivery

Q17 - Chao is a new program manager working in the Hunting organization. After he was appointed to manage a starting program, he spent some time with the program sponsor to understand how the funding will be for his program. The program sponsor informed him that the Hunting organization uses a tiered funding process with a series of go/no-go decisions at each major stage of the program. Chao was not happy with this information as he thought that the budget would be allocated according to the program total cost of ownership. What is your advice to Chao?

(a) I will advise Chao to ask the sponsor to allocate the total funds at the program startup
(b) I will advise Chao to struggle to allocate the total funds at the program startup to increase its success probability
(c) I will advise Chao to avoid using a tiered funding for his program
(d) I will advise Chao to accept a tiered funding principle in his program and to get management agreement on an overall financial management plan

Question Category: Difficult
The right answer is Option (D)
The Standards for Program Management - 4th Edition - reference: Chapter (8), Program Activities, 8.1.2.3 PROGRAM COST ESTIMATION, pages 113
Clarification and Tips:
Many organizations use a tiered funding process with a series of go/no-go decisions at each major stage of the program. They agree to an overall financial management plan and commit to a budget only for the next stage at each governance milestone.
Therefore, Option (D) is the right answer.
Please note that Option (B) is wrong in principle.
Domain: Life Cycle Management
Phase or Element: Definition

Q18 - All the following artifacts are expected in the program work breakdown structure (WBS), except:

(a) Program management plans, procedures, standards, and processes
(b) Out of scope items
(c) Program management deliverables
(d) Program management office (PMO) support deliverables

Question Category: Easy
The right answer is Option (B)
The Standards for Program Management - 4th Edition - reference: Chapter (8), Program Activities, 8.1.2.12 PROGRAM SCOPE MANAGEMENT PLANNING, pages 123
Clarification and Tips:
Elements not in the program WBS are outside the scope of the program. The program WBS

includes, but is not limited to, program management artifacts such as plans, procedures, standards, processes, program management deliverables, and program management office (PMO) support deliverables.

Options (A), (C), and (D) are part of the program work breakdown structure, but Option (B) is not. Therefore, the right answer is Option (B).

Domain: Life Cycle Management
Phase or Element: Definition

Q19 - On your new program, you started to fill-in your stakeholder register. Which of the following is not considered an Internal Stakeholder?

- (a) Portfolio governance body
- (b) Program team
- (c) Investors
- (d) Departments Managers

Question Category: Easy
The right answer is Option (C)
The Standards for Program Management - 4th Edition - reference: Chapter (5), Program Stakeholder Engagement, General
Clarification and Tips:
Investors are considered external stakeholders, but the rest of the options are all internal stakeholder, so the right answer is Option (C)
Domain:
Domain: Stakeholder Engagement
Phase or Element: General

Q20 - What is the difference between program payment schedules and component payment schedules?

- (a) The component payment schedules and the program payment schedules indicate how and when contractors are paid in accordance with the contract provisions
- (b) No difference, they are the same
- (c) The component payment schedules identify the schedules and milestone points where funding is received by the funding organization. The program payment schedules indicate how and when contractors are paid in accordance with the contract provisions.
- (d) The program payment schedules identify the schedules and milestone points where funding is received by the funding organization. The component payment schedules indicate how and when contractors are paid in accordance with the contract provisions.

Question Category: Difficult
The right answer is Option (D)
The Standards for Program Management - 4th Edition - reference: Chapter (8), Program Activities, 8.2.3.1 PROGRAM COST BUDGETING, pages 129
Clarification and Tips:
The program payment schedules identify the schedules and milestones where funding is received by the funding organization.
The component payment schedules indicate how and when contractors are paid in accordance with the contract provisions.
Therefore, Option (D) is the right answer.
Domain: Life Cycle Management
Phase or Element: Delivery

Q21 - What is the risk Watch List?

(a) Risk Watch List contains the list of all Black Swan risks
(b) Risk Watch List contains all the important and high probable risks to be monitored
(c) Risk Watch List contains the risks with obviously low ratings of probability and impact and they are not retained for additional work
(d) Risk Watch List contains all risks that were emerged as a result of executing risk responses

Question Category: Difficult
The right answer is Option (C)
The Standards for Program Management - 4th Edition - reference: Chapter (8), Program Activities, 8.2.8 PROGRAM RISK MONITORING AND CONTROLLING, General
Clarification and Tips:
Option (C) is the right description for the risk watch list.
Option (A) refers to "Black Swan Risk" which is a risk that is related to a few low probable events that will impact the program dramatically when all of them happen together.
Domain: Life Cycle Management
Phase or Element: Delivery

Q22 - Mustafa is managing a program in his organization, which is progressing well as planned. But, due to recent changes in a few environmental factors, the strategic objectives changed. Which of the following statement describes the most probable action that will be taken regarding this program?

(a) The program may be changed, put on hold, or canceled

(b) The program will not be canceled as it is well performed, but change management will be applied
(c) The program manager will call the steering committee as a second level of escalation to discuss how to absorb the change
(d) The change manager will call the change board to discuss the impact of the change

Question Category: Difficult
The right answer is Option (A)
The Standards for Program Management - 4th Edition - reference: Chapter (3), Program Strategy Alignment, 3.4.1 ENTERPRISE ENVIRONMENTAL FACTORS, page 38
Clarification and Tips:
The organization selected and prioritized the program according to how well it supports its strategic goals. However, in response to environmental factors, the strategic goals change. When this occurs, a change in the direction of the organization may cause the program to be out of alignment with the organization's revised strategic objectives. And when this happens, the program may be changed, put on hold, or cancelled regardless of how well it was performing. So the right answer is Option (A).
Domain: Strategy Alignment
Phase or Element: ENVIRONMENTAL ASSESSMENTS

Q23 - Ian defined his components cost estimation during the program Definition phase. Now during the Benefits delivery phase, Ian discovered that his estimation is not accurate enough for one of his components and he had to request more budget for this component. What is the best choice for Ian?

(a) Ian will create a change request to get the required additional budget
(b) Ian will record this issue in the log
(c) Ian should lower the scope of this component to accommodate the allocated budget
(d) Ian will communicate the subject to the component manager to find a solution

Question Category: Moderate
The right answer is Option (A)
The Standards for Program Management - 4th Edition - reference: Chapter (8), Program Activities, 8.2.3.2 COMPONENT COST ESTIMATION, pages 129
Clarification and Tips:
The best choice for Ian is to create a change request to get the required additional budget for his program component. Recording issue in the log for this lack of budget is an option that may come later, but de-scoping some items to fit the budget or transferring the problem to the component manager is a bad choice. Therefore, the right answer is Option (A).
Domain: Life Cycle Management
Phase or Element: Delivery

Q24 - The following risks are all related to the strategy alignment, except:

(a) Program objective not supportive of portfolio objectives
(b) Program resource requirements include scarce resources
(c) Program objectives not supportive of organizational objectives
(d) Program resource requirements out of sync with organizational capacity and capability

Question Category: Difficult
The right answer is Option (B)
The Standards for Program Management - 4th Edition - reference: Chapter (3), Program Strategy Alignment, 3.5.3 INITIAL PROGRAM RISK ASSESSMENT, page 42
Clarification and Tips:
Options (A), (C), and (D) are considered risk related to strategy alignment, but Option (B) is not. Therefore, Option (B) is the right answer.
Domain: Strategy Alignment
Phase or Element: General

Q25 - An organization whose personnel are the most directly involved in doing the work of the program is called:

(a) Receiving organization
(b) Performing organization
(c) External organization
(d) Internal organization

Question Category: Easy
The right answer is Option (B)
The Standards for Program Management - 4th Edition - reference: Chapter (5), Program Stakeholder Engagement, 5.1 PROGRAM STAKEHOLDER IDENTIFICATION, page 61
Clarification and Tips:
An organization whose personnel are the most directly involved in doing the work of the program is called a performing organization.
Domain: Stakeholder Engagement
Phase or Element: PROGRAM STAKEHOLDER IDENTIFICATION

Q26 - When a stakeholder has not been actively participating in your program activities, it may be that the stakeholder is confident in the program's direction or has lost interest in the program. What should you do to know the right reason for a non-participating stakeholder?

(a) I should call him in front of the program sponsor and ask him directly for the reason behind his reduced participation
(b) I should call him for a one-to-one meeting and ask him directly for the reason behind his reduced participation
(c) I should perform a thorough analysis to avoid incorrect assumptions about stakeholder behavior
(d) I should review the Power/Interest Grid to know his power and interest position

Question Category: Difficult
The right answer is Option (C)
The Standards for Program Management - 4th Edition - reference: Chapter (5), Program Stakeholder Engagement, 5.4 PROGRAM STAKEHOLDER ENGAGEMENT, page 65
Clarification and Tips:
When a stakeholder has not been actively participating, thorough analysis avoids incorrect assumptions about the stakeholder's behavior, so Option (C) is the right answer.
Option (B) is good but may come after executing Option (C).
Option (A) should be avoided as it will damage the relation more than fixing the situation.
Domain: Stakeholder Engagement
Phase or Element: PROGRAM STAKEHOLDER ENGAGEMENT

Q27 - All the following are considered intangible benefits, except:

(a) Goodwill
(b) Revenue increased
(c) Improved morale
(d) Perception of the organization

Question Category: Moderate
The right answer is Option (B)
The Standards for Program Management - 4th Edition - reference: Chapter (4), Program Benefits Management, 4.2 BENEFITS ANALYSIS AND PLANNING, page 48
Clarification and Tips:
Options (A), (C), and (D) are examples for intangible benefits, but Option (B) is an example of tangible benefits, so Option (B) is the right answer.
Domain: Benefits Management
Phase or Element: BENEFITS ANALYSIS AND PLANNING

Q28 - As a part of program governance plan development, Mohamed is creating effective risk and issue management processes and procedures.
How do you think the effective risk and issue management practices are important to the program?

(a) They ensure that all risks are mitigated and all issues are resolved
(b) They ensure that key risks and issues are escalated appropriately and resolved in a timely manner
(c) They ensure that all risks and issues are recorded in the respected log
(d) They ensure that all risks and issues have response plans

Question Category: Moderate
The right answer is Option (B)
The Standards for Program Management - 4th Edition - reference: Chapter (6), Program Governance, 6.1.6 PROGRAM RISK AND ISSUE GOVERNANCE, page 73
Clarification and Tips:
Effective risk and issue management practices ensure that key risks and issues are escalated appropriately and resolved in a timely manner, so Option (B) is the right answer.
Domain: Program Governance
Phase or Element: PROGRAM GOVERNANCE PRACTICES

Q29 - Which of the following will be included in the review to initiate a program component?

(a) Ensuring appropriate program-level communications of the component's closure to key stakeholders
(b) Confirming that the business case for the component has been sufficiently satisfied
(c) Assessing lessons learned of the component
(d) Authorizing the governance structure to track the component's progress against its goals

Question Category: Moderate
The right answer is Option (D)
The Standards for Program Management - 4th Edition - reference: Chapter (6), Program Governance, 6.1.11 PROGRAM COMPONENT INITIATION AND TRANSITION, page 77
Clarification and Tips:
Only Option (D) is expected to appear in the review to initiate a program component, so Option (D) is the right answer.
Options (A), (B), and (C) are expected to appear in the review to transition a program component.
Domain: Program Governance
Phase or Element: PROGRAM GOVERNANCE PRACTICES

Q30 - Lee is managing a program in his organization where he created a strong quality management plan and is performing on Quality control throughout the duration of the program. He was about to request an evaluation for fitness for use of the delivered products. Who should evaluate the fitness for use of the products delivered by the program?

   (a) The team who received these products
   (b) The team who tested these products
   (c) The team who developed these products
   (d) The program managers in the same organization

Question Category: Difficult
The right answer is Option (A)
The Standards for Program Management - 4th Edition - reference: Chapter (8), Program Activities, 8.2.6.1 PROGRAM QUALITY CONTROL, pages 132
Clarification and Tips:
The fitness for use of the benefits, product, or service delivered by the program is best evaluated by those who receive it, so Option (A) is the right answer.
Domain: Life Cycle Management
Phase or Element: Delivery

Q31 - Which of the following are not considered factors the organization should assume when defining the degree of autonomy given to the program manager for oversight of his program's components?

   (a) The complexity and sensitivity of the program to the organization
   (b) The experience level of the program manager
   (c) The number of the program milestones
   (d) The relation of this program to the different organization units

Question Category: Moderate
The right answer is Option (C)
The Standards for Program Management - 4th Edition - reference: Chapter (6), Program Governance, General
Clarification and Tips:
Options (A), (B), and (D) are factors the organization should consider when defining the degree of autonomy given to the program manager for oversight of his program's components, but Option (C) is not related. Therefore, the right answer is Option (C).
Domain: Program Governance
Phase or Element: General

Q32 - Which of the following actions should be taken first when a change occurs on the schedule of a program component?

(a) The program master schedule will be reviewed to assess the impact of component-level changes on other components and on the program itself
(b) The other component schedules will be reviewed to define the changes
(c) The program manager will call the steering committee to meet and discuss this change
(d) The component manager will raise a change request

Question Category: Difficult
The right answer is Option (A)
The Standards for Program Management - 4th Edition - reference: Chapter (8), Program Activities, 8.2.9 PROGRAM SCHEDULE MONITORING AND CONTROLLING, pages 136
Clarification and Tips:
The first action to be made is Option (A) in order to define the impact of the change, then you can discuss the change with the steering committee or request the component manager to raise a change request.
Therefore, Option (A) is the right answer.
Domain: Life Cycle Management
Phase or Element: Delivery

Q33 - Mustafa is evaluating the program component performance against applicable acceptance criteria, reviewing the operational and program process documentation, and reviewing the readiness assessment by receiving organization. In which program benefits management phase is Mustafa working?

(a) Benefits transition phase
(b) Benefits identification phase
(c) Benefits sustainment phase
(d) Benefits delivery

Question Category: Moderate
The right answer is Option (A)
The Standards for Program Management - 4th Edition - reference: Chapter (4), Program Benefits Management, 4.4 Benefits Transition, page 53
Clarification and Tips:
The activities mentioned in the questions are part of the benefits transition phase. Therefore, the right answer is Option (A).

Domain: Benefits Management
Phase or Element: General

Q34 - Brada is managing a program with ten components. He is currently planning for the program quality and is discussing with his team how to reduce the quality cost across the different program components. What is your advice to Brada?

- (a) I will advise him to build quality plans only for the important components
- (b) I will advise him to use the program quality management plan and apply it to all the components to reduce cost
- (c) I will advise him to analyze program quality in order to evaluate it across the program with the goal of combining quality tests and inspections where feasible
- (d) I will advise him to decrease the number of quality management staff to reduce cost

Question Category: Difficult
The right answer is Option (C)
The Standards for Program Management - 4th Edition - reference: Chapter (8), Program Activities, 8.1.2.8 PROGRAM QUALITY MANAGEMENT PLANNING, pages 118
Clarification and Tips:
It is beneficial to analyze program quality in order to evaluate it across the program with the goal of combining quality tests and inspections in order to reduce costs, where feasible. Therefore, Option (C) is the right answer.
Domain: Life Cycle Management
Phase or Element: Definition

Q35 - You are working as a program manager to manage a program that consists of five projects and two subsidiary programs. Three of the five projects created contracts with a service company called Jika, which is one of the leading service companies in this industry. You have similar procurement requests from the other two projects, what is your best choice to balance your risks?

- (a) I will use the same company, Jika, for the required recruitment of the other two projects
- (b) I will use the same company, Jika, for the required recruitment of the other two projects, but I will ensure that they are using different resources to minimize risks
- (c) I will encourage open competition in the procurement requirements for the other two projects
- (d) I will extend the contract with Jika of the three projects to include the other two projects

Question Category: Difficult
The right answer is Option (C)

The Standards for Program Management - 4th Edition - reference: Chapter (8), Program Activities, 8.1.2.7 PROGRAM PROCUREMENT MANAGEMENT PLANNING, pages 117

Clarification and Tips:

The program procurement management should determine the best program-wide approach to competition (for example, the risks of sole source contracts in one area of the program could be balanced with the different risks associated with full and open competition in other areas of the program).

Therefore, Option (C) is the best answer to balance program risks.

Please note the following:

Options (A) and (B) are not good for risk balancing.

Option (C) is a good option to get the best deal, but not good from the risk balancing view.

Domain: Life Cycle Management

Phase or Element: Definition

Q36 - Who in the following roles is responsible for securing funding for the program, ensuring program goals and objectives are aligned with the strategic vision and enabling the delivery of benefits?

(a) The program sponsor
(b) The component manager
(c) The program manager
(d) The program management office

Question Category: Moderate

The right answer is Option (A)

The Standards for Program Management - 4th Edition - reference: Chapter (6), Program Governance, 6.2.1 PROGRAM SPONSOR, page 80

Clarification and Tips:

The responsibilities of the program sponsor are to (1) Secure funding for the program and ensure program goals and objectives are aligned with the strategic vision, (2) Enable the delivery of benefits, and (3) Remove barriers and obstacles to program success.

Thus, Option (A) is the right answer.

Domain: Program Governance

Phase or Element: PROGRAM GOVERNANCE PRACTICES

Q37 - Anne-Marie is working in the risk management activities of one program in her organization. She repeated the risk identification three times while she was working in the program delivery phase. In the risk identification session, the participants attended are different. Which of the following statements describes the involvement of the participants in the risk identification correctly?

   (a) Risk identification is an iterative activity where the involvement of the participants or their variations has no influence on the sessions
   (b) Risk identification is an iterative activity where the involvement of the participants will be the same group in all sessions to keep consistency
   (c) Risk identification is an iterative activity where the involvement of participants may vary from one session to another
   (d) Risk identification is an iterative activity where the involvement of the participants has already identified as per the risk management plan

Question Category: Difficult
The right answer is Option (C)
The Standards for Program Management - 4th Edition - reference: Chapter (8), Program Activities, 8.2.8.1 PROGRAM RISK IDENTIFICATION, pages 134
Clarification and Tips:
Risk identification is an iterative activity. As the program progresses, new risks may evolve or become known. The frequency of iteration and involvement of participants may vary, but the format of the risk statements should be consistent.
Therefore, Option (C) is the right answer.
Please note the following:
Option (A) is wrong as the participants will help in risk identification.
Option (B) is wrong as the different risk categories and sources may need different participants.
Option (C) is wrong as such details are not expected to be in the risk management plan.
Domain: Life Cycle Management
Phase or Element: Delivery

Q38 - Who should plan the ongoing sustainment of program benefits?

   (a) The receiving organization
   (b) The program manager
   (c) The component project managers
   (d) The program manager and the component project managers

Question Category: Moderate
The right answer is Option (D)
The Standards for Program Management - 4th Edition - reference: Chapter (4), Program Benefits Management, 4.4 4.5 BENEFITS SUSTAINMENT, page 55
Clarification and Tips:
Ongoing sustainment of program benefits should be planned by the program manager and the component project managers during the performance of the program, so Option (D) is the right

answer.
Domain: Benefits Management
Phase or Element: BENEFITS SUSTAINMENT

Q39 - Program D-Com is executed in your organization where its main scope is to implement an ERP solution which is a product of the Nivada company.
Which of the following roles is not considered one of the common program management roles?

- (a) Program Governance Board Members
- (b) Nivada Account Manager
- (c) Program Team Members
- (d) Component Project Manager

Question Category: Easy
The right answer is Option (B)
The Standards for Program Management - 4th Edition - reference: Chapter (6), Program Governance, 6.2 PROGRAM GOVERNANCE ROLES, page 78
Clarification and Tips:
Nivada account manager is not considered one of the common program management roles as he is an external stakeholder. Therefore, the right answer is Option (B).
Domain: Program Governance
Phase or Element: PROGRAM GOVERNANCE ROLES

Q40 - You started to write the program communication management plan with the help of the program management office. You are defining the requirements clearly to facilitate the transfer of information between the program and its components and from the program to the appropriate stakeholders. Where should you record the communication requirements specific to particular stakeholders?

- (a) In the stakeholder register
- (b) In the information management plan
- (c) In the change management plan
- (d) In the stakeholder engagement plan

Question Category: Moderate
The right answer is Option (A)
The Standards for Program Management - 4th Edition - reference: Chapter (8), Program Activities, 8.1.2.2 PROGRAM COMMUNICATIONS MANAGEMENT PLANNING, pages 112
Clarification and Tips:
Communication requirements specific to particular stakeholders should be included in the

stakeholder register. Therefore, Option (A) is the right answer.
Domain: Life Cycle Management
Phase or Element: Definition

Q41 - Which of the following tools can help the program manager to remind his team of which stakeholders need to be engaged at various times in the program life cycle?

   (a) The power/interest grid
   (b) The stakeholder register
   (c) The stakeholder map
   (d) The salience model

Question Category: Difficult
The right answer is Option (C)
The Standards for Program Management - 4th Edition - reference: Chapter (5), Program Stakeholder Engagement, 5.2 PROGRAM STAKEHOLDER ANALYSIS, page 63
Clarification and Tips:
The power/interest grid groups stakeholders based on their level of authority power and their level of concern interest regarding the project outcomes.
The stakeholder register lists the stakeholders and categorizes their relationship to the program, their ability to influence the program outcome and their degree of support for the program.
The stakeholder map visually represents the interaction of all stakeholders' current and desired support and influence. The map serves as a tool to assess the impact of a change on the program community. It can be used to remind teams of which stakeholders need to be engaged at various times in the program life cycle.
The salience model describes classes of stakeholders based on assessments of their power, urgency, and legitimacy.
Therefore, the right answer is Option (C).
Domain: Stakeholder Engagement
Phase or Element: PROGRAM STAKEHOLDER ANALYSIS

Q42 - All the following are considered description for the program roadmap, except:

   (a) The program roadmap is an effective way to communicate the overarching plan and benefits to stakeholders to build and maintain advocacy.
   (b) The program roadmap is a chronological representation of a program's intended direction
   (c) The program roadmap defines program specific goals and objectives in alignment with the organization's strategic plan

(d) The program roadmap is graphically depicting dependencies between major milestones and decision points

Question Category: Moderate
The right answer is Option (C)
The Standards for Program Management - 4th Edition - reference: Chapter (3), Program Strategy Alignment, 3.3 PROGRAM ROADMAP, page 36
Clarification and Tips:
Options (A), (B), and (D) are considered descriptions for the program roadmap, but Option (C) is not considered a description for the roadmap, it is considered for the charter. Therefore, Option (C) is the right answer.
Domain: Strategy Alignment
Phase or Element: PROGRAM ROADMAP

Q43 - The following elements are included in the benefits register, except:

(a) List of planned benefits
(b) Person or group who will sustain the benefits
(c) Establishment of processes for measuring progress against the benefits plan
(d) Key performance indicators for evaluating benefits achievement

Question Category: Moderate
The right answer is Option (B)
The Standards for Program Management - 4th Edition - reference: Chapter (4), Program Benefits Management, 4.1.1 BENEFITS REGISTER, page 47
Clarification and Tips:
Options (A), (C), and (D) include elements of the benefits register, but Option (B) is not expected to appear in the benefits register. Therefore, Option (B) is the right answer.
Domain: Benefits Management
Phase or Element: BENEFITS IDENTIFICATION

Q44 - Why should the program manager ensure resources are released for other programs when they are no longer necessary for the current program?

(a) To save cost in the current program
(b) To make these resources available for other programs
(c) To increase the morale of the other resources within the current program
(d) All of the above

Question Category: Moderate
The right answer is Option (D)
The Standards for Program Management - 4th Edition - reference: Chapter (8), Program Activities, 8.2.7 PROGRAM RESOURCE MANAGEMENT, pages 133
Clarification and Tips:
Options (A), (B), and (C) are good reasons for the program manager to ensure resources are released for other programs when they are no longer necessary for the current program. Therefore, Option (D) is the right answer.
Domain: Life Cycle Management
Phase or Element: Delivery

Q45 - Which of the following statements are related to program benefit attributes?

(a) Benefits may be shared among multiple stakeholders
(b) Benefits are often defined in the context of the intended beneficiary
(c) Benefits are the gains and assets realized by the organization and other stakeholders as the result of outcomes delivered by the program
(d) All the above

Question Category: Moderate
The right answer is Option (D)
The Standards for Program Management - 4th Edition - reference: Chapter (4), Program Benefits Management, page 44
Clarification and Tips:
Options (A), (B), and (C) are descriptions related to the program benefits, so Option (D) is the right answer.
Domain: Benefits Management
Phase or Element: General

Q46 - While you were managing one program in your organization, you noticed that the funding organization, which is different from your organization, is trying to impose some skills in the program management team and suggested specific monitoring and controlling tools. What should be your best response to the funding organization?

(a) Neglect the request of the funding organization as their role is only to fund the program
(b) Establish an interactive communication with the funding organization to inform them that program management is out of their scope
(c) Establish an interactive communication with the funding organization and work hard to manage their expectations on the program management team

(d) Escalate the subject to the program sponsor and get his advice

Question Category: Difficult
The right answer is Option (C)
The Standards for Program Management - 4th Edition - reference: Chapter (8), Program Activities, 8.1.2.4 PROGRAM FINANCIAL FRAMEWORK ESTABLISHMENT, pages 114
Clarification and Tips:
Due to the large amount of money involved in most programs, the funding organization is rarely a passive partner but instead has significant inputs to program management and to decisions made by the business leads, technical leads and program manager. Due to this, communications with the program sponsor and other key stakeholders should be proactive and timely.
Therefore, Option (C) is the right answer.
Domain: Life Cycle Management
Phase or Element: Definition

Q47 - Mohamed, the program manager in your organization, is suffering from the time consumed in the communications with the different stakeholders; within the program and outside the program. The size of the program which has seven components and the number of identified key stakeholders took a lot of his program management time. He is looking for a solution and asked you for advice, what is your advice to Mohamed?

(a) I will advise him to minimize the communications and use the time in the rest of the other program activities
(b) I will advise him to assign a full-time manager to hold the communication responsibilities
(c) I will advise him to delegate some of his program management responsibilities to one of the component managers
(d) I will advise him to delegate some of the program management responsibilities to the sponsor

Question Category: Moderate
The right answer is Option (B)
The Standards for Program Management - 4th Edition - reference: Chapter (8), Program Activities, 8.2.2 PROGRAM COMMUNICATIONS MANAGEMENT, pages 126
Clarification and Tips:
Program Communications Management can be challenging and time-consuming and may require a full-time manager assigned to the task.
Therefore, Option (B) is the right answer.
Domain: Life Cycle Management
Phase or Element: Delivery

Q48 - Which of the following is the best approach to engage the stakeholders to address the change that the program will bring?

(a) Sending regular reports to the stakeholders
(b) Engaging stakeholders to assess their readiness for change, planning for the change, providing program resources and support for the change
(c) Involving the key stakeholders in the steering meetings
(d) Sending the change requests status regularly to the stakeholders

Question Category: Moderate
The right answer is Option (B)
The Standards for Program Management - 4th Edition - reference: Chapter (5), Program Stakeholder Engagement, page 60
<u>**Clarification and Tips:**</u>
The best approach to engage the stakeholders to address the change the program will bring is engaging stakeholders to assess their readiness for change, planning for the change, providing program resources and support for the change, so Option (B) is the right answer.
Options (A) and (D) may help, but Option (B) is much better.
Option (C) is not good as it is not the program manager's decision to include stakeholders in the steering committee.
Domain: Stakeholder Engagement
Phase or Element: General

Q49 - Kristin is the program manager in your organization. She was appointed to manage a critical program a few months ago. She is very keen on avoiding incorrect messages to the stakeholders, so she requested her program management team to review the communication that they will distribute to the key stakeholders with her first. What is the impact of an incorrect message to a stakeholder?

(a) An incorrect message to a stakeholder may make the stakeholder unhappy
(b) An incorrect message to a stakeholder may cause problems for the program and in some cases, lead to the stoppage of a program
(c) An incorrect message to a stakeholder will be reclaimed by another correct message
(d) An incorrect message to a stakeholder will be reclaimed by an apology from the program manager

Question Category: Moderate
The right answer is Option (B)
The Standards for Program Management - 4th Edition - reference: Chapter (8), Program

Activities, 8.2.2 PROGRAM COMMUNICATIONS MANAGEMENT, pages 126

Clarification and Tips:
Regardless of the distribution method, the information should remain in the program's control. An incorrect message to an audience may cause problems for the program and in some cases, lead to the stoppage of a program. Therefore, Option (B) is the right answer.
Please note the following:
Option (A) is a weak answer, Option (B) is much better.
Option (C) and (D) are weak answers and may help in some cases, but Option (B) is the better answer.
Domain: Life Cycle Management
Phase or Element: Delivery

Q50 - After Simon developed the program financial framework as part of the program planning activities, he found some changes that impact the original business case justifying the program. What should be done?

(a) The business case is created and approved, so there is no need to modify it
(b) The business case should not be updated after it is approved by the senior management
(c) The business case should be revised with full involvement of the decision makers
(d) The business case should be revised with the sponsor approval

Question Category: Difficult
The right answer is Option (C)
The Standards for Program Management - 4th Edition - reference: Chapter (8), Program Activities, 8.1.2.4 PROGRAM FINANCIAL FRAMEWORK ESTABLISHMENT, pages 114
Clarification and Tips:
As the program financial framework is developed and analyzed, changes may be identified that impact the original business case justifying the program. Based on these changes, the business case is revised with full involvement of the decision makers.
Therefore, Option (C) is the right answer.
Domain: Life Cycle Management
Phase or Element: Definition

Q51 - Chun is working in the program schedule management planning activities. She created the program high level schedule and is requesting the component managers to create their schedules as well. During these activities, she got a comment from the PMO asking her to create the program schedule first and then the component detail schedule. What is your advice to Chun?

(a) The initial program master schedule and the detailed schedules of the program components are created in parallel, so I will advise her to reject the PMO request
(b) The initial program master schedule is often created before the detailed schedules of the program components so it is better to keep this order
(c) The initial program master schedule is often created after the detailed schedules of the program components so it is better to keep this order
(d) Ask the PMO not to be involved with the program management role and responsibilities and concentrate on that of the PMO

Question Category: Difficult
The right answer is Option (B)
The Standards for Program Management - 4th Edition - reference: Chapter (8), Program Activities, 8.1.2.11 PROGRAM SCHEDULE MANAGEMENT PLANNING, pages 121
Clarification and Tips:
The initial program master schedule is often created before the detailed schedules of the individual components are available, so Option (B) is the right answer.
Please note that option (D) is totally wrong as the program management office is part of the program management team.
Domain: Life Cycle Management
Phase or Element: Definition

Q52 - Kim has finished his financial estimation of his Absolute program and he is waiting for the sponsoring organization to approve the program financial.
Which of the following will drive the funding decision?

(a) Program benefits to be realized
(b) Program budget versus the benefits to be realized
(c) The total cost of ownership relative to the expected benefit of the program
(d) The total of used resources relative to the expected program benefits

Question Category: Moderate
The right answer is Option (C)
The Standards for Program Management - 4th Edition - reference: Chapter (8), Program Activities, 8.1.2.3 PROGRAM COST ESTIMATION, pages 113
Clarification and Tips:
Calculating full life cycle costs and including transition and sustainment costs result in a total cost of ownership. The total cost of ownership is considered to be relative to the expected benefit of one program against another to derive a funding decision.
Therefore, Option (C) is the right answer.
Domain: Life Cycle Management
Phase or Element: Definition

Q53 - All the following are part of the program business case, except:

(a) The program milestones
(b) Cost benefit analysis,
(c) Time to market
(d) The extent to which the program aligns with the organization's strategic plan

Question Category: Moderate
The right answer is Option (A)
The Standards for Program Management - 4th Edition - reference: Chapter (3), Program Strategy Alignment, 3.1 PROGRAM BUSINESS CASE, page 35
Clarification and Tips:
Options (B), (C), and (D) are items expected to appear in the program business case, but Option (A) is not. Therefore, the right answer is Option (A).
Domain: Strategy Alignment
Phase or Element: PROGRAM BUSINESS CASE

Q54 - Which document is considered the baseline document that guides the delivery of benefits during the program's performance?

(a) The business case
(b) The benefits register
(c) The benefits management plan
(d) The program roadmap

Question Category: Moderate
The right answer is Option (C)
The Standards for Program Management - 4th Edition - reference: Chapter (4), Program Benefits Management, 4.2.1 BENEFITS MANAGEMENT PLAN, page 50
Clarification and Tips:
The benefits management plan is considered the baseline document that guides the delivery of benefits during the program's performance, so Option (C) is the right answer.
Domain: Benefits Management
Phase or Element: BENEFITS ANALYSIS AND PLANNING

Q55 - Kyra the program manager of the G5 program is reviewing one of the program agreements. She ensured that all deliverables have been satisfactorily completed, that all payments have been made and that there are no outstanding contractual issues. What is the next step to do with this agreement?

(a) Request an audit for the agreement
(b) Close out the agreement
(c) Financially close the agreement
(d) Ask the program sponsor for advice

Question Category: Difficult
The right answer is Option (B)
The Standards for Program Management - 4th Edition - reference: Chapter (8), Program Activities, 8.3.3 PROGRAM PROCUREMENT CLOSURE, page 140
Clarification and Tips:
Agreements of the program are formally close out after ensuring that all deliverables have been satisfactorily completed, that all payments have been made and that there are no outstanding contractual issues. Therefore, Option (B) is the right answer.
Domain: Life Cycle Management
Phase or Element: Closing

Q56 - Which of the following items are different in handling between the stakeholders and the risks?

(a) The impact may be positive or negative
(b) They should be identified, studied, categorized, and tracked
(c) They can be managed by the program team
(d) They may generate an issue

Question Category: Moderate
The right answer is Option (C)
The Standards for Program Management - 4th Edition - reference: Chapter (5), Program Stakeholder Engagement, General
Clarification and Tips:
Options (A), (B) and (D) have items that are shared between the stakeholders and the risks. Option (C) is valid for the risk and not valid for the stakeholders as the term used with stakeholders is "Stakeholder Engagement", or "Manage Stakeholder Expectations". Therefore, the right answer is Option (C).
Domain: Stakeholder Engagement
Phase or Element: General

Q57 - Santiago is creating a document that answers the following questions: Why is the program important and what does it achieve? What is the end state and how will it benefit the organization? and What are the key outcomes required to achieve the program vision and benefits?

Which document is this?

(a) The program roadmap
(b) The program business case
(c) The program charter
(d) The program benefits realization plan

Question Category: Moderate
The right answer is Option (C)
The Standards for Program Management - 4th Edition - reference: Chapter (7), Program Life Cycle Management, 7.1.2.1 PROGRAM FORMULATION, page 93
Clarification and Tips:
The document that answers the given questions is the program charter, so Option (C) is the right answer.
Domain: Life Cycle Management
Phase or Element: Definition

Q58 - You are requested to estimate the required resources to prepare the program business case and the program charter. Which of the following are not considered a program resource?

(a) Software
(b) Key stakeholders
(c) Office supplies and office space
(d) Data centers

Question Category: Moderate
The right answer is Option (B)
The Standards for Program Management - 4th Edition - reference: Chapter (8), Program Activities, 8.1.1.7 PROGRAM RESOURCE REQUIREMENTS ESTIMATION, pages 109
Clarification and Tips:
Options (A), (C), and (D) are considered program resources, but Option (B) is not. Therefore, Option (B) is the right answer.
Domain: Life Cycle Management
Phase or Element: Definition

Q59 - Simon and Jack are discussing the program roadmap. Simon says it is a chronological representation in a graphical form of a program's intended direction. But Jack says that it is graphically depicting dependencies between major milestones and decision points, which reflects the linkage between the business strategy and the program work. What is the right description of the program roadmap?

(a) Simon's description is right
(b) Jack's description is right
(c) The program roadmap is both a chronological representation in a graphical form of a program's intended direction and is graphically depicting dependencies between major milestones and decision points, which reflects the linkage between the business strategy and the program work.
(d) Both are wrong, the program roadmap is chronologically representing the program major delivery

Question Category: Moderate
The right answer is Option (C)
The Standards for Program Management - 4th Edition - reference: Chapter (3), Program Strategy Alignment, 3.3 PROGRAM ROADMAP, page 36
Clarification and Tips:
The right description for the program roadmap is Option (C). Both options (A) and (B) are partial correct relative to option (C).
Therefore, the right answer is Option (C).
Domain: Strategy Alignment
Phase or Element: PROGRAM ROADMAP

Q60 - During the formulation subphase, who will work to develop an initial risk assessment?

(a) The sponsor
(b) The sponsoring organization
(c) The program manager
(d) The sponsor, sponsoring organization, and the program manager work closely together

Question Category: Moderate
The right answer is Option (D)
The Standards for Program Management - 4th Edition - reference: Chapter (7), Program Life Cycle Management, 7.1.2.1 PROGRAM FORMULATION, page 92
Clarification and Tips:
The sponsor, sponsoring organization, and the program manager work closely together to develop an initial risk assessment.
Therefore, Option (D) is the right answer.
Domain: Life Cycle Management
Phase or Element: Definition

Q61 - Simon is working on developing the program change management plan for his first time. He was not sure about the main focus of the change plan and asked you to help him. What will be your best answer?

   (a) The plan should focus on how to evaluate the impact of a change on the program time, cost and quality
   (b) The plan should focus on how to evaluate the impact of a change on the components time, cost and quality
   (c) The plan should focus on how to evaluate the impact of a change on the time, cost and quality of both the program and its components
   (d) The plan should focus on how to evaluate the impact of a change to the program outcomes and therefore on the benefits expected by the stakeholders

Question Category: Difficult
The right answer is Option (D)
The Standards for Program Management - 4th Edition - reference: Chapter (8), Program Activities, 8.1.2.1 PROGRAM CHANGE MANAGEMENT PLANNING, pages 112
Clarification and Tips:
the plan should focus on how to evaluate the impact of a change (e.g., change in a component, change in the roadmap, change in technology, etc.) to the program outcomes and therefore on the benefits expected by the stakeholders.
Therefore, Option (D) is the right answer.
Domain: Life Cycle Management
Phase or Element: Definition

Q62 - Cindy is appointed as a program manager and she started to create her first draft of the stakeholder engagement plan, which of the following should not be part of this stakeholder engagement plan?

   (a) The strategy for effective stakeholder engagement
   (b) The metrics used to measure the performance of stakeholder engagement activities
   (c) Name and position of each stakeholder
   (d) The guidelines for project-level stakeholder engagement

Question Category: Moderate
The right answer is Option (C)
The Standards for Program Management - 4th Edition - reference: Chapter (5), Program Stakeholder Engagement, 5.3 PROGRAM STAKEHOLDER ENGAGEMENT PLANNING, page 64
Clarification and Tips:

Options (A), (B), and (D) are expected to appear in the stakeholder engagement plan, but Option (C) is expected to appear in the stakeholder register. Therefore, the right answer is Option (C).
Domain: Stakeholder Engagement
Phase or Element: PROGRAM STAKEHOLDER ENGAGEMENT PLANNING

Q63 - The program manager interacts with stakeholders in the following ways, except:

(a) Includes stakeholders in program activities
(b) Engages stakeholders by assessing their attitudes and interests toward the program and their change readiness
(c) Hides the news of negative impacts that are expected by the program from reaching them
(d) Uses communications targeted to their needs, interests, requirements, expectations, and wants

Question Category: Moderate
The right answer is Option (C)
The Standards for Program Management - 4th Edition - reference: Chapter (5), Program Stakeholder Engagement, page 59
Clarification and Tips:
Options (A), (B), and (D) are valid ways for the program manager to interact with the stakeholders, but Option (C) is not valid as it is unethical and against the PMI standards. Therefore, Option (C) is the right answer.
Domain: Stakeholder Engagement
Phase or Element: General

Q64 - Adam is writing his program governance and is adding some elements related to the program funding. To which degree should the program governance facilitate program funding?

(a) Program governance facilitates program funding to the degree of the program scope
(b) Program governance facilitates program funding to the degree of the program scope and the approved change requests
(c) Program governance facilitates program funding to the degree necessary to support the approved business case
(d) Program governance facilitates program funding to the degree of the program budget

Question Category: Difficult
The right answer is Option (C)
The Standards for Program Management - 4th Edition - reference: Chapter (6), Program Governance, 6.1.3 PROGRAM APPROVAL, ENDORSEMENT, AND DEFINITION, page 72
Clarification and Tips:

Program governance facilitates program funding to the degree necessary to support the approved business case, so Option (C) is the right answer.
Domain: Program Governance
Phase or Element: PROGRAM GOVERNANCE PRACTICES

Q65 - George is working in the risk management planning. He is creating a document which is a living document that is updated as program risks and risk responses change during program delivery. Which document is this?

    (a) The risk response plan
    (b) The program roadmap
    (c) The risk management plan
    (d) The risk register

Question Category: Moderate
The right answer is Option (D)
The Standards for Program Management - 4th Edition - reference: Chapter (8), Program Activities, 8.1.2.10 PROGRAM RISK MANAGEMENT PLANNING, pages 120
Clarification and Tips:
The program risk register is a living document that is updated as program risks and risk responses change during program delivery.
Therefore, Option (D) is the right answer.
Domain: Life Cycle Management
Phase or Element: Definition

Q66 - You requested your program team to collect and log stakeholder issues and concerns, and then manage them to closure. If the number of stakeholders in your program is small, what is the suitable tool to be used by your team to document, prioritize, and track issues relevant to the stakeholders?

    (a) A simple spreadsheet may be an adequate tracking tool
    (b) A table in MS words may be more than sufficient
    (c) A sophisticated tracking and prioritization mechanism using a developed application
    (d) No tool is required

Question Category: Moderate
The right answer is Option (A)
The Standards for Program Management - 4th Edition - reference: Chapter (5), Program Stakeholder Engagement, 5.4 PROGRAM STAKEHOLDER ENGAGEMENT, page 65
Clarification and Tips:

When the list of stakeholders is small, a simple spreadsheet may be an adequate tracking tool to document, prioritize, and track issues related to the stakeholders, so Option (A) is the right answer.
Option (B) is hard to use as handling tables in MS Words are not easy like Excel.
Option (C) is more suitable for programs with complex risks and issues affecting large numbers of stakeholders.
Domain: Stakeholder Engagement
Phase or Element: PROGRAM STAKEHOLDER ENGAGEMENT

Q67 - Ahmed the program manager for the Falcon program used to review the stakeholder metrics with the project managers and subsidiary program managers on a weekly basis. Why should the program manager review stakeholder metrics regularly?

- (a) To ensure that there are no missing stakeholders
- (b) To identify potential risks caused by a lack of participation from stakeholders
- (c) To ensure that new stakeholders are considered in the engagement plan
- (d) To deal with the changing environment around the program

Question Category: Difficult
The right answer is Option (B)
The Standards for Program Management - 4th Edition - reference: Chapter (5), Program Stakeholder Engagement, 5.4 PROGRAM STAKEHOLDER ENGAGEMENT, page 65
Clarification and Tips:
The program manager should review stakeholder metrics regularly to identify potential risks caused by a lack of participation from stakeholders, so Option (B) is the right answer.
Options (A), (C), and (D) are not good reasons for the program manager to review stakeholder metrics regularly.
Domain: Stakeholder Engagement
Phase or Element: PROGRAM STAKEHOLDER ENGAGEMENT

Q68 - You want to initiate your first program component in the Geely program. You have prepared two slides to represent the request to initiate the program component to the steering committee in order to get their approval. Why do you need the steering committee approval?

- (a) Because the new component includes benefits to be realized
- (b) To assure that the program component has still required benefits and do not become obsolete
- (c) Because the new component has the introduction of additional governance structures that are responsible for monitoring and managing the component

(d) Because the new component status will be presented regularly during the steering committee

Question Category: Difficult
The right answer is Option (C)
The Standards for Program Management - 4th Edition - reference: Chapter (6), Program Governance, 6.1.11 PROGRAM COMPONENT INITIATION AND TRANSITION, page 76
Clarification and Tips:
Program steering committee approval is usually required prior to the initiation of individual components of the program because the authorization of a component requires resource commitment from the organization. It is also required because of the introduction of additional governance structures that are responsible for monitoring and managing the component.
Therefore, Option (C) is the right answer.
Options (A) and (D) are wrong as the given reason is weak.
Options (B) is wrong as there is no need to reassure the benefits of the new component unless there is a change affecting the business case.
Domain: Program Governance
Phase or Element: PROGRAM GOVERNANCE PRACTICES

Q69 - Omar is working in the program delivery phase in the financial activities. Which of the following activities are considered part of the financial management activities?

(a) Identify any critical assumptions upon which the estimates are made
(b) Monitoring contract expenditures to ensure funds are disbursed in accordance with the contracts
(c) Identify the program's financial sources
(d) Integrate the budgets of the program components

Question Category: Moderate
The right answer is Option (B)
The Standards for Program Management - 4th Edition - reference: Chapter (8), Program Activities, 8.2.3 PROGRAM FINANCIAL MANAGEMENT, pages 128
Clarification and Tips:
Option (B) is part of the financial management activities.
Option (A) is part of the cost estimation activities.
Option (C) and (D) are part of the financial planning activities.
Therefore, Option (B) is the right answer.
Domain: Life Cycle Management
Phase or Element: Delivery

Exam 2 - Questions and Answers

Q70 - What is the primary objective of the stakeholder engagement?

(a) The primary objective is to gain and maintain stakeholder register for future use
(b) The primary objective is to ensure the alignment with the organization strategic objectives
(c) The primary objective is to gain and maintain stakeholder buy-in for the program's objectives and benefits
(d) The primary objective is to communicate the program status and get their feedback

Question Category: Moderate
The right answer is Option (C)
The Standards for Program Management - 4th Edition - reference: Chapter (5), Program Stakeholder Engagement, General
<u>**Clarification and Tips:**</u>
Option (A) is wrong as the stakeholder register is an input for the stakeholder engagement and not an objective.
Option (B) is wrong as the alignment with the organization strategic objectives is an objective of the strategy management and not the engagement management.
Option (C) is the right answer.
Option (D) is wrong as communicating the program status to the stakeholders and getting their feedback is a part of the stakeholder engagement activities and not a key objective.
Domain: Stakeholder Engagement
Phase or Element: General

Q71 - Your organization is preparing for a large program that will enhance the two major products with respect to your organization revenue. The funding organization, which is a government entity, requested to share in the decision of appointing the program manager. How should your organization decision makers deal with this request?

(a) They should accept this request from the funding organization and ask them to interview the candidate program manager as part of the approval process
(b) They should reject this request from the funding organization as they are the responsible organization in executing the program
(c) They should limit their involvement in the program only to the funding and financial issues
(d) They should raise this request as an issue in the steering meeting with the government senior management

Question Category: Difficult
The right answer is Option (A)
The Standards for Program Management - 4th Edition - reference: Chapter (8), Program Activities, Program Management Supporting Processes, 8.1.2.11 PROGRAM SCHEDULE

MANAGEMENT PLANNING, page 123
Clarification and Tips:
Due to the large amount of money involved in most programs, the funding organization is rarely a passive partner but instead has significant inputs to program management and to decisions made by the business leads, technical leads and program manager.
Therefore, Option (A) is the right answer.
Domain: Life Cycle Management
Phase or Element: Definition

Q72 - How is the program selected and prioritized within the organization?

(a) The program is selected and prioritized according to how well it supports the strategic goals of the organization
(b) The program is selected and prioritized according to the benefits to be realized
(c) The program is selected and prioritized according to the resource requirements
(d) The program is selected and prioritized according to the completion schedule date

Question Category: Difficult
The right answer is Option (A)
The Standards for Program Management - 4th Edition - reference: Chapter (3), Program Strategy Alignment, 3.4.1 ENTERPRISE ENVIRONMENTAL FACTORS, page 38
Clarification and Tips:
Although the benefits are to be realized and the resource requirements are important to the program, the program is selected and prioritized mainly according to how well it supports the strategic goals of the organization. Thus, the main focus of prioritizing the program is the alignment with the organizational strategic goals. So the right answer is Option (A).
Domain: Strategy Alignment
Phase or Element: ENVIRONMENTAL ASSESSMENTS

Q73 - Mustafa is a program manager executing a program whose main objective is to develop a car that can be driven on the roads and on the sea. During the program phase-gate review, the program steering meeting found that the program benefits deviate from the original plan. What decision should be taken by the steering meeting?

(a) The steering meeting should take the hard decision to terminate the program
(b) The steering meeting should initiate recommendations for adaptive changes to the program's plan to improve the program's ability to pursue and deliver its intended benefits
(c) The steering meeting should ensure that this deviation is registered in the issue register

(d) The steering meeting should initiate a program health check

Question Category: Difficult
The right answer is Option (B)
The Standards for Program Management - 4th Edition - reference: Chapter (6), Program Governance, 6.1.9 PROGRAM GOVERNANCE REVIEWS, page 76
Clarification and Tips:
Through the conduct of reviews, the program steering committee has the opportunity to confirm its support for the continuation of the program as defined or to initiate recommendations for adaptive changes to the program's strategy, improving the program's ability to pursue and deliver its intended benefits.
Therefore, the right answer is Option (B).
Option (A) is wrong as program termination decision may be taken when the program is no longer expected to fulfill the planned benefits, cannot be supported at the investment level required or should no longer be pursued as determined in a portfolio review.
Option (C) is wrong as having the issue recorded in the register is good but is not going to resolve the deviation.
Option (D) is wrong as health check concentrates on the program delivery of value in order to see if the expected outcome was achieved or not.
Domain: Program Governance
Phase or Element: PROGRAM GOVERNANCE PRACTICES

Q74 - Sam is a new program manager who is asking himself why he had spent all of these long hours working with the stakeholder to obtain key information. Why do you think these hours spent with stakeholders are valuable to the program?

(a) For better understanding the organizational culture and politics concerning the program
(b) For better understanding, the concerns related to the program
(c) For better understanding the overall impact of the program
(d) All the above

Question Category: Easy
The right answer is Option (D)
The Standards for Program Management - 4th Edition - reference: Chapter (5), Program Stakeholder Engagement, General
Clarification and Tips:
Options (A), (B), and (C) are valid reasons to spend hours with the stakeholders to gather key information. Thus, the right answer is Option (D).
Domain: Stakeholder Engagement
Phase or Element: General

Q75 - Aisa is writing a document in her program that records all of the program's financial aspects; including funding schedules and milestones, initial budget, contract payments and schedules, and the financial metrics.
Which document is this?

(a) The program financial framework
(b) The financial management plan
(c) The stakeholder engagement plan
(d) The cost management plan

Question Category: Moderate
The right answer is Option (B)
The Standards for Program Management - 4th Edition - reference: Chapter (8), Program Activities, 8.1.2.4 PROGRAM FINANCIAL FRAMEWORK ESTABLISHMENT, pages 114
Clarification and Tips:
The program financial management plan documents all of the program's financial aspects; funding schedules and milestones, initial budget, contract payments and schedules, financial reporting activities and mechanisms, and the financial metrics.
Therefore, Option (B) is the right answer.
Please note that:
"Cost management plan" is not a valid term in the PMI standards for program management.
Domain: Life Cycle Management
Phase or Element: Definition

Q76 - James is managing a program where no transition to operation is included. How could this happen?

(a) When the chartered program is no longer of value to the organization
(b) When the charter has been fulfilled and operations are not necessary to continue realization of ongoing benefits
(c) When the program is completed earlier than planned
(d) Options (A) and (B)

Question Category: Difficult
The right answer is Option (D)
The Standards for Program Management - 4th Edition - reference: Chapter (4), Program Benefits Management, 4.4 BENEFITS TRANSITION, page 54
Clarification and Tips:
The program may not have transition to operation if it becomes with no value to the

organization or if the charter has been fulfilled and operations are not needed to continue realization of ongoing benefits. So the right answer is Option (D).
Domain: Benefits Management
Phase or Element: BENEFITS TRANSITION

Q77 - The past and future customers who will be watching intently to see how well the program delivers the stated benefits are called _____

- (a) New customers
- (b) Old customers
- (c) Potential customers
- (d) Senior customers

Question Category: Easy
The right answer is Option (C)
The Standards for Program Management - 4th Edition - reference: Chapter (5), Program Stakeholder Engagement, 5.1 PROGRAM STAKEHOLDER IDENTIFICATION, page 61
Clarification and Tips:
The past and future customers who will be watching intently to see how well the program delivers the stated benefits are called potential customers, so Option (C) is the right answer.
Domain: Stakeholder Engagement
Phase or Element: PROGRAM STAKEHOLDER IDENTIFICATION

Q78 - In the program management environment, which entity holds the responsibilities to provide governance support for the program, ensure program goals and planned benefits align with organizational strategic and operational goals, and endorse or approve program recommendations and changes?

- (a) The program management office
- (b) The project management office
- (c) The steering committee
- (d) The group of component managers

Question Category: Moderate
The right answer is Option (C)
The Standards for Program Management - 4th Edition - reference: Chapter (6), Program Governance, 6.2.2 PROGRAM STEERING COMMITTEE, page 81
Clarification and Tips:
The program sponsor holds the responsibilities to provide governance support for the program, ensure program goals and planned benefits align with organizational strategic and operational

goals, and endorse or approve program recommendations and changes, so Option (C) is the right answer.
Domain: Program Governance
Phase or Element: PROGRAM GOVERNANCE PRACTICES

Q79 - Sam is a program manager assigned to a New-Tech program after the first program manager left the New-Tech program due to personal reasons.
Sam found in the benefits register an item regarding the employee moral improvement. Sam felt uncomfortable about this uncertain benefit and he thinks about removing it out of the benefits register. What is your advice for Sam?

(a) I will advise Sam to work on removing it out of the benefits register as it is an uncertain outcome
(b) I will tell Sam that some benefits may be less easily quantifiable and may produce an uncertain outcome, and I will advise him to keep this benefit
(c) I will advise Sam to investigate first how this benefit was added to the register
(d) I will advise Sam to escalate the subject to the steering committee and get their advice

Question Category: Moderate
The right answer is Option (B)
The Standards for Program Management - 4th Edition - reference: Chapter (4), Program Benefits Management, 4.2 BENEFITS ANALYSIS AND PLANNING, page 48
Clarification and Tips:
Some benefits may be less easily quantifiable and may produce somewhat uncertain outcomes, such as improvement in employee morale or customer satisfaction. Therefore, the right answer is Option (B).
Domain: Benefits Management
Phase or Element: BENEFITS IDENTIFICATION

Q80 - Anne-Marie is at a critical stage in the program where she will have a phase-gate review and a decision is going to be made at this decision point to move forward and continue with the program or to terminate the program. Which of the following cases may lead to program termination?

(a) The program is not likely to deliver its expected benefits
(b) The program has many open issues with high impact
(c) The program has many open risks with high impact and high probability
(d) The program is suffering a high number of change requests

Question Category: Moderate
The right answer is Option (A)
The Standards for Program Management - 4th Edition - reference: Chapter (6), Program Governance, 6.1.9 PROGRAM GOVERNANCE REVIEWS, page 76
Clarification and Tips:
The program may be terminated when it is determined for any number of reasons that the program is not likely to deliver its expected benefits, cannot be supported at the investment level required or should no longer be pursued as determined in a portfolio review, so Option (A) is the right answer.
Domain: Program Governance
Phase or Element: PROGRAM GOVERNANCE PRACTICES

Q81 - Omar is a program manager for the Z-Tech program. He noticed that one of the key stakeholders is not supporting the program. What should Omar do?

(a) Omar should escalate the subject in the next steering committee
(b) Omar should escalate the subject to the program sponsor
(c) Omar should spend extensive time and energy with this stakeholder to ensure all points of view have been considered and addressed and get his interest in the program
(d) Omar should review the program governance plan and react accordingly

Question Category: Moderate
The right answer is Option (C)
The Standards for Program Management - 4th Edition - reference: Chapter (5), Program Stakeholder Engagement, Page 57
Clarification and Tips:
It is the responsibility of the program manager to spend extensive time and energy with all known stakeholders to ensure all points of view have been considered and addressed. Thus, the right answer is Option (C).
Options (A) and (B) are wrong as it is early for the program manager to escalate the subject before doing his job.
Option (D) is wrong as exerting effort to engage the stakeholders is part of the responsibilities of the program manager and is not expected to be resolved by reviewing the program governance plan.
Domain: Stakeholder Engagement
Phase or Element: General

Q82 - Adron was a good project manager who proven himself through many completed successful projects. A month ago, he was promoted to be a program manager and appointed to manage one program in your organization. Adron thinks that the communication in program management is similar to the that in project management. He came asking you for advice in this regard, what you will tell him?

(a) Program communications management is similar to project communications management
(b) Program communications management requires more dedication than project communication as the number of stakeholders is higher
(c) Program communications management is more complicated than project communications management as it affects a wider array of stakeholders with widely varying communication needs and different communication approaches
(d) Project Communications management is more complicated than program communications management

Question Category: Moderate
The right answer is Option (C)
The Standards for Program Management - 4th Edition - reference: Chapter (8), Program Activities, 8.1.1.2 PROGRAM COMMUNICATIONS ASSESSMENT, pages 107
Clarification and Tips:
Program communications management is different from project communications. Since it affects a wider array of stakeholders with widely varying communication needs, different communication approaches and methods of delivery are required.
Therefore, Option (C) is the right answer.
Domain: Life Cycle Management
Phase or Element: Definition

Q83 - How should the program management work with the resource interdependencies?

(a) The program manager should neglect the interdependencies and work with the resources according to the resource management plan
(b) The program manager should work to ensure that the interdependencies do not cause a delay in benefits delivery
(c) The program manager should work to ensure that his program is free from resource interdependencies
(d) The program manager should work to ensure that the interdependencies do not cause a delay in any of the component activities

Question Category: Difficult
The right answer is Option (B)
The Standards for Program Management - 4th Edition - reference: Chapter (8), Program Activities, 8.2.7 PROGRAM RESOURCE MANAGEMENT, pages 133
Clarification and Tips:
Resources are often shared among different components within a program. The program

manager should work to ensure that the interdependencies do not cause a delay in benefits delivery.
Therefore, Option (B) is the right answer.
Domain: Life Cycle Management
Phase or Element: Delivery

Q84 - Which of the following may be considered a key aspect of conducting a program level procurement?

(a) To save budget that can be utilized for other program activities
(b) To set standards for the components like; qualified seller lists, pre-negotiated contracts, blanket purchase agreements and formalized proposal evaluation criteria
(c) To increase quality
(d) To avoid the unethical use of budget

Question Category: Moderate
The right answer is Option (B)
The Standards for Program Management - 4th Edition - reference: Chapter (8), Program Activities, 8.2.5 PROGRAM PROCUREMENT MANAGEMENT, pages 131
<u>**Clarification and Tips:**</u>
The question is asking for the "key" aspect of conducting program level procurement. Option (B) is the "key" aspect, but options (A) and (C) are not considered "key", although they may be considered reasons or benefits of conducting a program level procurement. Therefore, the right answer is Option (B).
Option (D) can be neglected as it is wrong.
Domain: Life Cycle Management
Phase or Element: Delivery

Q85 - To which level should the program manager control the scope of the program?

(a) To the program level only and not look for components
(b) To the program level and to the allocated level for components
(c) To the program level and going down to control the component scope
(d) To the program level and going down to update the WBS levels of the program components

Question Category: Difficult
The right answer is Option (B)
The Standards for Program Management - 4th Edition - reference: Chapter (8), Program Activities, 8.2.10 PROGRAM SCOPE MONITORING AND CONTROLLING, pages 137

Clarification and Tips:
Program managers should restrict their activities to managing scope only to the allocated level for components and should avoid controlling component scope that has been further decomposed by the project manager or by subsidiary program managers.
Therefore, Option (B) is the right answer.
Domain: Life Cycle Management
Phase or Element: Delivery

Q86 - You are managing your first program in the Fing organization. You joined this organization recently and you do not know yet the different stakeholders and the right way to deal with them. It comes to your knowledge that you will have many stakeholders in this program with different communication requirements. What should you do to assess the stakeholder's communication requirements?

(a) Survey program stakeholders to identify their expectations for program outcome and their interests in staying informed and involved during the program delivery
(b) Meet with a sample of the different stakeholders and identify their expectations for program outcome and their interests in the program communication
(c) Get an old program communication assessment that was performed earlier in the organization and then use it as a guide in my new program
(d) Apply the PMI best practices and my best experience when dealing with different stakeholders with different opinions

Question Category: Difficult
The right answer is Option (A)
The Standards for Program Management - 4th Edition - reference: Chapter (8), Program Activities, 8.1.1.2 PROGRAM COMMUNICATIONS ASSESSMENT, pages 107
Clarification and Tips:
It is useful as part of program formulation to survey program stakeholders to identify their expectations for its outcome and their interests in staying informed and involved during its delivery, so Option (A) is the right answer.
Options (B) and (C) are not good enough to address the issue expressed in the question and Option (D) is vague.
Domain: Life Cycle Management
Phase or Element: Definition

Q87 - Yung wonders what the meaning of stakeholder risk tolerance is, how can you help him?

(a) It is the risk which was accepted by the stakeholder as part of the response planning

(b) It is the threshold or attitude of the stakeholder towards the positive effects of risks on the program or generally on the organization

(c) It is the threshold or attitude of the stakeholder towards the positive or negative effects of risks on the program or generally on the organization

(d) It is the threshold or attitude of the stakeholder towards the negative effects of risks on the program or generally on the organization

Question Category: Difficult
The right answer is Option (C)
The Standards for Program Management - 4th Edition - reference: Chapter (8), Program Activities, 8.2.8 PROGRAM RISK MONITORING AND CONTROLLING, General
Clarification and Tips:
The stakeholder risk tolerance is well described in Option (C), the descriptions in the rest of the options are wrong.
Therefore, Option (C) is the right answer.
Domain: Life Cycle Management
Phase or Element: Delivery

Q88 - The following organizational factors are considered when performing a program feasibility study, except:

(a) The organization's constraint profile
(b) The organization's sourcing
(c) The organization's culture
(d) The organization's complexity

Question Category: Moderate
The right answer is Option (C)
The Standards for Program Management - 4th Edition - reference: Chapter (3), Program Strategy Alignment, 3.4.2.2 FEASIBILITY STUDIES, page 40
Clarification and Tips:
Options (A), (B), and (D) are factors that the organization may consider during the feasibility study process to decide on the proposed program, but Option (C) is not one of these factors. Therefore, the right answer is Option (C).
Domain: Strategy Alignment
Phase or Element: ENVIRONMENTAL ASSESSMENTS

Q89 - Sam qualifies the incremental delivery of the program benefits to measure the planned benefits during the performance of the program. Why is this measurement important?

(a) Measuring the incremental delivery of the program benefits helps in establishing the benefits management plan
(b) Measuring the incremental delivery of the program benefits helps the program manager define risks as early as possible
(c) Measuring the incremental delivery of the program benefits helps the program manager determine whether benefits are delivered in a timely manner
(d) Measuring the incremental delivery of the program benefits helps the program manager and stakeholders determine whether benefits exceed their control thresholds and whether they are delivered in a timely manner

Question Category: Difficult
The right answer is Option (D)
The Standards for Program Management - 4th Edition - reference: Chapter (4), Program Benefits Management, 4.2 BENEFITS ANALYSIS AND PLANNING, page 48
Clarification and Tips:
Meaningful measures of incremental delivery of benefits help the program manager and stakeholders determine whether benefits exceed their control thresholds and whether they are delivered in a timely manner, so Option (D) is the right answer.
Option (A) is wrong as the benefits management plan is created before this step.
Options (B) and (C) may be partial correct, but Option (D) is a complete and better answer.
Domain: Benefits Management
Phase or Element: BENEFITS ANALYSIS AND PLANNING

Q90 - When does the budget become the primary financial target that the program is measured against?

(a) When the program charter is created
(b) When the budget is allocated
(c) When the budget is baselined
(d) When there is no change request on the baseline budget

Question Category: Moderate
The right answer is Option (C)
The Standards for Program Management - 4th Edition - reference: Chapter (8), Program Activities, 8.2.3.1 PROGRAM COST BUDGETING, page 129
Clarification and Tips:
The baselined program budget is the primary financial target that the program is measured against. Therefore, the right answer is Option (C).
Domain: Life Cycle Management
Phase or Element: Delivery

Exam 2 - Questions and Answers

Q91 - Ming is managing the GUME program in one of the leading companies in the Oil and Gas industry. Ming is facing conflicting stakeholders' expectations regarding the new explored gas field in the north of the country. He found that the expectations of the office group are close to the program benefits, but the expectation of the field engineers are contradicting. What is the best action that Ming should do?

(a) Ming should encourage the office group expectations
(b) Ming should facilitate negotiation sessions among stakeholder groups to work on the expectations conflict
(c) Ming should request a meeting with the steering committee to describe the conflict and ask them to take a decision
(d) Ming should discourage the field engineering expectations

Question Category: Difficult
The right answer is Option (B)
The Standards for Program Management - 4th Edition - reference: Chapter (5), Program Stakeholder Engagement, 5.4 PROGRAM STAKEHOLDER ENGAGEMENT, page 65
Clarification and Tips:
Large programs with diverse stakeholders may require facilitated negotiation sessions among stakeholders or stakeholder groups when their expectations conflict, so Option (B) is the right answer.
Option (A) and (D) are weak actions and don't resolve the situation.
Option (C) is wrong as the program manager should do his job first with the stakeholders and not escalate the conflict to the steering committee until he finished all the required activities to resolve the conflict.
Domain: Stakeholder Engagement
Phase or Element: PROGRAM STAKEHOLDER ENGAGEMENT

Q92 - You may create all the following elements as part of program financial management planning, except:

(a) Component payment schedules,
(b) Program financial metrics
(c) Program funding schedules
(d) Program cost management plan

Question Category: Moderate
The right answer is Option (D)
The Standards for Program Management - 4th Edition - reference: Chapter (8), Program Activities, 8.1.2.5 PROGRAM FINANCIAL MANAGEMENT PLANNING, pages 116
Clarification and Tips:

Options (A), (B), and (C) are part of program financial management planning, but Option (D) is not as it is not part of the program management standards, so Option (D) is the right answer.
Domain: Life Cycle Management
Phase or Element: Definition

Q93 - What is the main goal of linking the program to the organization's strategic plan?

(a) To ensure that the program goals and objectives are not contradicting with the organization strategy
(b) To help in creating the program business case and program charter
(c) To satisfy the stakeholders need
(d) To help the organization achieve its strategic goals and objectives

Question Category: Difficult
The right answer is Option (D)
The Standards for Program Management - 4th Edition - reference: Chapter (3), Program Strategy Alignment, 3.1 PROGRAM BUSINESS CASE, page 35
Clarification and Tips:
The goal of linking the program to the organization's strategic plan is to plan and manage a program that will help the organization achieve its strategic goals and objectives and to balance its use of resources while maximizing value.
Therefore, Option (D) is the right answer. Please note that Options (A) and (C) are also correct, but Option (D) is the better option as it is directly related to the question subject
Domain: Strategy Alignment
Phase or Element: PROGRAM BUSINESS CASE

Q94 - Amy is looking for a document that should help to get the list of the stakeholders who should be engaged and communicated with during the program's life cycle and governance activities. Which document should Amy look for?

(a) The stakeholders list
(b) The stakeholder map
(c) The benefits realization plan
(d) The program governance plan

Question Category: Difficult
The right answer is Option (D)
The Standards for Program Management - 4th Edition - reference: Chapter (6), Program Governance, 6.1.1.3 OTHER CONTENT, page 71
Clarification and Tips:

The program governance plan includes contents related to the stakeholder engagement which is the listing of the stakeholders who should be engaged and communicated with during the program's life cycle and governance activities. Therefore, Option (D) is the right answer.
Domain: Program Governance
Phase or Element: PROGRAM GOVERNANCE PRACTICES

Q95 - Which is the most important element with which the program manager should provide the decision-making stakeholders to help him in making the right decisions at the right time necessary to move the program forward?

(a) The company strategic objectives
(b) The program business case
(c) The program status in a timely manner
(d) The adequate information

Question Category: Difficult
The right answer is Option (D)
The Standards for Program Management - 4th Edition - reference: Chapter (5), Program Stakeholder Engagement, 5.5 PROGRAM STAKEHOLDER COMMUNICATIONS, page 66
Clarification and Tips:
It is important that decision-making stakeholders are provided with adequate information to make the right decisions at the right time necessary to move the program forward. Therefore, within the given options, Option (D) is the most suitable option.
Domain: Stakeholder Engagement
Phase or Element: PROGRAM STAKEHOLDER COMMUNICATIONS

Q96 - You are assigned to execute a critical program in your organization, the program infrastructure includes a quality manager who was appointed by the governing body. When you started your meeting to develop a program resource plan, the quality manager requested to attend to verify that quality activities and controls are applied in the planning phase. What is your reply to him?

(a) I will welcome the quality manager to attend and to do his job in the program planning activities
(b) I will ask the quality manager to concentrate on the deliverables and services and not on the program management activities
(c) I will speak to the governing body to let the quality manager concentrating on his job only

(d) I will escalate the subject to his department manager in the organization to let him concentrate on his job only

Question Category: Difficult
The right answer is Option (A)
The Standards for Program Management - 4th Edition - reference: Chapter (8), Program Activities, 8.1.2.8 PROGRAM QUALITY MANAGEMENT PLANNING, pages 118
Clarification and Tips:
Quality management should be considered when defining all program management activity as well as for every deliverable and service.
Therefore, Option (A) is the right answer.
Domain: Life Cycle Management
Phase or Element: Definition

Q97 - During the Benefits Delivery phase, the resulting benefits review require analysis of the planned versus actual benefits across a wide range of factors. Which of the following aspect is the most important to be analyzed and assessed?

(a) Program components performance status
(b) Program schedule variance
(c) Change management status
(d) Strategic alignment

Question Category: Difficult
The right answer is Option (D)
The Standards for Program Management - 4th Edition - reference: Chapter (4), Program Benefits Management, 4.3 BENEFITS DELIVERY, page 52
Clarification and Tips:
The resulting benefits review require analysis of the planned versus actual benefits across a wide range of factors. The most important aspects to be analyzed and assessed in this manner are the strategic alignment and the value delivery, which focus on ensuring that the program delivers the promised benefits.
Therefore, the right answer is Option (D).
Domain: Benefits Management
Phase or Element: BENEFITS DELIVERY

Q98 - Where is the information, regarding the roles and responsibilities required to manage the program benefits, recorded?

(a) In the benefits register

(b) In the business case
(c) In the benefits management plan
(d) In the program roadmap

Question Category: Moderate
The right answer is Option (C)
The Standards for Program Management - 4th Edition - reference: Chapter (4), Program Benefits Management, 4.2.1 BENEFITS MANAGEMENT PLAN, page 50
Clarification and Tips:
The information regarding the roles and responsibilities required to manage the program benefits is recorded in the benefits management plan, so Option (C) is the right answer.
Domain: Benefits Management
Phase or Element: BENEFITS ANALYSIS AND PLANNING

Q99 - George is creating the program stakeholder engagement plan, which of the following attributes will not be considered for each stakeholder?

(a) Attitudes about the program and its sponsor
(b) The degree of support or opposition to the program benefits
(c) His culture to deal with his subordinates
(d) Organizational culture and acceptance of change

Question Category: Moderate
The right answer is Option (C)
The Standards for Program Management - 4th Edition - reference: Chapter (5), Program Stakeholder Engagement, 5.3 PROGRAM STAKEHOLDER ENGAGEMENT PLANNING, page 64
Clarification and Tips:
Options (A), (B), and (D) may be considered for each stakeholder as part of the engagement plan.
The stakeholder's culture and dealing with his subordinates are not relevant to the development of the stakeholder engagement plan. Therefore, the right answer is Option (C).
Domain: Stakeholder Engagement
Phase or Element: PROGRAM STAKEHOLDER ENGAGEMENT PLANNING

Q100 - You are managing a program in your organization which has five projects. The definition phase is completed and you are currently working in the delivery phase. When the component detailed planning started, one project surprised you, the ERP project, it has more scope than required and it is going to affect one more project because of the integration. What is the best action should you do?

(a) I should ask the ERP project manager to work closely with the project manager of the other affected project to close this issue
(b) I should stop the delivery phase execution and go back to the definition phase to complete the planning properly
(c) I should replan for the proper integration with the ERP project and realign to accommodate changes in program direction through adaptive change
(d) I should escalate the problem to the program sponsor and ask him for advice

Question Category: Difficult
The right answer is Option (C)
The Standards for Program Management - 4th Edition - reference: Chapter (7), Program Life Cycle Management, 7.1.3 PROGRAM DELIVERY PHASE, pages 95
Clarification and Tips:
The program manager needs to continually oversee the components throughout the delivery phase and when necessary, replan for their proper integration or realign to accommodate changes in program direction through adaptive change.
Therefore, Option (C) is the right answer.
Please note the following:
Option (A) is wrong as the program manager has the overall responsibility of the component integrations.
Option (B) is wrong as this kind of changes are expected during the delivery phase because of the uncertain nature of the program.
Option (D) is wrong as escalation is not the right action, I should expect such kind of changes in the program management due to the uncertain nature of the program.
Domain: Life Cycle Management
Phase or Element: Delivery

Q101 - Marcie is a program manager who is managing a program with four projects. The first project, which is managed by Anil, is currently in the planning phase. Marcie asked Anil to conduct a feasibility study. Why did Marcie request a feasibility study from Anil?

(a) She wants to understand why this project should be authorized
(b) She wants to verify that the project properly supports the program's outcomes and aligns with the strategy and ongoing work of the organization prior to authorization
(c) She wants to present the feasibility study in the coming steering committee
(d) She wants to verify that Anil can write a feasibility study for his project

Question Category: Difficult
The right answer is Option (B)
The Standards for Program Management - 4th Edition - reference: Chapter (7), Program Life Cycle Management, 7.1.3.1 COMPONENT AUTHORIZATION AND PLANNING, pages 96

Exam 2 - Questions and Answers

Clarification and Tips:
A number of activities are required to verify that a component properly supports the program's outcomes and aligns with the strategy and ongoing work of the organization prior to authorization. These activities may include performing a needs analysis, conducting a feasibility study, or creating a plan to ensure the projects realize their intended benefits.
Therefore, Option (B) is the right answer.
Domain: Life Cycle Management
Phase or Element: Delivery

Q102 - In which of the following does the program financial management plan expand upon the program financial framework?

(a) It includes more quality controls
(b) It describes the cost of items
(c) It describes the management of items
(d) Nothing, both are the same

Question Category: Moderate
The right answer is Option (C)
The Standards for Program Management - 4th Edition - reference: Chapter (8), Program Activities, 8.1.2.5 PROGRAM FINANCIAL MANAGEMENT PLANNING, pages 115
Clarification and Tips:
The program financial management plan expands upon the program financial framework and describes the management of items such as risk reserves, potential cash flow problems and international exchange rate fluctuations.
Therefore, Option (C) is the right answer.
Domain: Life Cycle Management
Phase or Element: Definition

Q103 - Khadija, the program manager of Aqsa program, is reviewing with her PMO the factors that, for planning purposes, are considered true, real, or certain to validate them and to ensure that they have not been invalidated by events or other program activities.
What analysis does Khadija execute?

(a) She executes historical information analysis
(b) She executes trend analysis
(c) She executes assumptions analysis
(d) She executes comparative advantage analysis

Question Category: Moderate
The right answer is Option (C)
The Standards for Program Management - 4th Edition - reference: Chapter (3), Program Strategy Alignment, 3.4.2.4 ASSUMPTIONS ANALYSIS, page 40
Clarification and Tips:
Assumptions are factors that, for planning purposes, are considered true, real, or certain. Assumptions analysis include validating the assumptions during the course of the program to ensure that the assumptions have not been invalidated by events or other program activities. Therefore, Option (C) is the right answer.
Domain: Strategy Alignment
Phase or Element: ENVIRONMENTAL ASSESSMENTS

Q104 - What do you call the group of participants representing various program-related interests with the purpose of supporting the program under its authority by providing guidance, endorsements, and approvals through the governance practices?

(a) Program steering committee
(b) Change control board
(c) Legal agencies
(d) Board of director

Question Category: Moderate
The right answer is Option (A)
The Standards for Program Management - 4th Edition - reference: Chapter (5), Program Stakeholder Engagement, 5.1 PROGRAM STAKEHOLDER IDENTIFICATION, page 61
Clarification and Tips:
The program steering committee is a group of participants representing various program-related interests with the purpose of supporting the program under its authority by providing guidance, endorsements, and approvals through the governance practices.
Therefore, Option (A) is the right answer.
Domain: Stakeholder Engagement
Phase or Element: PROGRAM STAKEHOLDER IDENTIFICATION

Q105 - All the following are considered risks of implementing the program benefits, except:

(a) New market entrants
(b) The amount of change being absorbed by the organization
(c) Realization of unexpected outcomes
(d) Stakeholder acceptance

Question Category: Moderate
The right answer is Option (A)
The Standards for Program Management - 4th Edition - reference: Chapter (4), Program Benefits Management, 4.2 BENEFITS ANALYSIS AND PLANNING, page 49
Clarification and Tips:
Options (B), (C), and (D) are considered risks of implementing the program benefits, but Option (A) is not. Therefore, Option (A) is the right answer.
Domain: Benefits Management
Phase or Element: BENEFITS ANALYSIS AND PLANNING

Q106 - If your program is part of the portfolio structure, which of the following entities should provide your program with a governance-supporting function?

  (a) The governing body
  (b) The portfolio
  (c) The steering committee
  (d) The PMO

Question Category: Difficult
The right answer is Option (B)
The Standards for Program Management - 4th Edition - reference: Chapter (6), Program Governance, page 68
Clarification and Tips:
For a program within a portfolio structure, the program governance should be aligned with the portfolio governance as this program is a portfolio component, so Option (B) is the right answer. Please note that the for stand-alone programs that are outside of a portfolio structure, a governing body provides governance-supporting functions.
Domain: Program Governance
Phase or Element: General

Q107 - Anne-Marie is expecting some changes to the environmental factors in which her program is executed. She discussed the subject with the program sponsor and ensured that some of these factors would affect the organization's strategic objectives. What should she do?

  (a) She should monitor the environmental factors to ensure the program remains aligned with the environmental factors
  (b) She should monitor the environmental factors to ensure the program remains aligned with the organization's strategic objectives
  (c) She should ignore the environmental factors as their effect on the strategy did not happen yet

(d) She should ask the sponsor for advice

Question Category: Difficult
The right answer is Option (B)
The Standards for Program Management - 4th Edition - reference: Chapter (3), Program Strategy Alignment, 3.4.1 ENTERPRISE ENVIRONMENTAL FACTORS, page 39
Clarification and Tips:
The ongoing management of a program should include continual monitoring of the environmental factors to ensure the program remains aligned with the organization's strategic objectives.
Therefore, Option (B) is the right answer.
Remember that program alignment is required with the organization's strategic objectives and not with the environmental factors as mentioned in Option (A).
Domain: Strategy Alignment
Phase or Element: ENVIRONMENTAL ASSESSMENTS

Q108 - Which of the following is not important to be considered by the program manager before starting the program transition?

(a) Confirm that the stakeholders have the latest program updates
(b) Confirm that all transition work was performed within the component transition
(c) Determine whether there is another program or sustaining activity that will oversee the ongoing benefits for which this program was chartered
(d) Ensure that the program has met all of the desired benefits

Question Category: Moderate
The right answer is Option (A)
The Standards for Program Management - 4th Edition - reference: Chapter (7), Program Life Cycle Management, 7.1.4 PROGRAM CLOSURE PHASE, page 97
Clarification and Tips:
Option (A) should be executed during the whole program life cycle and not particularly during the program transition.
Options (B), (C), and (D) should be considered before starting the program transition subphase. So the right answer is Option (A).
Domain: Life Cycle Management
Phase or Element: Closing

Q109 - You are managing a critical program in your organization. You spent many interviews and focus group sessions with the stakeholders to analyze the stakeholders and then to create the stakeholders' engagement plan that includes guidelines. With whom should you share these guidelines?

(a) The guidelines should be shared with the component projects only
(b) The guidelines should be shared with the component subsidiary programs only
(c) The guidelines should be shared with the component projects, subsidiary programs, and other program activities under the program
(d) The guidelines should be kept with the program management team only

Question Category: Moderate
The right answer is Option (C)
The Standards for Program Management - 4th Edition - reference: Chapter (5), Program Stakeholder Engagement, 5.3 PROGRAM STAKEHOLDER ENGAGEMENT PLANNING, page 64
Clarification and Tips:
The guidelines for stakeholder engagement should be provided to the component projects, subsidiary programs, and other program activities under the program, so Option (C) is the right answer.
Domain: Stakeholder Engagement
Phase or Element: PROGRAM STAKEHOLDER ENGAGEMENT PLANNING

Q110 - What is the difference between the contingency reserves at the program level and the component contingency reserve held at the component level?

(a) The program manager holds contingency reserves at the program level to support risk responses and uses this contingency as a substitute for the component contingency reserve
(b) The program manager holds contingency reserves at the program level to support risk responses, while the component contingency reserve is held at the component level
(c) There are no differences as in programs, contingency reserve is allowed only on the program level
(d) The component contingency reserve is calculated as part of the contingency reserve at the program level

Question Category: Difficult
The right answer is Option (B)
The Standards for Program Management - 4th Edition - reference: Chapter (8), Program Activities, 8.2.8.3 PROGRAM RISK RESPONSE MANAGEMENT, pages 135
Clarification and Tips:
The program manager may hold contingency reserves at the program level to support risk responses. The program contingency reserve is not a substitute for the component contingency reserve, which is held at the component level.

Therefore, Option (B) is the right answer.
Domain: Life Cycle Management
Phase or Element: Delivery

Q111 - Cindy, the program manager in Hopton organization, started to quantify all the benefits added to the benefits register. Why are benefits quantified?

- (a) Benefits are quantified so sponsor approval can be obtained
- (b) Benefits are quantified so customer approval can be obtained
- (c) Benefits are quantified so risks can be mitigated
- (d) Benefits are quantified so that their realization can be measured over time

Question Category: Difficult
The right answer is Option (D)
The Standards for Program Management - 4th Edition - reference: Chapter (4), Program Benefits Management, 4.4 BENEFITS TRANSITION, page 53
Clarification and Tips:
Benefits are quantified so that their realization can be measured over time, so Option (D) is the right answer.
Domain: Benefits Management
Phase or Element: BENEFITS TRANSITION

Q112 - After assigned as a program manager, Richard started to develop the program roadmap and the program management plan as part of the program Definition phase. Richard has uncertainty regarding the full suite of program components, he thinks that some of them may not be known in the program definition phase.
How should Richard accommodate this uncertainty?

- (a) Richard needs to continually oversee the components throughout the benefits delivery phase and when necessary, re-plan for their proper integration or changes in program direction
- (b) Richard needs to create a program issue regarding this subject in the issue log
- (c) Richard will transfer his uncertainty to his component managers to share the responsibility
- (d) Richard should not start the program delivery phase until he cleared this uncertainty

Question Category: Moderate
The right answer is Option (A)
The Standards for Program Management - 4th Edition - reference: Chapter (8), Program Activities, 8.2.3.2 COMPONENT COST ESTIMATION, pages 129

Clarification and Tips:
Option (A) has the right solution to accommodate the uncertainty regarding the full suite of program components.

Options (B), (C), and (D) are not helping in clearing this uncertainty. Therefore, the right answer is Option (A).

Domain: Life Cycle Management
Phase or Element: Delivery

Q113 - Tom is working in the risk management activities in his ORA program. He is creating a fallback plan and getting some help from the industry subject matter experts in his program. What is the purpose of using the fallback plan?

(a) The fallback plan is for the risks that have been deliberately accepted
(b) The fallback plan is for the risks that are expected to remain after planned responses have been taken
(c) The fallback plan is used as a response to a risk that has occurred and the primary response proves to be inadequate
(d) The fallback plan is for addressing the positive risks

Question Category: Moderate
The right answer is Option (C)
The Standards for Program Management - 4th Edition - reference: Chapter (8), Program Activities, 8.2.8.3 PROGRAM RISK RESPONSE MANAGEMENT, pages 135

Clarification and Tips:
The fallback plan is used as a response to a risk that has occurred and the primary response proves to be inadequate, so Option (C) is the right answer.

Domain: Life Cycle Management
Phase or Element: Delivery

Q114 - Which of the following is not part of the historical information?

(a) Program risks
(b) Estimations from previous programs that may be relevant to the current program
(c) Portfolio capacity and capability management
(d) Program artifacts

Question Category: Easy
The right answer is Option (C)
The Standards for Program Management - 4th Edition - reference: Chapter (3), Program Strategy Alignment, 3.4.2.5 HISTORICAL INFORMATION ANALYSIS, page 40

Clarification and Tips:
Options (A), (B), and (D) are considered part of the historical information, but Option (C) is not as it is a portfolio related type of information. So, the right answer is Option (C).
Domain: Strategy Alignment
Phase or Element: ENVIRONMENTAL ANALYSIS

Q115 - On your new program, you started to fill-in your stakeholder register. Which of the following is not considered an External Stakeholder?

- (a) Business partners
- (b) Customers
- (c) Government and legal
- (d) Business operational team

Question Category: Easy
The right answer is Option (D)
The Standards for Program Management - 4th Edition - reference: Chapter (5), Program Stakeholder Engagement, General
Clarification and Tips:
The business operational team is considered an internal stakeholder, but the rest of the options are all external stakeholder, so the right answer is Option (D).
Domain: Stakeholder Engagement
Phase or Element: General

Q116 - James is working in the program closure. He provides the new supporting organization with documentation of operation and user guides, and he prepared a training session for some employees of the new supporting organization. Which activity in the program closure is he executing?

- (a) Program Procurement Closure
- (b) Program Financial Closure
- (c) Program Information Archiving and Transition
- (d) Program Resource Transition

Question Category: Moderate
The right answer is Option (C)
The Standards for Program Management - 4th Edition - reference: Chapter (8), Program Activities, 8.3.2 PROGRAM INFORMATION ARCHIVING AND TRANSITION, page 139
Clarification and Tips:
Proper information management during program closure includes the transfer of program

knowledge to support the ongoing sustainment of program benefits by providing the new supporting organization with documentation, training, or materials. Therefore, Option (C) is the right answer.
Domain: Life Cycle Management
Phase or Element: Closing

Q117 - Which of the following can be used as a quality control measurement?

(a) Quality control completed checklists
(b) Customer satisfaction surveys
(c) Quality control inspection reports
(d) Quality audits

Question Category: Moderate
The right answer is Option (B)
The Standards for Program Management - 4th Edition - reference: Chapter (8), Program Activities, 8.2.6.1 PROGRAM QUALITY CONTROL, pages 132
Clarification and Tips:
Programs often use customer satisfaction surveys as a quality control measurement, so Option (B) is the right answer.
Domain: Life Cycle Management
Phase or Element: Delivery

Q118 - The limiting factors that affect the execution of a project, program, portfolio, or process are called:

(a) Assumption
(b) Constraint
(c) Risk
(d) Issue

Question Category: Moderate
The right answer is Option (B)
The Standards for Program Management - 4th Edition - reference: Chapter (3), Program Strategy Alignment, 3.4.2.4 ASSUMPTIONS ANALYSIS, page 40
Clarification and Tips:
Assumptions are factors that, for planning purposes, are considered true, real, or certain. The constraint is a limiting factor that affects the execution of a project, program, portfolio, or process.

Program Risk is an uncertain event or condition that, if it occurs, has a positive or negative effect on the program.
The issue is a current condition or situation that may have an impact on the program objectives. Therefore, Option (B) is the right answer.
Domain: Strategy Alignment
Phase or Element: ENVIRONMENTAL ASSESSMENTS

Q119 - Antonin is reviewing his funding sources in the program that he was assigned to manage. He was surprised when he found that the program is funded by the government, and the program components are funded by a consortium of companies in the private sector. What is your advice to Antonin regarding the funding sources?

(a) There is no issue in funding sources as the program itself may be funded by one or more sources, and the program components may be funded by altogether different sources
(b) There is no issue in funding sources as the program itself is funded by the government which has the upper hand with respect to the component funding source
(c) There is a funding issue that Antonin should address to the program sponsor
(d) There is a funding issue that Antonin should address to the program steering committee

Question Category: Difficult
The right answer is Option (A)
The Standards for Program Management - 4th Edition - reference: Chapter (8), Program Activities, 8.1.2.4 PROGRAM FINANCIAL FRAMEWORK ESTABLISHMENT, pages 114
Clarification and Tips:
The program itself may be funded by one or more sources, and the program components may be funded by altogether different sources, so Option (A) is the right answer.
Option (B) is wrong as the given reason has no value.
Domain: Life Cycle Management
Phase or Element: Definition

Q120 - You are in the delivery phase of your critical program. You noticed that the program costs exceed the budget. What is expected to happen in your program?

(a) The program sponsor will need to increase the budget
(b) The program will continue after changing the program manager
(c) The program will have a hard steering meeting
(d) The program may no longer satisfy the business case used to justify it and may be subject to cancellation

Question Category: Difficult
The right answer is Option (D)
The Standards for Program Management - 4th Edition - reference: Chapter (8), Program Activities, 8.2.3 PROGRAM FINANCIAL MANAGEMENT, pages 127
Clarification and Tips:
A program whose costs exceed the planned budget may no longer satisfy the business case used to justify it and may be subject to cancellation. Even minor overruns are subject to audit and management oversight and should be justified.
Therefore, Option (D) is the right answer.
Domain: Life Cycle Management
Phase or Element: Delivery

Q121 - Mustafa is the program manager who has confirmed with his team that the program charter is fulfilled. Which of the following statements describes the benefits status after the charter is fulfilled?

(a) When a program has fulfilled its charter, its benefits may have been fully realized or benefits may continue to be realized and managed as part of organizational operations
(b) When a program fulfills its charter, its benefits will be fully realized
(c) When the program charter is fulfilled, the program benefits will be either realized or canceled
(d) There is no relation between the benefits realization and the charter. The benefits are realized according to the benefits management plan

Question Category: Moderate
The right answer is Option (A)
The Standards for Program Management - 4th Edition - reference: Chapter (7), Program Life Cycle Management, 7.2.2.5 PROGRAM CLOSEOUT, page 102
Clarification and Tips:
Option (A) has the right description for the benefits after the program charter is fulfilled. The rest of the options are just noise.
Domain: Life Cycle Management
Phase or Element: Closing

Q122 - Richard is a program manager, he is currently monitoring the organizational environment, program objectives, and benefits realization to ensure that the program remains aligned with the organization's strategic objectives. He is also initiating, performing, transitioning, closing components, and managing the interdependencies among them.
With respect to the benefits management domain, which phase is Richard executing?

(a) Benefits Identification phase
(b) Benefits Delivery phase
(c) Benefits Transition phase
(d) Benefits Sustainment

Question Category: Moderate
The right answer is Option (B)
The Standards for Program Management - 4th Edition - reference: Chapter (4), Program Benefits Management, 4.3 BENEFITS DELIVERY, page 51
Clarification and Tips:
It is clear from the description that Richard is in the Benefits Delivery phase. Review the given reference in the Standard Guide if you still need help.
Domain:
Domain: Benefits Management
Phase or Element: BENEFITS DELIVERY

Q123 - Which of the following may be considered part of the stakeholders' engagement metrics?

(a) Stakeholder level of power
(b) Positive contribution to the realization of the program's objectives and benefits
(c) Stakeholder level of interest
(d) Stakeholder level of influence

Question Category: Moderate
The right answer is Option (B)
The Standards for Program Management - 4th Edition - reference: Chapter (5), Program Stakeholder Engagement, 5.4 PROGRAM STAKEHOLDER ENGAGEMENT, page 65
Clarification and Tips:
Options (A), (C) and (D) are considered as attributes of the stakeholder based on his role and responsibility and not to be used as part of the stakeholders' engagement metrics.
Option (B) is considered a part of the stakeholders' engagement metrics. Thus, the right answer is Option (B).
Domain: Stakeholder Engagement
Phase or Element: PROGRAM STAKEHOLDER ENGAGEMENT

Q124 - Pari is managing a long running program with six components. One of the components is managed by the project manager Chao. Pari noticed that Chao monitors the project schedule to identify the slippage and does not pay attention to the probable opportunity in the schedule.

What should Pari do?

(a) Pari should ask Chao to identify not only schedule slippages but also opportunities to accelerate the component schedule
(b) Pari should ask Chao to continue his good job
(c) Pari should ask Chao to come to him for consultancy on how to control the component schedule
(d) Pari should ask Chao to do a better job and ask for schedule review by the PMO

Question Category: Difficult
The right answer is Option (A)
The Standards for Program Management - 4th Edition - reference: Chapter (8), Program Activities, 8.2.9 PROGRAM SCHEDULE MONITORING AND CONTROLLING, pages 136
Clarification and Tips:
Schedule control involves identifying not only slippages, but also opportunities to accelerate program or component schedules
Therefore, Option (A) is the right answer.
Domain: Life Cycle Management
Phase or Element: Delivery

Q125 - Question Set (1/2) - Mohamed focuses on having a complete and accurate program information repository, although it took a good amount of time from him and his program team. What is the importance of the program information repository?

(a) It can be an invaluable aid to other program activities
(b) It will help when there is a need to refer to past decisions
(c) It will help when there is a need to prepare analyses based on trends
(d) All of the above

Question Category: Easy
The right answer is Option (D)
The Standards for Program Management - 4th Edition - reference: Chapter (8), Program Activities, 8.2.3.2 COMPONENT COST ESTIMATION, pages 129
Clarification and Tips:
The program information repository can be an invaluable aid to other program activities, particularly when there is a need to refer to past decisions or prepare analyses based on trends reflected in the historical program information.
Therefore, Option (D) is the right answer.
Domain: Life Cycle Management
Phase or Element: Delivery

Q126 - Question Set (2/2) - Mohamed focuses on having a complete and accurate program information repository, even though it took a good amount of time from him and his program team. When should the program team make the program information available to support program communications and management?

(a) It should be made available at the program closure for archiving
(b) It should be made available in the planning subphase to build accurate program plans
(c) It should be made available throughout the program life cycle
(d) It should be made available in the definition phase to have correct program startup

Question Category: Moderate
The right answer is Option (C)
The Standards for Program Management - 4th Edition - reference: Chapter (8), Program Activities, 8.2.3.2 COMPONENT COST ESTIMATION, pages 129
Clarification and Tips:
Managing this information and making it available to support program communications, program management or archiving is a significant and continuous task, so it is executed throughout the program life cycle.
Therefore, Option (C) is the right answer.
Domain: Life Cycle Management
Phase or Element: Delivery

Q127 - Jacob is managing a project as part of the program. He has analyzed his project risks, but the program manager asked him to do further analysis. What is the most probable reason behind the program manager request?

(a) To determine if they will have impacts outside of the component that may influence the program
(b) To make sure that the impact and probability are correct
(c) To use more qualitative and quantitative technique in risk analysis
(d) To consult more SME in risk analysis

Question Category: Moderate
The right answer is Option (A)
The Standards for Program Management - 4th Edition - reference: Chapter (8), Program Activities, 8.2.8.2 PROGRAM RISK ANALYSIS, General
Clarification and Tips:
The program manager may ask the component manager to do further analysis for the identified

risks to determine if they will have impacts outside of the component that may influence other components or the whole program.
The other reasons mentioned in options (B), (C), and (D) are not good enough. Therefore, the right answer is Option (A).
Domain: Life Cycle Management
Phase or Element: Delivery

Q128 - You are pleased to be promoted to manage your first program in your organization. You started to execute the environmental assessment and you need to convince your team why the environmental assessments are conducted, which of the following options will help you?

- (a) The environmental assessments are conducted to ensure ongoing stakeholder alignment
- (b) The environmental assessments are conducted to ensure the program's continued alignment with the organization's strategic goals and objectives
- (c) The environmental assessments are conducted to ensure overall program success
- (d) The environmental assessments are conducted to ensure ongoing stakeholder alignment, the program's continued alignment with the organization's strategic goals and objectives, and overall program success

Question Category: Easy
The right answer is Option (D)
The Standards for Program Management - 4th Edition - reference: Chapter (3), Program Strategy Alignment, 3.4 ENVIRONMENTAL ASSESSMENTS, page 38
Clarification and Tips:
Option (D) is a completed answer with respect to the other options which have a partial answer. Therefore, the right answer is Option (D).
Domain: Strategy Alignment
Phase or Element: ENVIRONMENTAL ASSESSMENTS

Q129 - Peter is a newly assigned program manager in your organization, he has created the stakeholder register and he was about to grant access to all the stakeholders listed in the register.
What is your advice to Peter?

- (a) Peter should restrict the access to the register as the stakeholder register may contain politically and legally sensitive information.
- (b) Peter should be transparent and provide access to all the stakeholders mentioned in the register
- (c) Peter should grant access only to the high-power stakeholders

(d) Peter should not grant access to any of the stakeholders in the register

Question Category: Moderate
The right answer is Option (A)
The Standards for Program Management - 4th Edition - reference: Chapter (5), Program Stakeholder Engagement, 5.1 PROGRAM STAKEHOLDER IDENTIFICATION, page 60
Clarification and Tips:
The stakeholder register may contain politically and legally sensitive information, so it is advisable to restrict the access to the register and allow certain stakeholders to view a specific part of the register. Therefore, the right answer is Option (A).
Domain: Stakeholder Engagement
Phase or Element: PROGRAM STAKEHOLDER IDENTIFICATION

Q130 - Which of the following can be described as the program governance?

(a) Program Governance is the performance domain that enables and performs program decision making, establishes practices to support the program and maintains program oversight
(b) Program governance comprises the framework, functions and processes by which a program is monitored, managed and supported in order to meet organizational strategic and operational goals
(c) Program Governance refers to the systems and methods by which a program and its strategy are defined, authorized, monitored, and supported by its sponsoring organization
(d) All the above

Question Category: Easy
The right answer is Option (D)
The Standards for Program Management - 4th Edition - reference: Chapter (6), Program Governance, page 67
Clarification and Tips:
Options (A), (B) and (C) are valid descriptions of the program governance, so the right answer is Option (D).
Domain: Program Governance
Phase or Element: General

Q131 - Which of the following options describe the stakeholders in a more precise statement?

(a) Stakeholders represent all those who will interact with the program as well as those who will be affected by the implementation of the program

(b) Stakeholders represent all organization key staff who will interact with the program as well as those who will be affected by the implementation of the program
(c) Stakeholders represent all internal who will interact with the program, as well as external who will be affected by the implementation of the program
(d) Stakeholders represent all internal or external who will interact with the program

Question Category: Difficult
The right answer is Option (A)
The Standards for Program Management - 4th Edition - reference: Chapter (5), Program Stakeholder Engagement, General
Clarification and Tips:
Option (A) is the more precise statement for the description of the stakeholders.
Option (B) is wrong as it limits the stakeholders to the organization staff only.
Option (C) is wrong as it differentiates between internal and external in a wrong way.
Option (D) is wrong as it limits the stakeholders to interact with the program only.
Therefore, Option (A) is the right answer.
Domain: Stakeholder Engagement
Phase or Element: General

Q132 - Which of the following assessments can be executed in the decision-point review?

(a) Strategic alignment of the program and its components with the intended goals of both the program and the organization
(b) Program resource needs and organizational commitments in addition to capabilities for fulfilling them
(c) Program compliance with organizational quality or process standards
(d) All the above

Question Category: Easy
The right answer is Option (D)
The Standards for Program Management - 4th Edition - reference: Chapter (6), Program Governance, 6.1.9 PROGRAM GOVERNANCE REVIEWS, page 75
Clarification and Tips:
Options (A), (B), and (C) are elements that can be executed in the decision-point reviews, so Option (D) is the right answer.
Domain: Program Governance
Phase or Element: PROGRAM GOVERNANCE PRACTICES

Q133 - Mustafa is executing a process that assesses the feasibility of his program within the organization's financial, sourcing, complexity, and constraint profile. Which environmental analysis is he performing?

(a) Assumptions analysis
(b) SWOT analysis
(c) Feasibility studies
(d) Comparative advantage analysis

Question Category: Moderate
The right answer is Option (C)
The Standards for Program Management - 4th Edition - reference: Chapter (3), Program Strategy Alignment, 3.4.2.2 FEASIBILITY STUDIES, page 40
Clarification and Tips:
Using the business case, organizational goals, and other existing initiatives as a base, the feasibility study assesses the feasibility of the program within the organization's financial, sourcing, complexity, and constraint profile.
Therefore, Option (C) is the right answer.
Domain: Strategy Alignment
Phase or Element: ENVIRONMENTAL ASSESSMENTS

Q134 - Mohamed is currently in the program closure phase, he is executing the benefits transition activities. He realized three opened risks that may affect the transitioned benefit, how should he deal with these risks?

(a) He should ignore these risks as the program is closing
(b) He should add these risks to the lessons learned
(c) He should transfer these risks to the receiving organization
(d) He should report these risks to the steering committee

Question Category: Difficult
The right answer is Option (C)
The Standards for Program Management - 4th Edition - reference: Chapter (4), Program Benefits Management, 4.4 BENEFITS TRANSITION, page 54
Clarification and Tips:
Should any remaining risks affecting the transitioned benefit remain open, the program manager should transfer the risk to the appropriate organization, so Option (C) is the right answer.
Option (A) is wrong in principle.
Option (B) is not sufficient, Option (C) is much better.
Option (D) will not help.
Domain: Benefits Management
Phase or Element: BENEFITS TRANSITION

Q135 - Which of the following are confirmed during the program transition?

(a) Program charter development is completed
(b) The program has met all of the desired benefits and that all transition work has been performed within the component transition
(c) Program charter and business case are aligned
(d) Alignment of the program roadmap with the benefits management plan

Question Category: Moderate
The right answer is Option (B)
The Standards for Program Management - 4th Edition - reference: Chapter (7), Program Life Cycle Management, 7.1.4 PROGRAM CLOSURE PHASE, page 97
Clarification and Tips:
Only Option (B) has an element to be confirmed during the program transition. Therefore, Option (B) is the right answer.
Domain: Life Cycle Management
Phase or Element: Closing

Q136 - Which of the following statements has the most important reason to have programs?

(a) Programs are designed to realize a group of agreed upon benefits
(b) Programs are designed to align with the organizational strategy and to facilitate the realization of organizational benefits
(c) Programs are designed to manage its components in a coordinated manner to obtain benefits not available from managing them individually
(d) Programs are designed to achieve specific objectives

Question Category: Difficult
The right answer is Option (B)
The Standards for Program Management - 4th Edition - reference: Chapter (3), Program Strategy Alignment, page 33
Clarification and Tips:
Programs are designed to align with the organizational strategy and to facilitate the realization of organizational benefits, so Option (B) is the right answer.
Option (A) and (D) may be right answers, but Option (B) is much better.
Option (C) includes the program definition which is not the purpose of having a program.
Domain: Strategy Alignment
Phase or Element: General

Q137 - Jacob started to audit the Zaro program just after it was completed and he noticed that the cost is continued even after the program is closed. Which of the following cases may be a valid reason to have cost incurred for a closed program?

(a) Program costs may continue after program closeout to complete the opened change requests
(b) Program costs may continue after program closeout as operational costs to sustain the benefits
(c) Program costs may continue after program closeout to reward the program team
(d) Program costs may continue after program closeout as operational costs to resolve the opened issues

Question Category: Difficult
The right answer is Option (B)
The Standards for Program Management - 4th Edition - reference: Chapter (4), Program Benefits Management, 4.2 BENEFITS ANALYSIS AND PLANNING, page 48
Clarification and Tips:
Program costs may continue after program closeout as operational costs to sustain the benefits, so Option (B) is the right answer.
Option (A) and (D) are wrong as a program is closed after all change requests are closed or canceled and all issues are resolved.
Option (C) is wrong as rewarding the program team will not continue adding cost after the program is closed.
Domain: Benefits Management
Phase or Element: BENEFITS ANALYSIS AND PLANNING

Q138 - Which of the following activities will have the focus of the financial effort after the program receives initial funding and begins paying expenses?

(a) Tracking, monitoring and controlling the program's funds and expenditures
(b) Preparing for financial change requests
(c) Recording financial issues and assumptions in the issue log
(d) Checking the financial impact if the industry standards are changed in the future

Question Category: Moderate
The right answer is Option (A)
The Standards for Program Management - 4th Edition - reference: Chapter (8), Program Activities, 8.2.3 PROGRAM FINANCIAL MANAGEMENT, pages 127
Clarification and Tips:

Once the program receives initial funding and begins paying expenses, the financial effort moves into tracking, monitoring and controlling the program's funds and expenditures.
Therefore, the right answer is Option (A).
Domain: Life Cycle Management
Phase or Element: Delivery

Q139 - What is the relation between the program funding and the program components funding?

- (a) The program itself may be funded by one or more sources, and the program components may be funded by altogether different sources
- (b) The program and program components must be funded by the same sources whatever internal or external to the performing organization
- (c) The program may be funded by one or more sources internal or external to the performing organization, but the program components must be funded from internal sources
- (d) The program funding and the program components funding must be different

Question Category: Moderate
The right answer is Option (A)
The Standards for Program Management - 4th Edition - reference: Chapter (8), Program Activities, Program Management Supporting Processes, 8.1.2.4 PROGRAM FINANCIAL FRAMEWORK ESTABLISHMENT, page 114
Clarification and Tips:
The relation between the program funding and the program components funding are well defined in option (A). Therefore, Option (A) is the right answer.
Domain: Life Cycle Management
Phase or Element: Definition

Q140 - How is the program budget usually created?

- (a) Program budgets should include the costs for each individual component as well as costs for the resources to manage the program itself
- (b) Top-down cost aggregation is used to create the program budget
- (c) Bottom-up cost aggregation is used to estimate the program budget, then the top-down cost estimation is used to validate it
- (d) All the above

Question Category: Moderate
The right answer is Option (A)
The Standards for Program Management - 4th Edition - reference: Chapter (8), Program

Activities, 8.2.3.1 PROGRAM COST BUDGETING, pages 129
Clarification and Tips:
Since programs are by definition, composed of multiple components, program budgets should include the costs for each individual component as well as costs for the resources to manage the program itself.
Therefore, Option (A) is the right answer.
Domain: Life Cycle Management
Phase or Element: Delivery

Q141 - Cindy is working with her team to adapt to the multiple changes affecting her program as a result of recent unexpected regulation changes. Cindy is asking you about elements that may bound the changes authorized for a program. What should be your answer?

- (a) Organizational strategy
- (b) The business case
- (c) The components scope
- (d) Options (A) and (B)

Question Category: Difficult
The right answer is Option (D)
The Standards for Program Management - 4th Edition - reference: Chapter (6), Program Governance, 6.1.8 PROGRAM CHANGE GOVERNANCE, page 74
Clarification and Tips:
The extent to which a change can be authorized by program governance is bounded by the program business case and organizational strategy, so Option (D) is the right answer.
Please remember that programs are managed in a manner that accepts and adapts to change as necessary to optimize the delivery of benefits.
Domain: Program Governance
Phase or Element: PROGRAM GOVERNANCE PRACTICES

Q142 - Mohamed is writing a risk to the risk register that is expected to remain after planned responses have been taken. What is the name of this risk?

- (a) Black swan risks
- (b) Residual risks
- (c) Secondary risks
- (d) Negative risks

Question Category: Moderate
The right answer is Option (B)

The Standards for Program Management - 4th Edition - reference: Chapter (8), Program Activities, 8.2.8.3 PROGRAM RISK RESPONSE MANAGEMENT, pages 135

Clarification and Tips:
A black swan risk is a risk that is related to a few low probable events that will impact the portfolio dramatically when all of them happen together.
Residual risks are expected to remain after planned responses have been taken, as well as those that have been deliberately accepted.
Secondary risks that arise as a direct outcome of implementing the risk response.
The negative risk is the risk with negative impact.
Therefore, Option (B) is the right answer.

Domain: Life Cycle Management
Phase or Element: Delivery

Q143 - Who issues the program charter?

(a) The program manager
(b) The program sponsor
(c) The program management office
(d) The EPMO

Question Category: Easy
The right answer is Option (B)
The Standards for Program Management - 4th Edition - reference: Chapter (3), Program Strategy Alignment, page 33

Clarification and Tips:
The program sponsor issues the project charter, so Option (B) is the right answer.

Domain: Strategy Alignment
Phase or Element: General

Q144 - As per the last steering committee actions, the program manager, Anil, will include the program forecast in the steering committee's presentation.
What does the program forecast mean?

(a) It means to assess the likelihood of the final product success
(b) It means to assess the likelihood of achieving the planned program financial
(c) It means to assess the likelihood of achieving planned outcomes of the program
(d) It means to assess the likelihood of achieving the stakeholders' expectations

Question Category: Moderate
The right answer is Option (C)

The Standards for Program Management - 4th Edition - reference: Chapter (7), Program Life Cycle Management, 7.2.2.3 PROGRAM PERFORMANCE MONITORING AND CONTROLLING, page 101

Clarification and Tips:
Forecasts enable the program manager and other key stakeholders to assess the likelihood of achieving planned outcomes and to provide predictions of the program's future state based on the current information and knowledge available.
Therefore, the right answer is Option (C).
Domain: Life Cycle Management
Phase or Element: Delivery

Q145 - Zenon is a new program established between the Ministry of Housing and a private company called Elite to develop 10,000 housing units.
The newly assigned program manager Luis was confused to which steering committee he should report; the Ministry of Housing steering committee, or the Elite company steering committee. What is your advice to Luis?

(a) He should report to the Elite company steering committee
(b) He should report to the two steering committees; the Ministry of Housing steering committee and the Elite company steering committee
(c) He should report to the Ministry of Housing steering committee
(d) He should assume the responsibility of the steering committee to avoid this conflict

Question Category: Difficult
The right answer is Option (B)
The Standards for Program Management - 4th Edition - reference: Chapter (6), Program Governance, 6.2.2 PROGRAM STEERING COMMITTEE, page 82
Clarification and Tips:
Option (B) is the right answer as some programs may need to report to multiple steering committees; for example, programs that are sponsored and overseen jointly by private and governmental organizations.
Domain: Program Governance
Phase or Element: PROGRAM GOVERNANCE ROLES

Q146 - As part of the program change assessment activity, you started to identify the sources of change in your environment to help develop the program's business case and the program's charter.
What should you do with the identified sources of change?

(a) Estimate the likelihood of the changes that could arise from these sources

(b) Estimate the possible impacts of the changes that could arise from these sources
(c) Propose measures that could be taken to enable the program to respond to such changes in a positive way
(d) All the above

Question Category: Moderate
The right answer is Option (D)
The Standards for Program Management - 4th Edition - reference: Chapter (8), Program Activities, 8.1.1.1 PROGRAM CHANGE ASSESSMENT, pages 107
Clarification and Tips:
Regarding the identified sources of change, Sam should estimate the likelihood and possible impacts of the changes that could arise from these sources and he should propose measures that could be taken to enable the program to respond to such changes in a positive, rather than disruptive, way. Therefore, Option (D) is the right answer.
Domain: Life Cycle Management
Phase or Element: Definition

Q147 - Which of the following bounds the changes authorized for a program?

(a) The program scope
(b) The components scope
(c) The business case
(d) The organization risk appetite

Question Category: Difficult
The right answer is Option (C)
The Standards for Program Management - 4th Edition - reference: Chapter (6), Program Governance, 6.1.8 PROGRAM CHANGE GOVERNANCE, page 74
Clarification and Tips:
The extent to which a change can be authorized by program governance is bounded by the program business case and organizational strategy, so Option (C) is the right answer.
Please remember that programs are managed in a manner that accepts and adapts to change as necessary to optimize the delivery of benefits.
Domain: Program Governance
Phase or Element: PROGRAM GOVERNANCE PRACTICES

Q148 - Many organizations have programs with specific objectives to achieve, and planned benefits to realize. On what basis did the organizations evaluate, select, and authorize the programs?

(a) Organizations evaluated, selected, and authorized the programs based on value added by the programs to the community
(b) Organizations evaluated, selected, and authorized the programs based on organization's limiting factors
(c) Organizations evaluated, selected, and authorized the programs based on their alignment and support to achieve the organization's strategic plan
(d) Organizations evaluated, selected, and authorized the programs based on required resources

Question Category: Difficult
The right answer is Option (C)
The Standards for Program Management - 4th Edition - reference: Chapter (3), Program Strategy Alignment, 3.1 PROGRAM BUSINESS CASE, page 35
Clarification and Tips:
Programs are formally evaluated, selected, and authorized based on their alignment and support to achieve the organization's strategic plan, so Option (C) is the right answer.
Domain: Strategy Alignment
Phase or Element: PROGRAM BUSINESS CASE

Q149 - James is working on tools that are used to collect, integrate and communicate information critical to the effective management of one or more organizational programs. Which tools are these?

(a) Visual management tools
(b) Program information management tools
(c) The program management information system (PMIS)
(d) Internet-based group communication tools

Question Category: Difficult
The right answer is Option (C)
The Standards for Program Management - 4th Edition - reference: Chapter (7), Program Life Cycle Management, 7.2.2.1 PROGRAM INFRASTRUCTURE DEVELOPMENT, pages 100
Clarification and Tips:
A PMIS consists of tools used to collect, integrate and communicate information critical to the effective management of one or more organizational programs, so Option (C) is the right answer.
Domain: Life Cycle Management
Phase or Element: Definition

Q150 - James is working with the program risk manager to define the minimum level of risk exposure for a risk to be included in the risk register. What does James define?

(a) The program risk exposure
(b) The program risk threshold
(c) The program risk appetite
(d) Risk category

Question Category: Moderate
The right answer is Option (B)
The Standards for Program Management - 4th Edition - reference: Chapter (3), Program Strategy Alignment, 3.5.2 PROGRAM RISK THRESHOLDS, page 41
Clarification and Tips:
Risk exposure is an aggregate measure of the potential impact of all risks at any given point in time in a project, program, or portfolio.
Risk threshold is the measure of the degree of acceptable variation around a program objective that reflects the risk appetite of the organization and program stakeholders.
Risk appetite is an assessment of the organization's willingness to accept and deal with risks.
Risk category s a group of potential causes of risk.
Therefore, the right answer is Option (B).
Domain: Strategy Alignment
Phase or Element: PROGRAM RISK MANAGEMENT STRATEGY

Q151 - The benefits transition activities include all the following except:

(a) Evaluating opportunities and threats affecting benefits
(b) Verifying that the integration of the program and its components meet or exceed the benefit realization criteria
(c) Verifying that the transition and closure of the program and its components meet or exceed the benefit realization criteria
(d) Developing a transition plan

Question Category: Moderate
The right answer is Option (A)
The Standards for Program Management - 4th Edition - reference: Chapter (4), Program Benefits Management, 4.4 BENEFITS TRANSITION, page 53
Clarification and Tips:
Options (B), (C), and (D) are activities related to the benefits transition, but Option (A) is not.
Therefore, Option (A) is the right answer.
Domain: Benefits Management
Phase or Element: BENEFITS TRANSITION

Q152 - Anil was assigned to a three year program for building a Dam. After the first year passed. Once he joined the program, he reviewed the program benefits register and found that the benefits are realized only at the program closure, what should Anil do?

(a) Anil should call for a meeting with the program sponsor to review the whole benefits register
(b) Anil should call for a meeting with the program team to review the whole benefits register
(c) It is regular for large public work programs to realize the benefits at the end of the program. So, Anil should continue without stopping at this point
(d) Anil should call for a meeting with the governance board to review the approved program governance plan

Question Category: Difficult
The right answer is Option (C)
The Standards for Program Management - 4th Edition - reference: Chapter (4), Program Benefits Management, page 45
Clarification and Tips:
It is regular for large public work programs like Dams, Roads or Bridges to realize the benefits at the end of the program, so, the right answer is Option (C).
Domain: Benefits Management
Phase or Element: BENEFITS IDENTIFICATION

Q153 - Which of the following statements is not correct to describe the program roadmap?

(a) The roadmap outlines major program events for the purposes of planning
(b) The program roadmap summarizes the program status in a chronological order
(c) The roadmap outlines major program events for the purposes of developing more detailed schedules
(d) The program roadmap provides a high-level view of key milestones and decision points

Question Category: Difficult
The right answer is Option (B)
The Standards for Program Management - 4th Edition - reference: Chapter (3), Program Strategy Alignment, 3.3 PROGRAM ROADMAP, page 36
Clarification and Tips:
Options (A), (C), and (D) can be used to describe the program roadmap, but option (B) is not as it is referring to the program status. So the right answer is Option (B).
Domain: Strategy Alignment
Phase or Element: PROGRAM ROADMAP

Q154 - Amy is working on the preparation for the program reporting to send to the stakeholders as per the communication plan. Program reporting aggregates information from all the program components.

Amy needs to communicate this information to a group in order to provide them with general and background information about the program. Which group is this?

(a) The program management office
(b) The program steering committee
(c) The program team members and its constituent components
(d) The program managers in the same organization

Question Category: Moderate
The right answer is Option (C)
The Standards for Program Management - 4th Edition - reference: Chapter (8), Program Activities, 8.2.2.2 PROGRAM REPORTING, pages 127
Clarification and Tips:
The program reporting is conveyed to the stakeholders by means of the information distribution activity to provide them with the needed status and deliverable information. Additionally, this information is communicated to program team members and its constituent components to provide them with general and background information about the program.
Therefore, Option (C) is the right answer.
Please note the following:
Option (A) is partially right and it is part of Option (C) which is the complete right answer.
Option (B) is expected to be part of the key stakeholders to review the program reporting.
Option (D) is just to create confusion.
Domain: Life Cycle Management
Phase or Element: Delivery

Q155 - What is your best approach as a program manager, in handling the stakeholder register, when you have changes in your program scope that may involve the crafting department, as a new stakeholder?

(a) I should review the stakeholder register only when any required scope change is approved
(b) I should have the stakeholder register fixed during the program life cycle
(c) I should review the stakeholder register regularly and update it as the work of the program progresses and more stakeholders are engaged
(d) I should have the stakeholder register fixed during the Benefits Delivery phase

Question Category: Moderate
The right answer is Option (C)
The Standards for Program Management - 4th Edition - reference: Chapter (5), Program Stakeholder Engagement, 5.1 PROGRAM STAKEHOLDER IDENTIFICATION, page 60
Clarification and Tips:
When there are changes in the program scope that may involve a new department of the organization, the program manager should review the stakeholder register and update it with this new involved department.
The stakeholder register is not a fixed list, but it should be reviewed and updated regularly as the work of the program progresses and more stakeholders are engaged.
Therefore, the right answer is Option (C).
Domain: Stakeholder Engagement
Phase or Element: PROGRAM STAKEHOLDER IDENTIFICATION

Q156 - How should the program team deal with the stakeholders' issues and concerns?

(a) The program team should select the important issues and concerns only to record
(b) The program team should review the stakeholders' issues and concerns with the program manager before logging them
(c) The program team should accept and log the stakeholders' issues and concerns and should manage them to closure
(d) The program team should neglect the less important issues and concerns to save time for the project

Question Category: Moderate
The right answer is Option (C)
The Standards for Program Management - 4th Edition - reference: Chapter (5), Program Stakeholder Engagement, 5.4 PROGRAM STAKEHOLDER ENGAGEMENT, page 65
Clarification and Tips:
The program team should accept and log stakeholders' issues and concerns and should manage them to closure. They should not filter them, neglect some of them or consult the program manager before recording them. Therefore, the right answer is Option (C).
Domain: Stakeholder Engagement
Phase or Element: PROGRAM STAKEHOLDER ENGAGEMENT

Q157 - Sam is working with his program team to initiate his first program, he was discussing with the team the enterprise environmental factors and how they may affect the program. Which of the following program aspects may be influenced by the enterprise environmental factors?

(a) Program funding
(b) Program selection
(c) Program design
(d) All the above

Question Category: Moderate
The right answer is Option (D)
The Standards for Program Management - 4th Edition - reference: Chapter (3), Program Strategy Alignment, 3.4.1 ENTERPRISE ENVIRONMENTAL FACTORS, page 38
Clarification and Tips:
Options (A), (B), and (C) are program aspects that can be influenced by the change in the enterprise environmental factors.
Therefore, Option (D) is the right answer.
Domain: Strategy Alignment
Phase or Element: ENVIRONMENTAL ASSESSMENTS

Q158 - All the following are elements of the program governance plan, except:

(a) A schedule of anticipated program-related governance meetings
(b) The pace at which benefits are realized and serves as a basis for transition and integration of new capabilities
(c) A guidance for the scheduling of additional governance meetings or activities by defining criteria for their scheduling
(d) A definition of who will have accountability and authority with respect to key decision-making categories and responsibility boundaries

Question Category: Moderate
The right answer is Option (B)
The Standards for Program Management - 4th Edition - reference: Chapter (6), Program Governance, 6.1.1 PROGRAM GOVERNANCE PLAN, page 70
Clarification and Tips:
Options (A), (C), and (D) are elements that are expected in the program governance plan, but Option (B) is not part of a program governance plan. Therefore, Option (B) is the right answer.
Domain: Program Governance
Phase or Element: PROGRAM GOVERNANCE PRACTICES

Q159 - Rao had a long experience as a program manager in the local government where he executed more than five programs. Today, Rao was assigned as a program manager for a pharmaceutical development program called Pharma-1. When developing a program governance plan for Pharma-1, what should Rao do with his existing program governance plan that he developed and enhanced during the last period?

(a) Rao should use the old existing program governance plan as it is
(b) Rao should use the old governance plan as a template and start writing a new governance plan
(c) Rao should neglect his old program governance plan and he should start from scratch creating his new program governance plan
(d) Rao should apply the changes related to the pharmaceutical business needs, political, regulatory, technical and competitive environments to the existing program governance plan before using it for the Pharma-1 program

Question Category: Moderate
The right answer is Option (D)
The Standards for Program Management - 4th Edition - reference: Chapter (6), Program Governance, 6.3 PROGRAM GOVERNANCE DESIGN AND IMPLEMENTATION, page 85
Clarification and Tips:
Option (A) is wrong as there are different business needs, political, regulatory, technical, and competitive environments due to the business change.
Option (B) might work, but option (D) is more specific and is considered a complete answer.
Option (C) might work but is not efficient.
Domain: Program Governance
Phase or Element: PROGRAM GOVERNANCE DESIGN AND IMPLEMENTATION

Q160 - Michelle is a program manager in your organization, she controls all the component procurements at the program level. She came asking you for advice regarding the role of the component manager in contract administration in case the contract is controlled at the program level, what is your right advice?

(a) Component manager coordinates or reports contract issues
(b) Component manager reports contract changes
(c) Component manager reports deliverable acceptance
(d) All of the above

Question Category: Easy
The right answer is Option (D)
The Standards for Program Management - 4th Edition - reference: Chapter (8), Program Activities, 8.2.5.1 PROGRAM CONTRACT ADMINISTRATION, pages 131
Clarification and Tips:
Where contracts are administered at the program level, however, component managers coordinate or report deliverable acceptance, contract changes, and other contract issues with the program staff.

Therefore, Option (D) is the right answer.
Domain: Life Cycle Management
Phase or Element: Delivery

Q161 - Question Set (1/2) - You are the program manager in the Focus organization. You started to analyze the program stakeholders, but you have a large number of stakeholders; some with positive attitudes towards your program contribution and others with negative attitudes. Which of the following tools is the best to help you to solicit feedback from a large number of stakeholders?

- (a) Questionnaires and surveys
- (b) Interviews
- (c) Focus groups
- (d) Virtual meetings

Question Category: Moderate
The right answer is Option (A)
The Standards for Program Management - 4th Edition - reference: Chapter (5), Program Stakeholder Engagement, 5.2 PROGRAM STAKEHOLDER ANALYSIS, page 62
Clarification and Tips:
Questionnaires and surveys allow the program team to solicit feedback from a greater number of stakeholders than what is possible with interviews or focus groups, so Option (A) is the right answer.
Domain: Stakeholder Engagement
Phase or Element: PROGRAM STAKEHOLDER ANALYSIS

Q162 - Question Set (2/2) - You are the program manager in the Focus organization. You started to analyze the program stakeholders, but you have a large number of stakeholders; some have positive attitudes towards your program contribution and others have negative attitudes. How should you deal with the positive stakeholders and the negative stakeholders?

- (a) I should focus on activities related to mitigating the effect of negative stakeholders
- (b) I should establish a balance between activities related to mitigating the effect of negative stakeholders and encouraging the active support of positive stakeholders
- (c) I should focus on encouraging the active support of positive stakeholders and ignore the negative stakeholders
- (d) I should focus on encouraging the active support of positive stakeholders

Question Category: Moderate
The right answer is Option (B)

The Standards for Program Management - 4th Edition - reference: Chapter (5), Program Stakeholder Engagement, 5.2 PROGRAM STAKEHOLDER ANALYSIS, page 62

Clarification and Tips:
The program manager should establish a balance between activities related to mitigating the effect of stakeholders who view the program negatively and encouraging the active support of stakeholders who see the program as a positive contribution, so Option (B) is the right answer.

Domain: Stakeholder Engagement
Phase or Element: PROGRAM STAKEHOLDER ANALYSIS

Q163 - Matias is a program manager in your organization. He writes the information management plan. He determined the program's information management system, what is the next step he should do?

(a) Determine the program information distribution methods
(b) Determine the program information collection details
(c) Determine the program information retrieval details
(d) Options (B) and (C)

Question Category: Moderate
The right answer is Option (A)
The Standards for Program Management - 4th Edition - reference: Chapter (8), Program Activities, 8.1.2.6 PROGRAM INFORMATION MANAGEMENT PLANNING, pages 116

Clarification and Tips:
Program information distribution methods are determined once the program's information management system is determined, so Option (A) is the right answer.

Domain: Life Cycle Management
Phase or Element: Definition

Q164 - Who is responsible for ensuring alignment of individual project management plans with the program's goals and intended benefits?

(a) The project manager
(b) The PMO
(c) The project sponsor
(d) The program manager

Question Category: Moderate
The right answer is Option (D)
The Standards for Program Management - 4th Edition - reference: Chapter (3), Program Strategy Alignment, page 34

Clarification and Tips:
The program manager is responsible for ensuring alignment of individual project management plans with the program's goals and intended benefits to support the achievement of the organization's strategic goals and objectives.
Therefore, Option (D) is the right answer.
Domain: Strategy Alignment
Phase or Element: General

Q165 - Omar is the program manager who has five components in his project. Omar is asking the component managers for many details regarding component procurements to maintain visibility. What is the best reason for Omar to maintain visibility in the component procurements?

   (a) To ensure the program budget is being expended properly to obtain program benefits
   (b) To ensure the procurement is complying with the organization standards
   (c) To verify that procurement activities are executed as per the procurement management plan
   (d) To include the procurement progress in his regular reporting

Question Category: Moderate
The right answer is Option (A)
The Standards for Program Management - 4th Edition - reference: Chapter (8), Program Activities, 8.2.5.1 PROGRAM CONTRACT ADMINISTRATION, pages 131
Clarification and Tips:
The program manager maintains visibility in the procurements to ensure the program budget is being expended properly to obtain program benefits, so Option (A) is the right answer.
Please note the following:
Options (B), (C), and (D) may be right answers, but Option (A) is much better than all of them as it is directly related to the program benefits.
Domain: Life Cycle Management
Phase or Element: Delivery

Q166 - Khadija is managing the R3 program and she is currently writing the program governance with the program management office. Her aim is to create effective program governance.
In which of the following cases is the effective program governance especially important?

   (a) When the program environment is easy to manage, and it is necessary to respond rapidly to outcomes and information that becomes available during the course of the program

(b) When the program environment is easy to manage, and it is not necessary to respond rapidly to outcomes and information that becomes available during the course of the program
(c) When the program environment is highly complex or uncertain and it is necessary to respond rapidly to outcomes and information that becomes available during the course of the program
(d) When the program environment is highly complex or uncertain and it is not necessary to respond rapidly to outcomes and information that becomes available during the course of the program

Question Category: Moderate
The right answer is Option (C)
The Standards for Program Management - 4th Edition - reference: Chapter (6), Program Governance, page 69
Clarification and Tips:
Effective program governance is especially important in environments that are highly complex or uncertain when it is necessary to respond rapidly to outcomes and information that becomes available during the course of the program, so Option (C) is the right answer.
Domain: Program Governance
Phase or Element: General

Q167 - All the following options result from the approval of the program charter, except:

(a) Providing the program manager with authority to apply organizational resources to program activities
(b) Approving the program roadmap
(c) Connecting the program to the organization's ongoing work and strategic priorities
(d) Authorizing the commencement of the program

Question Category: Difficult
The right answer is Option (B)
The Standards for Program Management - 4th Edition - reference: Chapter (7), Program Life Cycle Management, 7.1.2.1 PROGRAM FORMULATION, page 92
Clarification and Tips:
Options (A), (C), and (D) may result from the approval of the program charter, but Option (B) is not as the program roadmap is approved after the program charter approval.
Domain: Life Cycle Management
Phase or Element: Definition

Q168 - Chao is managing a program in Bisco organization. He works in the program risk management and wants to determine whether proper risk management policies and procedures are being followed. Which risk activity does he work on?

- (a) Risk planning
- (b) Risk assessment
- (c) Risk identification
- (d) Risk monitoring

Question Category: Moderate
The right answer is Option (D)
The Standards for Program Management - 4th Edition - reference: Chapter (8), Program Activities, 8.2.8 PROGRAM RISK MONITORING AND CONTROLLING, pages 134
Clarification and Tips:
Risk monitoring is conducted to determine whether: 1) Program assumptions are still valid, 2) Assessed risk has changed from its prior state, 3) Proper risk management policies and procedures are being followed, and 4) Cost or schedule contingency reserves are modified in line with the risks of the program.
Therefore, Option (D) is the right answer.
Domain: Life Cycle Management
Phase or Element: Delivery

Q169 - Jack is assigned to manage the program Yen after it was running for six months and at the time it reached its delivery phase. Jack was reviewing the program documents to understand the program plans and progress. One of these documents includes definitions of roles and responsibilities, schedule of anticipated program-related governance meetings and scheduled expected decision-point reviews. Which document is this?

- (a) Program governance plan
- (b) Program roadmap
- (c) Benefits realization plan
- (d) Program business case

Question Category: Moderate
The right answer is Option (A)
The Standards for Program Management - 4th Edition - reference: Chapter (6), Program Governance, 6.1.1 PROGRAM GOVERNANCE PLAN, page 70
Clarification and Tips:
The program governance plan includes definitions of roles and responsibilities, schedule of anticipated program-related governance meetings, activities and key milestones, such as scheduled expected decision-point reviews, program health checks, and required audits.
Therefore, Option (A) is the right answer.

Domain: Program Governance
Phase or Element: PROGRAM GOVERNANCE PRACTICES

Q170 - Once the program steering committee approved the program change request, all the following activities will be executed, except:

(a) Reflect in updates to component plans
(b) Communicate the change request to appropriate stakeholders
(c) Define the minimum quality criteria and standards to be applied to the component level
(d) Record the change request in the program change log

Question Category: Moderate
The right answer is Option (C)
The Standards for Program Management - 4th Edition - reference: Chapter (6), Program Governance, 8.2.1 PROGRAM CHANGE MONITORING AND CONTROLLING, page 126
Clarification and Tips:
Options (A), (B), and (D) are activities that should be executed after the change request is approved, but Option (C) is not related to change request approval.
Therefore, Option (C) is the right answer.
Domain: Program Governance
Phase or Element: PROGRAM GOVERNANCE PRACTICES

Appendix (A) – Questions Mapping per Domain

1. Exam 1 – Question Reference

Question	Domain
Q3	Strategy Alignment
Q5	Strategy Alignment
Q13	Strategy Alignment
Q14	Strategy Alignment
Q28	Strategy Alignment
Q40	Strategy Alignment
Q50	Strategy Alignment
Q53	Strategy Alignment
Q54	Strategy Alignment
Q79	Strategy Alignment
Q86	Strategy Alignment
Q88	Strategy Alignment
Q91	Strategy Alignment
Q109	Strategy Alignment
Q110	Strategy Alignment
Q111	Strategy Alignment
Q112	Strategy Alignment
Q116	Strategy Alignment
Q119	Strategy Alignment
Q120	Strategy Alignment
Q144	Strategy Alignment
Q159	Strategy Alignment
Q160	Strategy Alignment
Q162	Strategy Alignment
Q169	Strategy Alignment

Exam 1 - Questions Mapping

Question	Domain	Question	Domain
Q4	Life Cycle Management	Q78	Life Cycle Management
Q6	Life Cycle Management	Q81	Life Cycle Management
Q7	Life Cycle Management	Q83	Life Cycle Management
Q8	Life Cycle Management	Q87	Life Cycle Management
Q10	Life Cycle Management	Q95	Life Cycle Management
Q11	Life Cycle Management	Q100	Life Cycle Management
Q12	Life Cycle Management	Q103	Life Cycle Management
Q16	Life Cycle Management	Q104	Life Cycle Management
Q18	Life Cycle Management	Q107	Life Cycle Management
Q20	Life Cycle Management	Q108	Life Cycle Management
Q23	Life Cycle Management	Q114	Life Cycle Management
Q25	Life Cycle Management	Q115	Life Cycle Management
Q27	Life Cycle Management	Q121	Life Cycle Management
Q30	Life Cycle Management	Q122	Life Cycle Management
Q31	Life Cycle Management	Q123	Life Cycle Management
Q32	Life Cycle Management	Q124	Life Cycle Management
Q35	Life Cycle Management	Q125	Life Cycle Management
Q36	Life Cycle Management	Q130	Life Cycle Management
Q37	Life Cycle Management	Q135	Life Cycle Management
Q43	Life Cycle Management	Q136	Life Cycle Management
Q45	Life Cycle Management	Q137	Life Cycle Management
Q47	Life Cycle Management	Q138	Life Cycle Management
Q51	Life Cycle Management	Q140	Life Cycle Management
Q55	Life Cycle Management	Q142	Life Cycle Management
Q56	Life Cycle Management	Q143	Life Cycle Management
Q58	Life Cycle Management	Q145	Life Cycle Management
Q59	Life Cycle Management	Q150	Life Cycle Management
Q60	Life Cycle Management	Q152	Life Cycle Management
Q61	Life Cycle Management	Q153	Life Cycle Management
Q62	Life Cycle Management	Q154	Life Cycle Management
Q63	Life Cycle Management	Q155	Life Cycle Management
Q65	Life Cycle Management	Q157	Life Cycle Management
Q66	Life Cycle Management	Q158	Life Cycle Management
Q70	Life Cycle Management	Q161	Life Cycle Management
Q71	Life Cycle Management	Q166	Life Cycle Management
Q73	Life Cycle Management	Q167	Life Cycle Management
Q76	Life Cycle Management	Q170	Life Cycle Management
Q77	Life Cycle Management		

Question	Domain
Q9	Benefits Management
Q38	Benefits Management
Q48	Benefits Management
Q67	Benefits Management
Q68	Benefits Management
Q69	Benefits Management
Q84	Benefits Management
Q90	Benefits Management
Q93	Benefits Management
Q96	Benefits Management
Q97	Benefits Management
Q102	Benefits Management
Q127	Benefits Management
Q131	Benefits Management
Q141	Benefits Management
Q148	Benefits Management
Q149	Benefits Management
Q151	Benefits Management
Q168	Benefits Management

Exam 1 - Questions Mapping

Question	Domain
Q1	Stakeholder Engagement
Q2	Stakeholder Engagement
Q17	Stakeholder Engagement
Q24	Stakeholder Engagement
Q26	Stakeholder Engagement
Q33	Stakeholder Engagement
Q52	Stakeholder Engagement
Q64	Stakeholder Engagement
Q72	Stakeholder Engagement
Q74	Stakeholder Engagement
Q89	Stakeholder Engagement
Q99	Stakeholder Engagement
Q106	Stakeholder Engagement
Q113	Stakeholder Engagement
Q117	Stakeholder Engagement
Q118	Stakeholder Engagement
Q126	Stakeholder Engagement
Q128	Stakeholder Engagement
Q129	Stakeholder Engagement
Q132	Stakeholder Engagement
Q133	Stakeholder Engagement
Q134	Stakeholder Engagement
Q139	Stakeholder Engagement
Q146	Stakeholder Engagement
Q156	Stakeholder Engagement
Q164	Stakeholder Engagement
Q165	Stakeholder Engagement

Exam 1 - Questions Mapping

Question	Domain
Q15	Program Governance
Q19	Program Governance
Q21	Program Governance
Q22	Program Governance
Q29	Program Governance
Q34	Program Governance
Q39	Program Governance
Q41	Program Governance
Q42	Program Governance
Q44	Program Governance
Q46	Program Governance
Q49	Program Governance
Q57	Program Governance
Q75	Program Governance
Q80	Program Governance
Q82	Program Governance
Q85	Program Governance
Q92	Program Governance
Q94	Program Governance
Q98	Program Governance
Q101	Program Governance
Q105	Program Governance
Q147	Program Governance
Q163	Program Governance

2. Exam 2 – Questions Reference

Qestion	Domain
Q1	Strategy Alignment
Q2	Strategy Alignment
Q8	Strategy Alignment
Q14	Strategy Alignment
Q22	Strategy Alignment
Q24	Strategy Alignment
Q42	Strategy Alignment
Q53	Strategy Alignment
Q59	Strategy Alignment
Q72	Strategy Alignment
Q88	Strategy Alignment
Q93	Strategy Alignment
Q103	Strategy Alignment
Q107	Strategy Alignment
Q114	Strategy Alignment
Q118	Strategy Alignment
Q128	Strategy Alignment
Q133	Strategy Alignment
Q136	Strategy Alignment
Q143	Strategy Alignment
Q148	Strategy Alignment
Q150	Strategy Alignment
Q153	Strategy Alignment
Q157	Strategy Alignment
Q164	Strategy Alignment

Exam 2 - Questions Mapping

Qestion	Domain
Q3	Life Cycle Management
Q5	Life Cycle Management
Q6	Life Cycle Management
Q7	Life Cycle Management
Q9	Life Cycle Management
Q10	Life Cycle Management
Q11	Life Cycle Management
Q15	Life Cycle Management
Q16	Life Cycle Management
Q17	Life Cycle Management
Q18	Life Cycle Management
Q20	Life Cycle Management
Q21	Life Cycle Management
Q23	Life Cycle Management
Q30	Life Cycle Management
Q32	Life Cycle Management
Q34	Life Cycle Management
Q35	Life Cycle Management
Q37	Life Cycle Management
Q40	Life Cycle Management
Q44	Life Cycle Management
Q46	Life Cycle Management
Q47	Life Cycle Management
Q49	Life Cycle Management
Q50	Life Cycle Management
Q51	Life Cycle Management
Q52	Life Cycle Management
Q55	Life Cycle Management
Q57	Life Cycle Management
Q58	Life Cycle Management
Q60	Life Cycle Management
Q61	Life Cycle Management
Q65	Life Cycle Management
Q69	Life Cycle Management
Q71	Life Cycle Management
Q75	Life Cycle Management
Q82	Life Cycle Management
Q83	Life Cycle Management

Qestion	Domain
Q84	Life Cycle Management
Q85	Life Cycle Management
Q86	Life Cycle Management
Q87	Life Cycle Management
Q90	Life Cycle Management
Q92	Life Cycle Management
Q96	Life Cycle Management
Q100	Life Cycle Management
Q101	Life Cycle Management
Q102	Life Cycle Management
Q108	Life Cycle Management
Q110	Life Cycle Management
Q112	Life Cycle Management
Q113	Life Cycle Management
Q116	Life Cycle Management
Q117	Life Cycle Management
Q119	Life Cycle Management
Q120	Life Cycle Management
Q121	Life Cycle Management
Q124	Life Cycle Management
Q125	Life Cycle Management
Q126	Life Cycle Management
Q127	Life Cycle Management
Q135	Life Cycle Management
Q138	Life Cycle Management
Q139	Life Cycle Management
Q140	Life Cycle Management
Q142	Life Cycle Management
Q144	Life Cycle Management
Q146	Life Cycle Management
Q149	Life Cycle Management
Q154	Life Cycle Management
Q160	Life Cycle Management
Q163	Life Cycle Management
Q165	Life Cycle Management
Q167	Life Cycle Management
Q168	Life Cycle Management

Exam 2 - Questions Mapping

Qestion	Domain
Q13	Benefits Management
Q27	Benefits Management
Q33	Benefits Management
Q38	Benefits Management
Q43	Benefits Management
Q45	Benefits Management
Q54	Benefits Management
Q76	Benefits Management
Q79	Benefits Management
Q89	Benefits Management
Q97	Benefits Management
Q98	Benefits Management
Q105	Benefits Management
Q111	Benefits Management
Q122	Benefits Management
Q134	Benefits Management
Q137	Benefits Management
Q151	Benefits Management
Q152	Benefits Management

Qestion	Domain
Q19	Stakeholder Engagement
Q25	Stakeholder Engagement
Q26	Stakeholder Engagement
Q41	Stakeholder Engagement
Q48	Stakeholder Engagement
Q56	Stakeholder Engagement
Q62	Stakeholder Engagement
Q63	Stakeholder Engagement
Q66	Stakeholder Engagement
Q67	Stakeholder Engagement
Q70	Stakeholder Engagement
Q74	Stakeholder Engagement
Q77	Stakeholder Engagement
Q81	Stakeholder Engagement
Q91	Stakeholder Engagement
Q95	Stakeholder Engagement
Q99	Stakeholder Engagement
Q104	Stakeholder Engagement
Q109	Stakeholder Engagement
Q115	Stakeholder Engagement
Q123	Stakeholder Engagement
Q129	Stakeholder Engagement
Q131	Stakeholder Engagement
Q155	Stakeholder Engagement
Q156	Stakeholder Engagement
Q161	Stakeholder Engagement
Q162	Stakeholder Engagement

Exam 2 - Questions Mapping

Qestion	Domain
Q4	Program Governance
Q12	Program Governance
Q28	Program Governance
Q29	Program Governance
Q31	Program Governance
Q36	Program Governance
Q39	Program Governance
Q64	Program Governance
Q68	Program Governance
Q73	Program Governance
Q78	Program Governance
Q80	Program Governance
Q94	Program Governance
Q106	Program Governance
Q130	Program Governance
Q132	Program Governance
Q141	Program Governance
Q145	Program Governance
Q147	Program Governance
Q158	Program Governance
Q159	Program Governance
Q166	Program Governance
Q169	Program Governance
Q170	Program Governance

Made in the USA
Columbia, SC
16 May 2023